Wordsmith

A Guide to Paragraphs and Short Essays

D1404775

Taken from:

Wordsmith: A Guide to Paragraphs and Short Essays,
Third Edition
by Pamela Arlov

Learning Solutions

New York   Boston   San Francisco
London   Toronto   Sydney   Tokyo   Singapore   Madrid
Mexico City   Munich   Paris   Cape Town   Hong Kong   Montreal

Cover Art: *Old Typewriter Shop 02,* by Michael Lary

Taken from:

Wordsmith: A Guide to Paragraphs and Short Essays, Third Edition
by Pamela Arlov
Copyright © 2007, 2004, 2000 by Pearson Education, Inc.
Published by Prentice Hall
Upper Saddle River, New Jersey 07458

Pearson Learning Solutions, 501 Boylston Street, Suite 900, Boston, MA 02116
A Pearson Education Company
www.pearsoned.com

Printed in the United States of America

14 15 16 17 V0ZN 14 13 12 11

2007420423

KH/MR

ISBN 10: 0-536-09357-1
ISBN 13: 978-0-536-09357-8

Copyright
Acknowledgments

Contents

Chapter 3   Writing Paragraphs: Topic Sentences   29

Chapter 4   Writing Paragraphs: Support   41

Chapter 5   Writing Paragraphs: Unity and Coherence   59

Chapter 6   Revising, Proofreading, and Formatting   75

Chapter 22   Words Commonly Confused   361

Chapter 23   Word Choice   371

Chapter 24   Commas   383

Chapter 25   Other Punctuation   395

Preface

To the Instructor

Thank you for choosing *Wordsmith: A Guide to Paragraphs and Short Essays, Third Edition,* as your textbook.

Like you, I am a teacher of writing. Like you, I struggle to find the best way to teach a subject that, on its surface, seems as simple as touching pen to paper. Yet writing is remarkably complex, incorporating the personality and experience of each writer and each reader. It requires adherence to agreed-upon rules of grammar, punctuation, and form. It is, in fact, a craft that might be best taught to a small group of students in a series of unhurried sessions and individual conferences over an extended period of time. But our reality is the fifty-minute hour, the class of twenty or more, the term that is measured in weeks. How best to handle that reality?

Most of us constantly refine our teaching methods, striving to make difficult concepts clear and tedious details interesting. Most of all, we try to ignite the spark that will help our students see writing as a meaningful, life-enriching activity. A good textbook should reinforce our efforts. I have spent considerable time trying to analyze what a good textbook should do, above and beyond presenting information in a given field. Here is what I have come up with: The book should be orderly and user-friendly, with a flexible format. Explanations should be clear and supported by numerous exercises and examples. The book should contain much more than is strictly necessary: it should be a smorgasbord, not just a meal. Finally, if it includes a little bit of fun, so much the better—for us and for our students. I have written *Wordsmith* with those principles in mind.

Features of *Wordsmith: A Guide to Paragraphs and Short Essays*

- A three-part layout allows the freedom to mix and match writing chapters, grammar chapters, and readings.
- A structured yet flexible approach to writing encourages clarity and creativity.
- A direct, conversational, student-friendly approach is used throughout.
- Lighthearted chapter openings promote a positive and playful approach to learning.

Although each of you will use the book in a different way and adapt it to your own students' needs, the following overview of each section may give you some ideas. For more ideas and for sample ten- and fifteen-week syllabi, check the Instructor's Guide in the back of the book.

Part 1   Composition

Part 1, Composition, takes the paragraph as its primary focus but provides an extensive chapter (Chapter 10) on the five-paragraph essay and a chapter (Chapter 11) on the summary report. Include or omit these chapters, as you prefer. The book begins with an overview of the writing process (Chapter 1), followed by a chapter on prewriting (Chapter 2). Planning and drafting, the next two steps in the writing process, are addressed in Chapters 3, 4, and 5. Chapter 6 addresses revising and proofreading.

Chapters 7, 8, and 9 address methods of development. I have sacrificed some flexibility by grouping the methods, so let me explain why. The first reason is philosophical. I believe it is more realistic to group the modes, since they are seldom used in isolation in "real-world" writing. Modes with a similar purpose are grouped together, and the optional "Mixed Methods" assignments at the end of the chapter show how the modes can be used together in a single piece of writing. The second reason for grouping modes is more practical. No matter how hard I try, I can never cover nine rhetorical modes in one term. Grouping them allows me to assign a chapter containing three modes and address only one or two in depth. If all three rhetorical modes chapters are assigned, students are exposed to all nine modes even if they practice only a few.

Special Features of Part 1 Composition

- A student paragraph is presented in all drafts and stages along with a transcript of a student writing group's discussion of the work in progress. (Chapter 1)
- A section "For Right-Brained Writers" gives tips for students who tend to think in terms of "the whole" rather than in terms of a step-by-step process. (Chapter 1)
- The five steps in the writing process are presented in the order in which most writers address them: prewriting, planning, drafting, revising, and proofreading. (Chapters 1–6)
- Methods of development are grouped into three chapters to highlight their relationship to one another and to allow students to read about all methods even if they use only a few. (Chapters 7, 8, and 9)
- Two paragraphs provide models for each method of development. (Chapters 7, 8, and 9)
- Throughout Part 1, topics for paragraph, essay, and journal writing provide a basis for assignments and encourage further practice.
- Students are introduced to academic writing in Chapter 11, "Writing Summary Reports."

Part 2 Grammar

Part 2, Grammar, can be used in a variety of ways: with direct, in-class instruction, in a lab setting, as a supplement, or for independent study. Part 2, Grammar, also works well for instructors who want to address more difficult grammar topics in class while assigning easier material or review material for independent study.

In the grammar chapters, explanations are clear and each topic is taken one skill at a time, with numerous practice exercises for each skill. At the end of each chapter are review exercises in increasing order of difficulty, ending with a paragraph-length editing exercise.

Special Features of Part 2 Grammar

- Explanations are clear, logical, and user-friendly.
- Step-by-step, easy-to-understand presentation is suitable for classroom discussion or independent study.

- An abundance of practice exercises allows instructors to assign as much or as little as they wish, without the need for supplemental exercises.
- Text boxes—Real-World Writing, Building Connections, Grammar Alert, and Punctuation Pointers—add liveliness and interest.
- Practice exercises allow immediate review of each skill, while review exercises at the end of each chapter allow practice on increasing levels of difficulty.

Part 3   Readings

Part 3, Readings, offers essays by professional writers. In any craft, the works of accomplished artisans can inspire the apprentice. These essays model writing at its best: entertaining, challenging, and thought-provoking. Each reading is followed by a comprehension exercise that includes questions about content, questions about the writer's techniques, and related topics for discussion and writing. Diversity in authorship, subject matter, and rhetorical method is emphasized.

Special Features of Part 3   Readings

- High-interest readings provide professional models, reinforce reading skills, and serve as springboards for discussion and assignments.
- Questions help students understand both the content of the essays and the writer's techniques.
- Suggested topics for journal, paragraph, and essay writing connect students' writing to ideas they have explored in the readings.

Instructor Resources

Instructor's Edition. Once again, *Wordsmith* has an Instructor's Edition. The IE contains in-text answers to help instructors best prepare for class and a built-in instructor's guide bound directly into the back. Written by Pam Arlov, the Instructor's Edition provides sample syllabi, teaching tips, and additional chapter-specific assignments. ISBN: 0-13-194987-X

Instructor's Resource Manual. The Instructor's Resource Manual contains additional sample syllabi and two chapter tests for each of the

28 chapters in the text. For each chapter there is one short answer and one multiple-choice test for instructors to choose from. There is also a grammar pretest and posttest. All are ready for easy duplication. ISBN: 0-13-199193-0

The Prentice Hall Writing Skills Test Bank. Written as a source of extra tests for instructors, this printed test bank includes over 50 additional quizzes for instructors to give students. Covering the writing process, patterns of development and grammar, the Prentice Hall Writing Skills Test Bank offers two quizzes for each skill—one multiple choice and one short answer. Designed to be used with any Prentice Hall writing text. ISBN: 0-13-111628-2

Student Resources

College instructors can package any two of the below student resources for their students. To add value to your textbook order by packaging one or two of these items, contact your local Prentice Hall representative or call Faculty Services at 1-800-526-0485.

MyWritingLab (www.mywritinglab.com): Where Better Practice Makes Better Writers. ISBN: 0-13-224426-8

This complete learning system is the first that will truly help students become successful writers—and therefore, successful in college and beyond.

- **A Comprehensive Writing Program:** MyWritingLab includes over 9,000 exercises in grammar, writing process, paragraph development, essay development, and research.

- **A Customized Learning Path:** Based on their text in use, students are automatically provided with a customized learning path that complements their textbook table of contents and extends textbook learning.

- **Diagnostic Testing:** MyWritingLab includes a comprehensive diagnostic test that thoroughly assesses students' skills in grammar. Based on the diagnostic test results, the students' learning path will reflect the areas where they need help the most and those areas that they have mastered.

- *Recall, Apply, and Write Exercises:* The heart of MyWritingLab is this progression of exercises within each module of the learning path. In completing the *Recall, Apply, and Write* exercises, students move from literal (*Recall*) to critical comprehension (*Apply*) to demonstrating concepts to their own writing (*Write*). This recursive learning process, not available in any other online resource, enables students to truly master the skills and concepts they need to be successful writers.

- **Progress Tracker:** All student work in MyWritingLab is captured in the site's Progress Tracker. Students can track their own progress and instructors can track the progress of their entire class in this flexible and easy-to-use tool.

Other resources for students in MyWritingLab: access to an interactive **Study Skills website,** access to **Research Navigator**™, and a complimentary subscription to our **English Tutor Center,** which is staffed by live, college instructors. Instructors who adopt MyWritingLab for their course are eligible to receive a complimentary subscription to **MyDropBox,** a leading online plagiarism detection service.

For more information and to view a demo, go to <u>www.mywritinglab. com</u>!

The New American Webster Handy College Dictionary. ISBN: 0-13-032870-7

The New American Roget's College Thesaurus In Dictionary Form. ISBN: 0-13-045258-0

The Prentice Hall Grammar Workbook, Second Edition. This 20-chapter workbook is a comprehensive source of instruction and practice for students who need additional grammar, punctuation, and mechanics instruction. Each chapter provides ample explanation, examples, and exercise sets. Review Tests reinforce concepts after every five chapters. ISBN: 0-13-194771-0

The Prentice Hall ESL Workbook, Second Edition. This 148-page workbook is divided into seven major units, providing explanations and exercises in the most challenging grammar topics for non-native speakers. With over 80 exercise sets, this guide provides ample instruction and practice in nouns, articles, verbs, modifiers, pronouns, prepositions, and sentence structure. ISBN: 0-13-194759-1

The Prentice Hall Editing Workbook. This 20-chapter workbook is a comprehensive source of instruction and practice for students who need additional grammar, punctuation, and mechanics instruction. Each chapter provides ample explanation, examples, and exercise sets. All exercises are in paragraph form, prompting students to identify errors in context. ISBN: 0-13-189352-1

Applying English to Your Career. This 320-page workbook addresses 25 key writing and grammar topics through workplace examples from 7 specific career fields. Career fields include Allied Health, AutoCAD, Automotive Technology, Criminal Justice, Electronics, Information Technology, and Paralegal Studies. ISBN: 0-13-192115-0

The Prentice Hall THEA Writing Study Guide. Written specifically for students in Texas, this guide prepares students for the writing portion of the

Texas Higher Education Assessment. In addition, it familiarizes the reader with the elements of the test and provides strategies for success. There are exercises for each part of the exam, and then a full-length practice test with answer key so students can gauge their own progress. ISBN: 0-13-041585-5

The Prentice Hall Florida Exit Test Study Guide for Writing. Written specifically for students in Florida, this guide is designed to prepare students for the writing section of the Florida Exit test. It also acquaints readers with the parts of the test and provides strategies for success. ISBN: 0-13-111652-5

The Prentice Hall Writer's Journal. A true writing journal, this spiral bound, 128-page blank book includes access to the Tutor Center. ISBN: 0-13-184900-X

A Prentice Hall Pocket Reader: Patterns. Twenty-seven readings organized by the nine patterns of development. ISBN: 0-13-144352-6

A Prentice Hall Pocket Reader: Themes. Eighteen essays grouped into six themes: People, Places, Animals, Technology, Language, and Advertisements. ISBN: 0-13-144355-0

A Prentice Hall Pocket Reader: Argument. Eighteen argument essays organized by theme: Arguments about People and Places, Arguments about Politics, Policy and Social Change, and Reflecting on Argument as a Process. ISBN: 0-13-189525-7

A Prentice Hall Pocket Reader: Writing Across the Curriculum. Twenty-three essays organized by theme: The Environment, The Media, The Arts, Technology, Gender and Race, Literature and Language. ISBN: 0-13-194210-7

A Prentice Hall Pocket Reader: Literature. Thirty-one selections in Fiction, Poetry, and Drama. ISBN: 0-13-189558-3

Acknowledgments

I could not have written this book without the help, support, and collaboration of a great many people. I owe thanks to all the staff at Prentice Hall, including Craig Campanella, Executive Editor, English, whose talents I admire more with each passing year; Joan Polk, Editorial Assistant, whose photo must appear beside the entry for "indispensable" in some dictionary somewhere; and Kate Mitchell, Marketing Manager, who is new to her position and already a powerhouse. I also thank my wonderful Project Manager, Shelley Creager, of TechBooks; Permissions Specialist, Diane Kraut; and Copy Editor, Sheryl Rose, whose eagle eye and considerable charm cannot be denied, even if she *isn't* a Braves fan.

In addition, I offer profound thanks to Cindy Gierhart of nSight, Inc. and Kerin Foley of nSight, Inc. for their expert assistance.

Also, I thank the reviewers, whose comments helped to shape the most recent edition of the *Wordsmith* series:

Jennifer Annick	El Camino College
Laura Apfelbeck	University of Wisconsin—Manitowol
Bruce Bennett	College of Southern Idaho
Graham Benton	California State University-Maritime
Roy Bond	Richland College
Virginia Brooks	Palm Beach Community College
Joyce Cheney	Santa Monica College
Patricia Colella	Bunker Hill Community College
Janet Cutshall	Sussex Community College
Margaret Fox	Oregon State University
Elizabeth Gilliland	San Jose State University
Betty Hufford	Glendale Community College
Anastasia Lankford	Eastfield College
Deborah Naquin	Northern Virginia Community College
Dianne Pearce	Irvine Valley College
Virginia Smith	Carteret Community College
Darlene Smith-Washington	Pitt Community College
Denton Tulloch	Miami Dade College
Maria Villar-Smith	Miami Dade College

I also thank Larry Fennelly, Chair of the Division of Learning Support at Macon State College, for his support as a department chair and as a friend; Deb Brennan, my declutter buddy and friend, for setting a disgustingly good example; and especially Nick Arlov, my dear husband, for his love and support, and for the sacrifices he made so many years ago so that I could attend college. I will always be grateful.

Pamela Arlov
Macon State College

Preface

To the Student

A Look at the Future

Outside the classroom window, two students pass by, laughing and clutching graduation robes packaged in plastic bags. But inside, the atmosphere is tense as the professor passes out term papers. These papers count as one-third of the course grade.

The professor sweeps by and drops a paper on the desk of Carl, who sits next to you. Carl opens his paper, then rubs his temples as if he has a sudden headache. You shoot him a questioning look. He unfolds his paper, and you see the large red F and the scrawled words. "Your writing skills are unacceptable!" You think of graduation, and realize that Carl will probably not march.

The professor sweeps by again, this time dropping a paper on your desk. Holding your breath, you open it and look at your grade.

No Time Like the Present

Writing is not the only skill you need in college, but it's one of the more important ones. In the classroom and beyond, the people who do well are most often those who think logically, who consider all the possibilities, and who communicate clearly. Writing can help you develop those skills.

In the college classroom, those who stand out also tend to be good writers. They write clearly, they state their ideas completely, and they don't embarrass themselves with poor grammar or misspelled words.

Perhaps, like most people, you feel there's room for improvement in your writing skills. Maybe you feel that your grammar is not up to par, or you're just never sure where to put commas. Or perhaps you go blank when you see an empty page in front of you, waiting to be filled.

But there's good news. Whether your writing needs a little help or a lot, you can be a better writer. Writing is not a talent bestowed by fate, it is a skill, like driving a car, playing a guitar, or designing a Web page on the computer. It is built through your own hard work and improved by practice.

How can you become a better writer? You're in the right place, enrolled in a writing course, and you are holding the right object in your hand—this textbook. But the real key is not the course, the textbook, or even your instructor. The key is you. If you take guitar lessons but never practice, how well will you play? Or think of weight training—if you buy a book about it but never exercise your muscles, how much change will occur? You have a book on writing and a "personal trainer"—your instructor—ready to help you, so exercise your writing muscles as much as possible. If you work at it, you will amaze yourself.

There's no time like the present to shape your future.

How This Textbook Can Help

Wordsmith: A Guide to Paragraphs and Short Essays, Third Edition, is designed to help you on your journey to becoming the writer you want to be, the writer your future demands. Read on to find out how each section can help you develop your writing skills.

Part 1   Composition

Part 1, Composition, gives you an overview of the writing process and provides step-by-step instructions for writing a paragraph, the basic building block for any longer piece of writing. Part 1 also presents nine methods of paragraph development: description, narration, example, definition, classification, process, comparison-contrast, cause-effect, and argument. Finally, it introduces the essay, perhaps the most flexible and adaptable form of writing that you will ever learn. Shrunk down a bit, it can be used to answer a question on an essay test. Expanded a bit, it can be used to write a research paper, a term paper, or even a master's thesis.

Part 2   Grammar

Part 2, Grammar, provides wide coverage of grammar and punctuation. Some of the concepts covered are probably review for you while others are new. The chapters are user-friendly and take a step-by-step approach, so that you can work with them in class or on your own.

Feel free to use the chapters in this section as a reference. If you aren't sure of a comma rule, look it up. If you aren't sure of your subject-verb agreement, check it out in the chapter entitled "Subject-Verb Agreement." You will gain knowledge as you improve your writing.

You can also use the chapters as a way to improve your grammar. If your instructor marks several sentence fragments on your paper, don't wait until the topic is covered in class. Work through the chapter on sentence fragments on your own so that you can correct the problem now.

Part 3   Readings

Part 3, Readings, contains readings from professional writers. You will notice differences between the journalistic writing of these professionals and the academic form you are encouraged to use. Topic sentences are not always placed at the beginning of each paragraph. The language is often informal. But these are merely differences of audience—writing in the academic world is expected to be more formal than journalistic essays written for a general audience. You will see similarities, too. The essays have the same qualities you are encouraged to incorporate in your paragraphs: direction, unity, coherence, and support.

Good readers make good writers. The more you read, the better your writing will become.

Just the Beginning

Writing is hard work. But it is also worthwhile. The more you write, the more skilled you become. Whatever your major, whatever your vocation, writing will serve you well. May this book mark just the beginning of your journey as a writer.

PART 1

Composition

The Writing Process

*Your ideas may seem scattered, disorganized,
jumbled, and downright messy,
but the writing process can
help you funnel them
and shape them
into real*

*W
R
I
T
I
N
G*

Writing is not a single act, but a process composed of several steps. As with most processes—swinging a baseball bat, playing the clarinet, or surfing the Internet—it is sometimes easier to do than to analyze. When people try to analyze how they write, their descriptions of the process are uniquely their own. Yet from a sea of individual accounts, the same steps emerge.

3

One writer, Antonio, describes the process this way:

> Well, first, I need time to think. If I have a while before the paper is due, I never start right away. Some people might call it procrastination, but it works for me. After the ideas have had time to percolate, I sit at the computer and just start writing. I just let my ideas flow, good or bad. If that doesn't work, sometimes I try a more organized approach, jotting down an outline. It's all a part of finding my focus. Then, once I know what I want to say, I just write. I am a slow writer because I try to get it right the first time. But I never do. If I look at it the next day, I see where the holes are—where I've left out details. I'm bad about that. So my second draft is always better than my first. When I'm finished, I check to make sure my commas are in the right place and my grammar is okay. Then I'm ready to turn it in.

The Writing Process

Though everyone approaches writing a little differently, most people follow a process similar to the one just described. The writer in the example above may not be aware of it, but he is following all of the steps in the writing process: prewriting, planning, drafting, revising, and proofreading.

Prewriting

> "... first, I need time to think."

Prewriting covers a range of activity from casually thinking about your topic to going through a prewriting exercise to get your thoughts on paper. You will probably find yourself doing some form of prewriting throughout the writing process. When you are sitting at a traffic light and the perfect example to illustrate your point pops into your head, you are prewriting. When you realize that your paragraph isn't working the way you wanted and you stop to list ideas or figure out another approach, you are returning to the prewriting stage. Prewriting *is* thinking, and the more thought you put into your paper, the stronger it will be.

Planning

"It's all a part of finding my focus."

Careful and thoughtful planning makes a paragraph easier for you to write and easier for your readers to read. Your plan may include a topic sentence, your statement of the main idea. Because it states the main idea, the topic sentence forms the cornerstone of your paragraph. Besides a topic sentence, your planning will probably include an informal outline. An outline can be as simple as a list of the points you will develop in a paragraph. Don't be afraid that planning will waste your time. Careful planning—or lack of it—always shows in the final draft.

Drafting

"I just write."

Sometimes drafting is a quick process, with ideas flowing faster than you can get them down on paper. At other times, the process is slow and difficult. Your thoughts grind to a standstill and you become frustrated, thinking you have nothing to say. If you get stuck during the drafting process, don't quit in frustration. The creative process is still at work. What is happening to you happens to all writers. *Write through* the problem, or, if necessary, return to the planning or prewriting stage.
As you draft your paper, you should not worry about grammar, spelling, or punctuation. Stopping to look up a comma rule will only distract you. Concentrate on ideas and save the proofreading for later.

Revising

"I see where the holes are."

In its Latin roots, the word *revising* means "seeing again." Revising is difficult because it is hard to see your work with the eyes of a reader. Writers often see what they *meant* to say rather than what they really said. Sometimes they take for granted background knowledge that the reader may not have. Because of these difficulties, it helps to put your draft aside for a day or so before trying to revise it. With twenty-four hours between writing and revising, you will see your paper more clearly. It is also helpful to ask someone else to look at your work—a friend, classmate, or relative.

Ask the person to focus on the *content* of your paper rather than on grammar, spelling, or punctuation. Ask which ideas are clear and which ones need more explanation. Ask how well your examples illustrate your points. A reader's comments can help you see your paper in a new light.

One word of advice—if you don't know how to use a computer, learn. Writing multiple drafts is much easier on a computer. Once you learn to write on a computer, the paragraphs, essays, term papers, and reports you will write in college will look much less intimidating.

Proofreading

"I check to make sure my commas are in the right place and my grammar is okay."

Proofreading is the final polish that you put on your paragraph. When you proofread, consider such things as grammar, spelling, and word choice. Replace vague words with specific words. Take out words that are not carrying their weight. Look at connections, making sure ideas flow smoothly from one sentence to the next. Because the stages of the writing process overlap, you have probably done some minor proofreading along the way. Before the final proofreading, set your paragraph aside for a while. Then proofread it once more to give it the luster of a finished piece.

An Important Point

If you go through the writing process expecting the steps to fall in order, like the steps involved in changing the oil in your car, you may think the process is not working. However, writing a paragraph is not a sequential process. It is a repetitive process, more like driving a car than changing its oil.

If you take a two-hundred-mile trip, the steps you follow might be described as "Turn on the ignition. Put the car in drive. Accelerate. Brake. Put the car in park. Turn off the ignition." Yet it is not that simple. During a two-hundred-mile drive, you repeat each step not once but several times, and you may even stop for rest or fuel.

Writing a paragraph works in the same way. You may list the steps as "prewrite, plan, draft, revise, proofread," but it is not that simple. You may change the order of the sentences as you write the first draft or correct a spelling mistake as you revise. Sometimes you repeat a step several times. You may even stop for rest or fuel, just as you do when you drive. Eventually, both processes will get you where you want to go.

EXERCISE 1 THE WRITING PROCESS

Answer the questions below to review your knowledge of the writing process.

1. The five steps in the writing process are _____, _____, _____, _____, and _____.

2. The "thinking step" in the writing process is called _____.

3. The part of the writing process that involves correcting grammar and punctuation is called _____.

4. Major changes would most likely be made during the _____ step in the writing process.

5. True or false? The steps in the writing process often overlap. _____

The Writing Process: Stephanie's Paragraph

The next section follows the development of one writer's paragraph from start to finish. In writing her paragraph, Stephanie went through several forms of prewriting, made two different outlines, conferred with members of her writing group and her instructor, and wrote two rough drafts. (Only the first of the two drafts is shown here because the final draft reflects all of the changes Stephanie made.) Before turning in her final draft, Stephanie also proofread the paragraph once from top to bottom and twice from bottom to top. Then she asked a member of her writing group to look over the final draft for any mistakes she had overlooked.

The steps that Stephanie goes through are steps that you will take as you learn the writing process. You will also share some of her frustrations. But, like Stephanie, you will find that what seems difficult at first is attainable, one step at a time.

Stephanie's Assignment

Stephanie's instructor handed out a list of three paragraph topics. Stephanie chose to write on this one: "Write about a piece of music or art that has a message for you. Don't just describe the piece of music or art; tell your reader how it affected you."

Stephanie's instructor suggested that the students prewrite, then make an outline. Earlier, the class had been divided into writing groups of four or five people who would help one another during the term. The instructor suggested that the writing groups meet to discuss each student's outline. Then, students would write a rough draft to bring to individual writing conferences with the instructor.

Stephanie's Prewriting

In class, Stephanie did a form of prewriting called *freewriting*. (For more information on freewriting and other forms of prewriting, see Chapter 2.) In this prewriting, Stephanie did not worry about grammar or spelling, but focused on gathering ideas. Stephanie's prewriting is reproduced here without correction.

> I remember the day my art class went to an exhibit at the museum and I saw a piece of art — I don't know what to call it. Not a painting or a drawing, but something the artist had put together. Built. I was trailing behind the class and something just pulled me over into the corner where it was. It was just me and that piece of art, and when I lifted the curtain — Wow! I was so knocked out. I remember my art teacher used to talk about what art meant, and I never understood until that day. I felt all sorts of emotion. I think I'll go over to the Tubman this weekend and see if it's still there.

Later, Stephanie visited the museum and took the following notes:

> ### "Beauty Standard" by Ce Scott
>
> Black frame, masks placed at top & bottom. Each side has female figure tied at ankles, wrist, and eyes with golden cord. They have bodies like models — thin & beautiful. Masks are just blank — no real features. Frame has tiny words repeated over and over "dark brown eyes big full lips flat wide nose." Velvet curtain — very mysterious hangs there. Golden tassels hang down. "Mirror" embroidered on. Card says "Lift the curtain to see the image by which each of us should be judged."

Stephanie's Rough Draft

Ce Scott's artwork <u>Beauty Standard</u> is a piece of art with a message. It hangs in the Tubman African American Museum. It has a black frame decorated with female figures bound at the wrists, ankles, and eyes with golden cord. They have bodies like models, thin and beautiful. At the center of the frame is a black velvet curtain embroidered with the word "Mirror." On the frame, in small writing are the words "dark brown eyes big full lips flat wide nose." A card beside the work invites the viewer to lift the cloth and see "the image by which each of us should be judged." Underneath is a mirror—not the one held up by society, but one that reflects the image of whoever looked into it. The message is that the only beauty standard you need to meet is your own.

Stephanie's Writing Group Meets

Next, Stephanie met with her writing group. A transcript of the portion of the session dealing with Stephanie's outline appears below.

Transcript: Writing Group Session,
Monday, September 7

Eddie: Okay, who's the first victim? Tran?

Tran: I don't want to go first. Stephanie?

Stephanie: I may as well. I think I need major help. (Stephanie passes out copies of her prewriting and rough draft, and the group reads silently.)

Tran: I like it. You have good grammar and spelling.

Stephanie: You're just saying that because I got you off the hook. You didn't have to go first. (Laughter.)

Kelly: I like it, too. But your prewriting is really different from the rough draft.

Stephanie: Yeah, the prewriting doesn't have much detail. I had to go back to the museum to look at the piece again because I had forgotten a lot.

Eddie: Yes, but I like the prewriting. I can tell you were really excited about the painting.

Stephanie: It's not a painting. I'm not sure what you'd call it.

Eddie: Whatever. But in the prewriting, I can tell it really had an effect on you. In the rough draft, the excitement disappears. It's just a description.

Kelly: Eddie is right. I mean, it's a good description, but it needs more of you in it.

Stephanie: Yeah, I see what you mean.

Tran: I chose the same topic, except I'm doing my paragraph on music. Anyway, I remember that the assignment said to tell how the music or art affected you.

Stephanie: That's right! I do need to put more of my reaction in there somehow. But won't that make it too long?

Kelly: Well, you heard what Dr. Pettis said. Plenty of support.

Stephanie: Okay, guys. Thanks. You've been a big help. Anything else?

Tran: Yeah. Will you help me with my grammar? (Laughter.)

Stephanie's Final Draft

Stephanie wrote a second rough draft. Then, she met with her instructor for a conference before writing her final draft. Stephanie's final draft appears below.

Beauty Standard

I always thought of art as something to hang on a wall, never as something that had a message for me. Then last fall, at the Tubman African American Museum, I saw a piece of art called <u>Beauty Standard</u> by Ce Scott. It had a black frame decorated with female figures bound at the wrists, ankles, and eyes with golden cord. At the center of the frame hung a black velvet curtain embroidered with the word "Mirror." A card beside the work invited the viewer to lift the cloth and see "the image by which each of us should be judged." On the frame, in small writing were the words "dark brown eyes big full lips flat wide nose." The words made me think of the sixties slogan, "Black is beautiful." It was a statement of pride and at the same time a demand to be included. At the time, society's beauty standard was a white one. And even though ideas of beauty now include different races, so many people are still left out—the old, those who are overweight, and even those who are just average. Suddenly, I felt angry and a little afraid to lift the velvet curtain. I looked at the bound female figures and understood that society binds me, too. Hesitantly, I lifted the curtain. My own face, skeptical and a bit defiant, looked back at me. It <u>was</u> a mirror—not the one held up by society, but one that reflected the image of whoever looked into it. As clearly as if she were in the room, the artist was telling me, "The only beauty standard you need to meet is your own."

Stephanie's Approach to Writing—and Yours

Stephanie's final draft is the product of many hours' thought and work, and it is at least partly a result of her willingness to listen to the advice and comments of others.

Writing is a process of trial and error, and sometimes it feels like mostly error. Even experienced writers often find writing difficult, often wonder if they have anything worthwhile to say or the ability to say it. If you fear writing, even if you dislike it, you are not alone. But writing is a skill that improves with practice, and if you give it serious effort, you will amaze yourself. The following list, "Five Quick Takes on Writing," may help you put the task of writing in perspective.

---

* Five Quick Takes on Writing

1. **Take it a step at a time.** Writing is often a slow process, and it always requires thought.
2. **Take it seriously.** The ability to write clearly and well will benefit you academically, professionally, and personally throughout your life.
3. **Take it easy.** Don't expect yourself to be perfect.
4. **Take it to the limit.** Stretch the limits of your imagination. Refuse to limit yourself by labeling yourself a poor writer.
5. **Take it with you.** Writing is a vital part of the real world. Make it a part of your life.

GROUP EXERCISE 1   The Ideal Conditions for Writing

In a group of three or four, discuss the ideal conditions for writing. Think about questions such as these: What tools do you enjoy working with? Do you write best with music or in absolute silence? Do you like having others around or do you prefer to be alone? Do you need coffee or snacks when you write? Do you need room to pace or do you think best seated in front of a desk or computer? After each group member has contributed, see what differences and similarities exist among members of your group. Have a spokesperson report your group's findings to the rest of the class.

Writing for Right-Brained Writers

This section is for those of you who rebel at the idea of a step-by-step approach like the one described in this chapter and outlined in the writing assignment at the chapter's end. Although prewriting, planning, drafting, revising, and proofreading are identifiable steps in the writing process, there's no law that says everyone has to approach them in exactly the same way.

For some people, a step-by-step approach does not come naturally. These people have a thinking style that is most often called "right-brained" or "holistic." The human brain is divided into two halves, or hemispheres, and most people are wired to rely heavily on the left hemisphere—the half responsible for logical, sequential, step-by-step thinking. Some people, however, rely more heavily on the right half of the brain, the part responsible for seeing the whole, for thinking in images, and for flashes of insight.

The following questions may help you decide if you are a right-brained thinker.

1. If you were asked to analyze how you write, would your answer be, "I don't know. I just do it"?
2. When you are required to turn in an outline, do you usually complete it *after* you have written the paper?
3. If you were asked to describe your usual prewriting technique, would you say, "I never prewrite"?
4. Do you often arrive at the right answer to math problems without following the steps?
5. Do you have a hard time getting detail into your writing?
6. Are you a "big-picture person" rather than a "detail person"?

If you answered "yes" to three or more of the questions above, you may have been seen as a rebel because you don't always follow a step-by-step, conventional approach to your work. But the chances are that whatever other characteristics you possess, you are also a right-brained writer.

Right-brained people are often intuitive, seeing the big picture before others do. They have a strong creative streak. They sometimes grasp ideas easily without knowing why or understanding how. But unlike their persistent, list-making, left-brained brothers and sisters, right-brained people often have trouble with the details. Planning isn't in their natures, and they tend not to have systems or specific steps to rely on. Whatever the task is, they "just do it."

If you are right-brained, does that mean that the methods in this text won't work for you? No. They *will* work. But you may have to work at them a bit harder. Give them a chance. Don't count them out until you have had enough experience with them to determine whether they work for you or not.

There are other strategies you can use, too. Unlike more conventional methods, the following tips were crafted with you in mind. These ideas may give you the extra boost you need to harness your creativity and let your right-brained way of thinking work for you, not against you. If your thinking style is left-brained, read on anyway. There may be something here that you can use along with the logical, step-by-step approach that works so well for you.

Tips for Right-Brained Writers

Find your most creative time and use it for writing. Some people find that they are at their best in the mornings. Others find that their creative juices begin to flow around 9:00 or 10:00 P.M. Writing will be easier if you schedule it during your natural period of creativity.

Use your rough draft as your prewriting. Since you think in terms of the whole, you may find it easier to do a rough draft than to prewrite. Consider your rough draft a form of prewriting, to be extensively revised before you turn it in.

Give your brain an assignment. When you have writing to do, let your right brain work on it while you are doing other things. At the beginning of the day, for instance, look over the assignment for a few minutes. Then come back to it in the evening and reap the benefits of having worked on the topic subconsciously. Or think about your topic before you go to sleep at night, then write in the morning. This technique can work not only in prewriting but also in revising.

Realize that doing the grunt work is a necessary evil. Right-brained people are less likely to put in the time it takes to master the basics because doing so may be tedious and boring to them. They are also less likely to plan. But even the most brilliantly creative people need self-discipline. It's a hard lesson to learn, but mastering the basics is essential to creative work. Singers spend endless time on breath control and scales. Artists learn anatomy and basic drawing. It is those efforts that set them free to do their best work. The payoff in mastering the basics is that once you learn them, you can forget about them. They will be second nature. The same goes for planning. Once you have made a plan, you are free to do the creative work. Doing the grunt work now always pays off in more freedom later.

Make a commitment to writing. Many professional writers are right-brained and face the same resistance that you do. Invariably, they say that the only way they can maintain the extended effort it takes to write books, plays, or novels is to have a routine and to write every day.

WRITING ASSIGNMENT 1   Writing and You

Write a paragraph describing your attitudes toward writing. Use the following steps.

Step 1: Prewrite. Jot down a few of the words that come to mind when you think of writing. Think of any significant experiences you have had that have shaped your attitude toward writing. Consider your writing habits. Are you organized? Do you procrastinate?

Step 2: Plan. Look over your prewriting. Try to sum up your attitude toward writing in a single word or phrase, and then construct an opening sentence for your paragraph using that word or phrase. Use one of the sentences below, filling in the blank with your word or phrase, or construct your own sentence.

My attitude toward writing is _____

_____

When I think about writing, I feel _____

_____

My feelings about writing have always been _____

_____

Once you have constructed an opening sentence, decide how to organize your paragraph. A couple of possibilities are listed below.

1. Take a historical approach, describing the influences that have shaped your writing. Use chronological (time) order.
2. Try a step-by-step approach, describing what you do and how you feel as you go through a writing assignment.

Complete the planning stage by making an outline that briefly lists the points you plan to make in support of your opening sentence.

Step 3: Draft. Write out a rough draft of your paragraph. Focus on expressing your ideas rather than on grammar and punctuation.

Step 4: Revise. Read over your rough draft. Have you left out anything important? Is each idea clearly expressed? Does the paragraph flow smoothly? Is the sequence of ideas logical and effective? If possible, ask a classmate to look over your rough draft with the same questions in mind. Then revise your paragraph, incorporating any necessary changes.

Step 5: Proofread. Check your paragraph for mistakes in spelling, grammar, or punctuation. Look at each sentence individually. Then proofread once more. You have now completed all the steps in the writing process.

CHAPTER 2

Preparing to Write

Just say

NO

to

~~Arachnophobia~~

WRITER'S BLOCK!

Many people suffer from arachnophobia—fear of spiders. Some people also develop a fear called "writer's block" when they are confronted with a blank sheet of paper or a blank computer screen. They fear that they will not be able to think of anything to say, or that if they do find something to say, it will be wrong. Writer's block happens to almost everyone at one time or another. It is not an indication of poor writing ability. In fact, writers who get writer's block are usually those who care about how they present themselves.

One of the best defenses against this kind of fear is prewriting. Prewriting is a playful "safety zone" that you can enter without fear. In prewriting, your purpose is to generate ideas, not to judge them, so you can't go wrong. Even if you don't have writer's block, prewriting can give your writing a jump-start.

Prewriting

Prewriting is the first step in the writing process. It is the act of sorting out your thoughts on a topic and finding out what you have to say about it. Depending on the assignment you are given, prewriting may also include narrowing your topic to a manageable size. Prewriting begins the moment you receive an assignment. Quietly, in the background, part of your mind begins to gather information. However, it usually takes a bit of effort to bring that information to the surface. The prewriting methods in this chapter can jump-start the writing process by helping you collect your thoughts on a topic and get them on paper.

Prewriting Methods

The aim of all prewriting methods is the same: to help you get ideas on paper. At this point in the writing process, it is not the quality of ideas that counts, but the quantity.

When you are ready to prewrite, sit at the computer or in a comfortable spot with pen and paper. Relax your mind and body, and remind yourself that prewriting is a playful exercise of the imagination and that it is okay to write down anything that comes to mind. As for the part of your mind that automatically jumps in to criticize what you think and say, give it some time off. Your purpose in prewriting is to put down every thought on your topic, no matter how ridiculous it seems. Later, you can discard what is not usable.

Some of the methods may feel awkward at first. But try them all. One will be right for you.

Brainstorming

Brainstorming, a listing technique, is one of the easiest prewriting techniques. To brainstorm, take a few minutes to list whatever comes to mind on your topic. Your purpose is not to censor or come up with the "right" items for your list, but to generate ideas.

Example

Here's how one writer, James, approached a brainstorming exercise on the topic "Describe a favorite holiday memory."

> Last 4th of July — family reunion
> Lake Sinclair
> plenty of food
> Aunt Mil's fried chicken
> baked beans
> over 100 relatives
> Mo's girlfriend!
> saw Grandaddy Bennett for the last time
> paper checkered tablecloths
> ants
> kids running and screaming
> fireworks over lake — color and noise
> Jim stretched out in back seat asleep on the way home

When James looked at his prewriting, he was not sure he could use it all, but he knew he had captured some of the vivid images and important memories from his Fourth of July family reunion.

EXERCISE 1   BRAINSTORMING

Brainstorm on one of the following topics; then see if you have an idea for a possible paragraph.

1. the importance of money
2. a holiday memory
3. an unexpected kindness
4. being an outsider
5. a bad habit

Freewriting

Freewriting is nonstop writing on a topic for a set time. The point of freewriting is that your flow of words never ceases; your pen never stops moving. If you have nothing to say, repeat your last thought again and again until a new thought replaces it. Do not worry about spelling, about clarity, or about whether your thoughts are logically connected. Just write.

Example

Emily did the following freewriting when her instructor asked the class to write on the topic "Discuss one of your pet peeves and why it annoys you."

> Let's see. Right now I am peeved about having to write about a pet peeve. Ha, ha! Seriously, I am an easygoing person and do not get too upset over anything. I don't like telephone salespeople. I don't like loud commercials. I don't like my ex-boyfriend. I don't like people who are late. I don't like it when a class or meeting is held up because some people are late. Yesterday, in Freshman Orientation, we had a quiz and when it was time for class to start, the instructor said, "We'll just wait a minute or two in case someone else comes in." Excuse ME, but I made it to class on time. Why should I wait for someone who is late? I can think of plenty of other examples. Is my ten minutes up yet? No. The minister at our church always starts services on time and it doesn't matter how many people come in late but when my cousin got married the ceremony was supposed to be at 7 PM and it did not start until 7:30. People just keep coming in, right up until about 7:25. I think spending a lot of money on a wedding is a waste — they should just buy furniture or something.

EXERCISE 2 FREEWRITING

Freewrite on one of the following topics; then see if you have a focus for a possible paragraph.

1. What is your pet peeve?
2. What is your favorite time of day?
3. Is honesty always the best policy?
4. What is your biggest complaint about college professors?
5. What can you tell about a person from the way he or she dresses?

Invisible Writing: A Computer Technique

Invisible writing is a freewriting technique especially for writing on a computer. Turn on your computer, and once you have a blank screen in front of you, type the words "Invisible Writing" at the top of the page. Then turn your monitor off or adjust the contrast button at the bottom of your screen until the words are no longer visible and your screen is completely dark.

Freewrite for five to ten minutes. It is especially important not to worry about spelling errors. With this method, you can hardly avoid them. At first, you may feel strange, even anxious, pouring your words into the dark computer screen. Soon, though, your fingers and your thoughts will fly.

EXERCISE 3   INVISIBLE WRITING

Prewrite by applying invisible writing to one of the following topics.

1. taking chances
2. superstitions
3. television or radio commercials
4. driving habits
5. ending a friendship

Clustering

Clustering is a technique designed to boost your creativity by stimulating both hemispheres of the brain. The left hemisphere, or "left brain," is used in logical tasks that move in 1-2-3 order. When you count to ten, write a sentence, or make an outline, you use your left brain. Your right brain, on the other hand, specializes in tasks involving visual images and intuition. Since clustering involves both listing (a left-brain task) and drawing (a right-brain task), it allows you to tap both your logical side and your creative side.

To cluster, begin with a circled word—your topic. From there, map out associations. Some people branch ideas from the central word like quills on a porcupine. Others group ideas when they cluster, with smaller clusters branching out from larger ones. When this type of cluster is finished, it resembles a biology textbook's diagram of a molecule.

What your diagram looks like does not matter. In clustering, what matters is that you get your thoughts on paper using both images and words.

Look at the following examples of clustering.

Example

Brandon did his "porcupine" cluster on the topic "your chosen career."

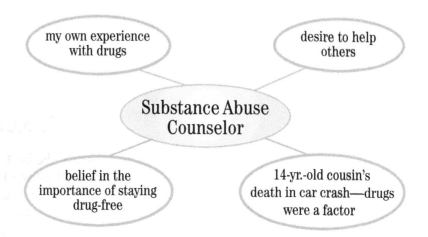

Example

Here is Kara's "molecule" cluster on the topic "Internet shopping."

EXERCISE 4 CLUSTERING

Draw a cluster diagram using one of the following topics.

1. credit cards
2. your favorite sport
3. your best or worst date
4. advantages or disadvantages of public transportation
5. your eating habits

Narrowing Your Topic: The Topic-Subtopic Method

If you are given a specific topic such as "Discuss the best way to make a positive impression on your instructor during the first week of class," your prewriting task is relatively easy. You can just begin thinking about the ways to make a good impression in class. In other words, you can begin thinking about supporting your paragraph. However, if you are given a general assignment such as "Write about something related to college," or "Write a paragraph about money," or even "Write a paragraph about a topic of your own choosing," then your task is a much larger one. Entire books have been written about college, and the books and magazines about money take up considerable shelf space in any bookstore. Therefore, you need to narrow and focus the topic so that it is manageable in a single paragraph.

For some writers, narrowing a topic becomes a natural part of the prewriting process. Others prefer to narrow their topics in a separate step or series of steps.

One way to narrow a topic is with a simple method called the topic-subtopic method.

Steps in the Topic-Subtopic Method

Step 1: Write down the topic.

Step 2: List possible subtopics.

Step 3: Look over the list of subtopics and pick the one you are most interested in. This subtopic now becomes your topic.

Step 4: Repeat the process until you have narrowed your topic to an appropriate size for a paragraph.

In the following example, the writer has taken a general topic, "animals," through three narrowings. In the first narrowing, she has made a list of subtopics. From that list, she has chosen the subtopic "pets." From there, she will repeat the process until she has narrowed the topic to the right size for the paragraph she wants to write.

General topic	Subtopics	
animals	wild animals	
	endangered species	
	pets	← (new topic)
	farm animals	
	animals raised for food	
	working animals (seeing-eye dogs, police dogs)	

"Pets" is narrower than "animals," but it is still a very broad topic. The writer does a second narrowing, this time with "pets" as the general topic.

General topic	Subtopics	
pets	dogs	← (new topic)
	cats	
	how to bathe a pet	
	pampered pets	
	mistreated pets	
	exotic pets (snakes, hedgehogs, etc.)	

Once the writer has decided on the topic "dogs," she decides to do a third narrowing of the topic:

Topic	Subtopics	
dogs	training	← (new topic)
	breeds	
	working dogs (drug-sniffing dogs, assistance dogs for blind)	
	feeding	

The writer decides to take the subtopic "training" and make it the subject of a paragraph. She is through with the narrowing process. Now, to flesh out the details of her paragraph, she does a brainstorming exercise. Her brainstorming follows.

Basic Training for Dogs

based on kindness and reward

no yelling or hitting

use food rewards

one trick or skill at a time

the basics — "down," "sit," "stay"

persistence and repetition

be consistent — don't say "down" one time and "get down" the next

---

EXERCISE 5   NARROWING A TOPIC

Take one of the following broad topics and narrow it to paragraph size, following the topic-subtopic method shown above. Take your topic through as many narrowings as are needed to bring it down to paragraph size.

1. the environment
2. alcohol
3. education
4. money
5. transportation

Outlining

Outlining is often the last step in the prewriting process. Once you have used one of the other prewriting methods, making an outline will take you one step further in the writing process. Forget about the formal outline with its Roman numerals, ABCs, and 123s. A short paragraph calls for a short outline. Your outline may be just a few words jotted on a page, or it may include a topic sentence and a brief listing of support. Below is Emily's outline of her paragraph describing her pet peeve.

Topic Sentence: I am an easygoing person, but it annoys me when a meeting, class, or other event does not begin on time because some people are late.

Freshman orientation class—quiz delayed because of people who were late.

Meeting with friends in restaurant—waited fifteen minutes to order until Kylie came.

Cousin's wedding—delayed a half hour because of late arrivals.

Summary sentence: Classes, meetings, and other gatherings should not be arranged for the convenience of latecomers, but for those who care enough to arrive on time.

EXERCISE 6   OUTLINING

Take one of the topics on which you have done a practice prewriting and make an outline for a paragraph.

Journal Writing

Journals are "daily writings"—the word *journal* comes from *jour,* the French word for *day.* Journals are usually composed of informal writings on a variety of subjects. Journal writing allows you to experiment with the techniques you are learning in your writing class. In a journal, the only form of writing you should avoid is "diary mode." An "I-got-up-I-fed-the-dog-I-went-to-school" format makes for dull writing and even duller reading. Write about issues that matter to you. Tell your dreams. Describe your grandfather's tool shed. Work toward detailed writing that follows a logical pattern.

Whether or not you receive credit for it in class, make journal writing a habit. Practice is the only thing that is guaranteed to make you a better writer. Courses and texts are of limited value without time spent alone with a word processor or pen and paper. If you think, "It won't matter. I'll never be a good writer," ask yourself this: How good a driver would you be if the only driving you had done was in a driver education course? You can be a better writer. Journal writing will start you on your way.

Journal Topics

1. What are some reasons for keeping a journal or diary?
2. If you had one day of your life to live over, which one would it be?
3. If you were cleaning out your mental closet, what would you most want to throw away?
4. Who is your role model? Why?
5. Is it better to have an assertive, in-your-face personality or to be laid-back and slow to show anger?
6. Other than food, water, and sleep, what *must* you have every day? Why?
7. If every job or career paid the exact same salary, what kind of work would you choose?
8. Discuss one item that fits this description: "It plugs into the wall, and I couldn't live without it."

9. If people had fur, what changes would take place in society?

10. If you had to live without television, how would you spend your extra time?

11. If you could have one talent that you do not now possess, what would it be? Singing.

12. If you could bring one fictional character to life (for whatever reason—to be your friend, to benefit humanity, or to solve a problem), who would it be?

13. If you could travel to any place in the world, where would you go?

14. Describe one effective method you use to reduce stress.

15. Describe the one place that, for you, is "heaven on earth."

16. What can you tell about people from the way they carry themselves—that is, the way they stand, sit, or move?

17. Is it better to have a wide circle of friends or just a few close friends?

18. Describe your general style of dealing with problems. Do you meet problems head-on, or do you hide your head in the sand and hope they will go away? Do you enlist the help of others, or try to solve your problems alone? Illustrate your journal entry with at least one example.

19. Which is more important, independence or security?

20. By the end of the twenty-first century, what change, development, or discovery would you most like to see? Why?

THE PROGRESSIVE WRITING ASSIGNMENT

How It Works

Begin by choosing one of the topics that follow; it will serve as the basis your first paragraph. In this chapter, you will complete prewriting for the paragraph. Throughout the next four chapters, each Progressive Writing Assignment will take you a step further toward a paragraph. By the time you have finished the final assignment, you will have completed all the steps in the writing process and will have a complete paragraph.

Progressive Writing Assignment: Prewriting

In this chapter, your Progressive Writing Assignment is a prewriting assignment. Choose one of the topics below—one you would like to write a paragraph about—and follow the instructions.

TIPS FOR PREWRITING

Prewrite on the topic, using one or several of the methods outlined in this chapter. As you prewrite, consider the different types of advice you have been offered: bad advice, good advice, advice that got you in trouble, or advice that cost you money. Consider the different people who have offered you advice. Taking a broad approach allows you to consider many different possibilities.

WHAT NOW?

After you have completed your prewriting, you should have more material than you will be able to use. To prepare for the next step in the Progressive Writing Assignment, choose the piece of advice that you want to focus on in your paragraph.

TIPS FOR PREWRITING

Prewrite on the topic, using one or several of the methods outlined in this chapter. As you prewrite, consider all the factors that surround your decision. What are they? Some people are motivated to attend college by the expectations of family or friends. Some are trying to put the past behind them, while others are trying to fulfill lifelong ambitions. Some people arrive certain of success; others fear failure. Consider everything surrounding your decision to attend college: your reasons, your expectations, the reaction of friends and family, and your own hopes and fears.

WHAT NOW?

After you have completed your prewriting, you should have more material than you will be able to use. To prepare for the next step in the Progressive Writing Assignment, decide which ideas you want to focus on.

TIPS FOR PREWRITING

Prewrite on the topic, using one or several of the methods outlined in this chapter. Consider that fears sometimes have a strong basis in reality: A person whose parents and grandparents died young may have a fear of not living long enough to see her children grow up. Just as often, though, fears seem irrational. A person with a steady job and a comfortable home may fear being homeless. Write down your fears, rational and irrational, and try to decide what lies behind them. Consider also how you deal with your fears. Do you have a specific method for coping with them, or do you just live with them?

WHAT NOW?

After you have completed your prewriting, you should have more material than you will be able to use. To prepare for the next step in the Progressive Writing Assignment, decide which ideas you want to focus on in your paragraph.

Topic 4: Discuss types of stress experienced by college students.

TIPS FOR PREWRITING

Prewrite on the topic, using one or several of the methods outlined in this chapter. Everyone experiences stress from many sources, such as overwork, family problems, or even boredom. However, there are some kinds of stress that may be specifically associated with college. In this paragraph, you will write about some of the types of stress experienced by college students. Thinking about your own stress is a good starting point, but imagine the kinds of stress experienced by students who may not be like you: older students, working students, students who have children. What kinds of stress are common to all college students, and which are particular to certain groups?

WHAT NOW?

After you have completed your prewriting, you should have more material than you will be able to use. To prepare for the next step in the Progressive Writing Assignment, decide which types of stress you want to focus on in your paragraph.

CHAPTER 3

Writing Paragraphs:
Topic Sentences

A Silly Riddle

How is a topic sentence like a compass?
   a. It always points to magnetic north.
   b. It's useful on a hiking expedition.
   *c. It shows exactly where you are
      headed.*

The riddle above may be silly, but the comparison it makes is valid.
A topic sentence *is* like a compass. It shows your reader exactly where
your paragraph is headed, and it also helps to keep you on track as you
write your paragraph. It gives **direction** to your paragraph.

   Direction is one of four characteristics of effective writing that you
will read about in this text and learn to develop in your own writing.

29

Before exploring the topic sentence further, look at the four characteristics of effective writing introduced below.

Characteristics of an Effective Paragraph

1. **Direction** means that the paragraph has a strong topic sentence that states the main idea and sets the course that the paragraph will follow.
2. **Unity** means that the paragraph makes one main point and sticks to that point.
3. **Coherence** means that the ideas in the paragraph are logically connected and easy to follow.
4. **Support** means that the paragraph contains specific and detailed discussion of the idea stated in the topic sentence.

Direction: Shaping the Topic Sentence of a Paragraph

A topic sentence provides direction by stating the main idea of a paragraph and answering the reader's unspoken question, "What is your point?"

Functions of a Topic Sentence

A topic sentence does two things. First of all, it tells the *general topic* of the paragraph. Second, it makes a *specific point about the topic.*

Example

✔ Carrying a homemade lunch instead of eating out has had unexpected benefits.

          topic   *specific point about the topic*

✔ Knowing how to research using a computer is an essential skill in college.

        topic   *specific point about the topic*

✔ There are many creative ways to hide thinning hair.

      specific point   *topic*

EXERCISE 1   ANALYZING TOPIC SENTENCES

In each of the topic sentences below, underline the topic and double-underline the specific point the writer is making about the topic.

1. <u>Praise</u> can be a powerful motivator.
2. <u>Saying "no" is a skill</u> that my brother Brian has never developed.
3. <u>Talk shows on television</u> are often offensive.
4. <u>My willpower</u> unravels at the sight of chocolate.
5. <u>Some of my coworkers</u> have little patience with machines.
6. <u>Stromboli's Italian Grill</u> is my favorite restaurant.
7. A successful letter of <u>complaint</u> has three essential elements.
8. <u>My brother's fondness for loud music</u> irritates the rest of the family.
9. <u>The woman who lives next door</u> is incurably nosy.
10. <u>Poor organization</u> can make studying difficult.

EXERCISE 2   ANALYZING TOPIC SENTENCES

In each of the topic sentences below, underline the topic and double-underline the specific point the writer is making about the topic.

1. <u>Gossip</u> can be hurtful.
2. <u>Listening</u> is difficult for some people.
3. <u>Watching television</u> is often a waste of time.
4. <u>Finding time to exercise</u> is difficult for me.
5. <u>Peer pressure</u> can weaken even the strongest will.
6. <u>My experience working at the Burger Basket</u> convinced me to avoid fast-food places.
7. <u>Trying to find information on the Internet</u> can be frustrating.
8. During the past year, <u>my cola habit</u> has gotten out of hand.
9. <u>Gas prices</u> vary in different parts of town.
10. <u>My vacation</u> will give me a chance to do some work around the house.

EXERCISE 3   COMPLETING TOPIC SENTENCES

Complete the topic sentences below. Then underline the topic once and double-underline the point about the topic.

1. Taking an aerobics class __is important__ (a good) healthy desicion.
2. __Air Conditioning__ is something no home should be without.
3. In the morning, __a warm coffee__ helps me prepare to face the day.
4. __The My red couch__ is my favorite piece of furniture.
5. To avoid last-minute cramming for tests, __I should study every day for 30 m.__

EXERCISE 4 WRITING TOPIC SENTENCES

Write five topic sentences. Underline the topic once. Then double-underline your point about the topic.

1. _Preparing for a triathlon, is good for me_

2. _Eating healthy is essential._

3. _One of my favorite thing to do is going shopping._

4. _____

5. _____

Writing Topic Sentences That Fit

A topic sentence also provides direction by precisely outlining the territory the paragraph will cover. A topic sentence that is *too broad* outlines more territory than a paragraph can comfortably cover. A topic sentence that is *too narrow* draws the boundaries of the paragraph uncomfortably small, usually by focusing on some fact that would make a good supporting detail but that does not lend itself to development.

Look at the following sample topic sentences on the subject "computers."

✗ Computers have changed modern society.

This topic sentence is too broad. It promises more than one paragraph can deliver. Think of all the ways computers have changed modern life: they have changed the way stores keep track of inventories, the way banks work, and the way groceries are checked out. They have created new jobs and made others obsolete. They have altered our ideas about what skills are essential and have raised new concerns about privacy and access to information. The topic "how computers have changed society" could easily be the subject of a book.

✗ My computer has a CD drive.

This topic is too narrow. It tells the reader that the writer will discuss a specific computer, her own, and that the focus will be the computer's CD drive. While the sentence might work as a supporting point in a paragraph, it is too narrow to be a topic sentence. A topic sentence that is too narrow is a dead-end statement, a fact that does not invite exploration. A good topic sentence opens a door to discussion.

✔   A computer can link a person who is disabled or homebound to the outside world.

This topic sentence is neither too broad nor too narrow. Within this paragraph, the writer can discuss how a computer helps a disabled person to bank or shop online. She can tell how a computer links a homebound person to people and information sources around the world. The sentence opens a door to an area of discussion and exploration that is neither too narrow nor too broad to develop in one paragraph.

EXERCISE 5 ANALYZING TOPIC SENTENCES

Each set of sentences below contains one topic sentence that is too broad, one that is too narrow, and one that would make a good topic sentence for a paragraph. In the blank to the left of each sentence, label it TB (too broad), TN (too narrow), or TS (topic sentence).

Set 1

_TB_ a.   The functions of a bank are many and varied.

_TS_ b.   Fees that banks charge seem to target lower-income customers.

_TN_ c.   My checking account is with First National Bank.

Set 2

_TB_ a.   My brother Simon often stays awake until 2:00 or 3:00 A.M.

_TN_ b.   My brother Simon is a night owl.

_TS_ c.   My brother Simon has different levels of energy at different times of the day, week, month, and year.

Set 3

_____ a.   Ordering merchandise by mail has several advantages.

_____ b.   I received a Lands' End catalog in today's mail.

_____ c.   Mail-order firms have been a vital part of American business for many decades.

Set 4

_____ **a.** Coping with my father's illness has been difficult for my family.

_____ **b.** Life has its ups and downs.

_____ **c.** Last year, my father had major surgery.

Set 5

_____ **a.** The commercials for Mercedes project a classy image.

_____ **b.** CNN and MSNBC are news channels.

_____ **c.** Television exerts a positive influence on American society.

EXERCISE 6   ANALYZING TOPIC SENTENCES

Each set of sentences below contains one topic sentence that is too broad, one that is too narrow, and one that would make a good topic sentence for a paragraph. In the blank to the left of each sentence, label it TB (too broad), TN (too narrow), or TS (topic sentence).

Set 1

_____ **a.** My cat has a marking on her back that looks like the number three.

_____ **b.** Training a dog to sit on command is a simple process.

_____ **c.** Pets are wonderful.

Set 2

_____ **a.** Housing costs vary widely across the United States.

_____ **b.** A one-bedroom apartment in the Aspen Forest apartment complex costs $570 per month.

_____ **c.** A first-time homebuyer should consider several factors when searching for a home.

Set 3

_____ **a.** Gasoline stations have been a part of the American landscape for almost a century.

_____ **b.** In my grandfather's time, gasoline cost fifty cents per gallon.

_____ **c.** The gasoline station of my grandfather's time offered services that are unheard of today.

Set 4

_____ **a.** Requiring fingerprints of citizens who obtain drivers' licenses is a bad idea.

_____ **b.** Many laws are unjust and should be repealed.

_____ **c.** In some states, a driver's license must bear the driver's fingerprint.

Set 5

_____ **a.** Fish are fascinating creatures.

_____ **b.** My sister's angelfish is named Gabriel.

_____ **c.** An aquarium is like a small entertainment center for the home.

GROUP EXERCISE 1   Writing a Topic Sentence
Confident? Go solo!

Have you had enough test *taking*? Form a test *making* team with two or three of your classmates and write an exercise similar to the one above. Choose three to five of the topics below, and for each topic, write a topic sentence that is too broad, one that is too narrow, and one that would fit a paragraph. Then trade tests with another group and see how your group's performance—as test makers and as test takers—stacks up to theirs.

Topics

1.	books	6.	furniture
2.	garbage	7.	nature
3.	beverages	8.	people
4.	music	9.	food
5.	schools	10.	television

Where Should a Topic Sentence Go?

If you look carefully at the paragraphs in textbooks, essays, and news stories, you will see that a topic sentence may appear anywhere in a paragraph. However, the most common position for a topic sentence is at or near the beginning of a paragraph. Placing the topic sentence at the beginning of a paragraph lets your reader know exactly where the paragraph is going and gives the impression that you have thought about the organization of your paragraph. And you *will* have thought about it.

The very act of constructing a topic sentence places your focus on the main idea of your paragraph and helps keep you on track in supporting that idea.

Topic Sentence First

Placing the topic sentence first is often your best choice. A topic sentence conveys your main idea and provides a strong, clear opening for your paragraph.

Example

Since I began carrying a homemade lunch to my part-time job at the mall, I have discovered the benefits of brown-bagging. The most obvious benefit is that bringing a lunch from home saves money. At the mall's food court, the price of a sandwich and chips or a slice of pizza and a soft drink can easily approach five dollars. But for less than ten dollars, I can buy a six-pack of soft drinks, a loaf of bread, and enough pimento cheese and peanut butter to make lunches for a week or more. Another benefit of brown-bagging—an unexpected one—is that I feel less rushed. Before I started bringing a lunch, my thirty-minute lunch break was consumed by a mad dash to the food court to stand in line, find a table, gulp down my food, and rush back to work. Now, I take a leisurely lunch in the employee break room, reading a magazine as I eat. Usually, I have an extra fifteen minutes to read and relax or take a stroll around the mall's upper level. I also benefit from the improved nutrition of my homemade lunches. Turkey on whole wheat or even peanut butter and jelly from home is lower in fat and calories than a hamburger or slice of pizza from the food court. For me, brown-bagging means that a healthier wallet, a more relaxed lunch break, and improved nutrition are "in the bag."

Topic Sentence after an Introductory Sentence

Sometimes, you may wish to include background material before you state the main point of your paragraph. In these instances, condense the background material to one introductory sentence. After your introductory sentence, state the topic sentence.

Example

Baldness runs in my family, and at thirty-five, I have come to accept my hair loss. **But as my hairline receded over the years, I discovered several creative ways to hide thinning hair.** My first solution to baldness was to wear a hat. Baseball caps in summer and knit caps in winter were only the beginning. During an "arty" phase in my mid-twenties, I wore a beret, and in the back of a closet somewhere, I still have a dashing Indiana-Jones-style hat. Another method I used to hide my thinning hair was the "comb-over"—combing hair over a bald spot. In the earliest stages of baldness, the method worked well for me. But as my hairline receded further, I stopped using the comb-over. I had seen too many men who looked ridiculous with just a few strands of foot-long hair covering a completely bald dome. The best method I have found to hide thinning hair is the one I use now. I have shaved my head completely. Now, no one can tell whether I am bald by nature or by choice. Shaving my head has helped me to get over my embarrassment at being bald. I have finally come to realize that bald is beautiful.

EXERCISE 7 FINDING TOPIC SENTENCES

One of the following paragraphs begins with an introductory sentence, while the other starts with the topic sentence. Underline the topic sentence in each paragraph.

Paragraph A

The glamour of Tyra Banks, Cindy Crawford, or Kate Moss may appeal to some, but my favorite models are not the ones who strut the runways for six figures a year. I like the real people who model the clothes in the Wal-Mart ads. In this week's Wal-Mart flyer, "Nellie, Associate" is modeling a red sweatshirt and matching sweatpants. She is not as thin or regal-looking as Tyra Banks, but I can tell her smile is real. She is looking up at Tequila, her daughter, who is modeling a powder-blue sweat outfit and reaching for her mother as she perches on the shoulders of "Calvin, Brother-in-Law of Nellie, Associate." On another page is "Brent, Tire and Lube Manager Trainee," a young man with a goatee and a shaved head. He wears a corduroy vest and a plaid shirt that looks ready to have its sleeves rolled up for some real work. In another section of the flyer, "Wendy, Customer Service Manager" models a cranberry-colored mock turtleneck. With her flying red hair, scrubbed, natural-looking skin, and ample frame, she doesn't look like a model. But a size-eighteen woman could look at the picture and have no doubt that she, like Wendy, would look really good in that top. The models in the Wal-Mart ads, real people who look good in real clothes, are much more appealing to me than the highly paid models whose only business is beauty.

Paragraph B

My brothers, Brad and Roy, are very different in their attitudes about money. Brad and his wife Lexie believe in living for today. They have a new house on the north side of town, a new sport utility vehicle, and a two-year-old Volvo. Their clothes are always designer labels in the latest fashions, and their home is a showplace of fine furniture. But they seldom have time to enjoy these things because they both work two jobs to pay off the massive debt they have accumulated. It is as though their possessions own them. My brother Roy goes a bit too far in the opposite direction. He puts every spare penny away for the future. Though he has a good job, he drives a thirteen-year-old car that rattles as if only habit is holding it together. He argues constantly with his wife, who simply wants decent clothes for herself and their children. Worse yet, he insists on buying nothing but practical gifts. I thought Andrea would divorce him when he gave her a hand-held vacuum for her birthday so that she could vacuum the inside of her car at home instead of taking it to the car wash. My two brothers agree on politics, football, and religion, but they will never agree about money.

PROGRESSIVE WRITING ASSIGNMENT

Progressive Writing Assignment: Topic Sentence

If your instructor has assigned the Progressive Writing Assignment, you have already completed your prewriting for one of the topics below. In this chapter, you will complete your topic sentence.

Topics and Tips for Writing a Topic Sentence

The Topics

Topic 1: Discuss the results of taking a specific piece of advice from a friend or family member.

Topic 2: Discuss your decision to attend college.

Topic 3: Discuss your greatest fear.

Topic 4: Discuss types of stress experienced by college students.

Tips for Writing a Topic Sentence

- Decide on the points you will cover in your paragraph and the order in which you will present them. Then write a tentative topic sentence.

- Make sure that the topic sentence presents a specific topic and makes a point about that topic.

- Check to make sure that your topic sentence is not too broad. For example, for Topic 4, "Discuss types of stress experienced by college students," the following topic sentence would be too broad:

  ✗   Everybody experiences stress at one time or another.

  The sentence is too broad because the paragraph is not about "everybody"; it is about college students. Two better topic sentences are shown below:

  ✔   College students are prone to certain kinds of stress.

  ✔   College students most often experience stress related to academic performance and lack of time.

- Check to make sure that your topic sentence is not too narrow. For example, for Topic 2, "Discuss your decision to attend college," the following topic sentence would be too narrow:

  ✗   I began college just two months ago.

    The sentence is too narrow because it does not address the idea of a decision to attend college. While the sentence might be appropriate as a supporting detail, it is too narrow to be a topic sentence. Two better topic sentences are shown below:

  ✔   Stuck in a dead-end job, I decided to attend college so that I could do something that will make a difference.

  ✔   Attending college will help me realize my lifelong dream of being a nurse.

Writing Paragraphs:
Support

Support:

STRONG

SOLID

Beautiful

Whether it is a column that holds up a roof or a sentence that helps to hold up a paragraph, support must be strong and solid. In fact, specific support is one of the keys to good writing. Before looking at paragraph support, review the following four principles of effective writing. The highlighted principle, support, is the focus of this chapter.

Characteristics of an Effective Paragraph

1. Direction means that the paragraph has a strong topic sentence that states the main idea and sets the course that the paragraph will follow.
2. Unity means that the paragraph makes one main point and sticks to that point.
3. Coherence means that the ideas in the paragraph are logically connected and easy to follow.
4. Support means that the paragraph contains specific and detailed discussion of the idea stated in the topic sentence.

Support: Using Specific Detail

A strong topic sentence, unity, and smooth transitions give a paragraph structure and style. Only support can give it life. Without specific details, a paragraph remains on a broad, general level. What is it like to read a paragraph without specific details? Imagine watching a movie, television show, or video that never shows a closeup but instead maintains a camera distance of ten feet from every character. You would probably feel detached and uninvolved. Readers feel the same way when a writer never gets close enough to the subject to describe it in detail.

The Difference Between Topic Sentences and Supporting Sentences

A topic sentence provides direction—the road map for a paragraph—but supporting sentences supply the scenery. While topic sentences are broad and general, large enough to encompass the entire paragraph, supporting sentences are specific, giving details and examples. The following exercise provides practice in distinguishing topic sentences from supporting details.

EXERCISE 1   DISTINGUISHING TOPIC SENTENCES FROM SUPPORTING DETAILS

Each numbered item contains three supporting details and one topic sentence. Write *SD* beside each of the three details and *TS* beside the topic sentence.

1. a. _____ Finally, he began throwing a tennis ball for his dog, who barked loudly in appreciation.

b. _____ Then he put on a CD by a group called the Funk Brigade and turned the volume up.

c. _____ First, he turned on the television to provide background noise.

d. _____ It was too quiet in the room, so Marcus decided to make some noise.

2. a. _____ In the second book, Harry meets Dobby, a house-elf who nearly kills Harry in an effort to help him.

b. _____ J. K. Rowling's popular *Harry Potter* books follow the adventures of a young wizard as he learns his craft.

c. _____ In the first book, Harry, who has always felt like the odd one out, finds out that he is a wizard and begins to discover his powers.

d. _____ The third book introduces Harry to a mysterious character named Sirius Black and to the soul-sucking guardians of Azkaban Prison.

3. a. _____ Being late is a harmful habit to acquire.

b. _____ People who are late to classes or meetings often miss important information.

c. _____ People who arrive late for appointments or meetings often anger those who have to wait.

d. _____ Although the impression may be inaccurate, people who are late are often perceived as rude or selfish.

4. a. _____ Tires that are not properly inflated can pose a danger to both driver and passengers.

b. _____ Windshield wipers that are excessively worn can pose a danger in rainy weather.

c. _____ Bald tires, worn tires, and tread that is unevenly worn can cause a car to lose traction on the road.

d. _____ Failure to take care of small details of car maintenance can make driving dangerous.

5. a. _____ The close companionship that arises between the adopted animal and its owner can benefit both animal and human.

b. _____ Shelter animals are euthanized if they are not adopted, so adopting a pet from the pound saves a life.

c. _____ Adopting a pet from the animal shelter can benefit both animal and owner.

d. _____ Pound puppies and kittens are usually spayed or neutered before adoption, saving the owner veterinary fees.

Recognizing Specific Detail

One of the most difficult tasks a writer faces is providing strong, specific supporting details. If a writer provides only vague, sketchy details, the picture presented to the reader will be fuzzy and out of focus. As details become sharper and more specific, the picture becomes clear. The following exercise will give you practice in recognizing sharp, clear detail.

EXERCISE 2   RECOGNIZING SPECIFIC DETAILS

Each of the following topic sentences is supported by three details. Place a check (✔) beside the two details that are sharp and specific. Place an ✗ beside the detail that needs to be more specific. Then, in the space provided, rewrite the vague sentence to make the supporting detail more specific.

1. All day long, Nicole was haunted by the number 8.

   _____ a. At the driver's license bureau, she pulled the number 8 out of a machine marked "Take a number."

   _____ b. At lunchtime, the first potato chip she pulled out of her bag was shaped like the number 8.

   _____ c. On her way home, yet another incident occurred involving the number 8.

   _____

   _____

2. Rodrigo's search for an apartment was long and difficult.

   _____ a. He looked at several apartments that were not suitable in terms of his financial situation.

   _____ b. Many of the apartments he could afford were too far away from work and school.

   _____ c. Finally, he found a small, affordable attic apartment close to his work and within walking distance of the college.

   _____

   _____

3. For several reasons, majoring in the health sciences is a good idea.

   _____ a. An aging population ensures that health-care professionals will be in demand for decades to come.

_____ **b.** A variety of fields from respiratory therapy to x-ray technology gives a student a wide range of choice.

_____ **c.** A nursing shortage means that anyone with a nursing degree has it made.

_____

_____

4. The small, crowded office was messy.

_____ **a.** In the corner, a trash can overflowed with paper and discarded soft-drink cans.

_____ **b.** The desk was also in disarray.

_____ **c.** Papers were spread in piles across the floor and around the desk, leaving little room for walking.

_____

_____

5. Elena worried that her memory was getting worse.

_____ **a.** She forgot an important appointment last week.

_____ **b.** She was constantly losing her glasses, her keys, and her wallet.

_____ **c.** She could no longer remember the items she needed at the grocery store without making a list, and she often forgot to bring the list.

_____

_____

Using Specific Words

Sometimes, a simple change in word choice makes all the difference. You paint a clearer picture for your reader when you use specific words and phrases: _four hours of research in the library_ instead of _a lot of work, Ella's Soul Food Café_ instead of _a restaurant, glared_ instead of _looked,_ or _a map of Florida, deck of cards, and two dollars in change_ instead of _things._

Making Nouns Specific

Consider the following sentence.

✗ Richard put _a heavy item_ in his trunk, then drove away from the _building._

Different readers will put different interpretations on this sentence. What did Richard put in his trunk? What kind of building did he leave? Specific detail would serve a twofold purpose: it would clearly convey the writer's meaning, and it would capture the reader's interest. Consider the revisions below.

✔ Richard put *a bulging briefcase* in his trunk, then drove away from *the law office.*

✔ Richard put *his ex-wife's body* in his trunk, then drove away from the *small white house where they had spent so many years together.*

✔ Richard put *a case of hymnals* in his trunk, then drove away from the *Harvest Religious Bookstore.*

Notice how the detail not only provides more specific information but also helps to characterize Richard. How does your impression of him change with each example?

EXERCISE 3   USING SPECIFIC WORDS

Create a new impression of Richard by varying what he puts in the trunk and the location described in the sentence.

1. Richard put _____ in his trunk, then drove away from the

   _____.

2. Richard put _____ in his trunk, then drove away from the

   _____.

3. Richard put _____ in his trunk, then drove away from the

   _____.

4. Richard put _____ in his trunk, then drove away from the

   _____.

5. Richard put _____ in his trunk, then drove away from the

   _____.

Practice in Making Vague Nouns Specific

Look at the following list. The nouns in the left-hand column provide little information, while those in the right-hand column are specific.

Notice, too, that the more specific term is often not simply a noun, but a phrase.

Vague Term	Specific Term
✗ course	✔ Introduction to Social Problems
✗ clothing	✔ man's herringbone jacket, size 42
✗ student	✔ Gloria Hollinger, first-year nursing student
✗ car	✔ 1965 Ford Mustang
✗ sandwich	✔ turkey on five-grain bread with mayonnaise

EXERCISE 4   CHOOSING SPECIFIC TERMS

From the three choices for each of the sentences below, circle the most specific choice to fill in the blank.

1. Carlos ate _____ at noon.
   a. a nutritious meal
   b. a tomato sandwich
   c. delicious food

2. When Larry took _____, he felt better.
   a. a pill
   b. two Excedrin tablets
   c. the advice of a respected physician

3. Ana said the _____ was breathtaking.
   a. spectacular view of the surrounding scenery
   b. works of some nineteenth-century poets
   c. ride on the Scream Machine

4. The vendor sold _____ from the back of a pickup truck.
   a. ripe peaches and black velvet art
   b. various wares in a wide range of colors
   c. electronic devices that may have been stolen

5. Melanie's mother said, "Would you help me _____?"
   a. complete a few simple household chores
   b. chop these onions
   c. do some errands

6. The little girl sat beside her mother in the veterinarian's waiting room, carefully holding _____.

    a. her animal companion

    b. a scrawny black kitten

    c. a cute, cuddly pet

7. On the refrigerator were _____.

    a. a child's drawing of a house, a grocery list, and a dentist's appointment card, held in place by colorful magnets

    b. photographs, papers, children's art, and reminders

    c. twelve magnets, along with the usual odds and ends that tend to accumulate under refrigerator magnets

8. Gerald's parents thought Kim was weird because _____.

    a. her appearance was unusual

    b. she had a pierced tongue and two-tone hair

    c. she did not look the way they thought a normal teenager should look

9. Because Harold did not believe in banks, he kept his money _____.

    a. in a place he thought was safe

    b. hidden away where no one who might want to steal it could find it

    c. in a waterproof plastic pouch buried under a rock

10. Pat believes she was straightforward and open, but other people saw her as _____.

    a. rude and tactless

    b. something else

    c. a person with an attitude that was often perceived negatively by those who had to be around her

EXERCISE 5   CHOOSING SPECIFIC TERMS

Three possible replacements follow each general term. One of the possible replacements is vague, while the other two are specific and thus would be acceptable substitutes. Circle the two specific terms in each of the following items.

1. tool

    a. hammer

    b. instrument

    c. spatula

2. test
   a. examination
   b. SAT
   c. math final

3. restaurant
   a. Vernon's Veggie Bar
   b. a hot dog stand on the corner
   c. an eatery

4. shoes
   a. sandals
   b. loafers
   c. footwear

5. noise
   a. sound
   b. earsplitting rock music
   c. click

6. pet
   a. animal companion
   b. Fluffy
   c. white hamster

7. home
   a. doublewide mobile home
   b. living space
   c. mansion

8. book
   a. telephone directory
   b. *War and Peace*
   c. published volume

9. ice cream
   a. delicious dessert
   b. pint of Rocky Road
   c. Ben & Jerry's Cherry Garcia

10. illness
    a. mumps
    b. disease
    c. food poisoning

Making Pronouns Specific

"I wanted to register today, but they wouldn't let me."

"Everybody says Ms. Torres is a tough teacher."

"The candidate says he will not increase taxes, but nobody believes him."

Sentences like these are common in conversation and usually go unchallenged. In writing, though, precision is necessary. Readers usually do not have access to the writers of the books, stories, and essays they read, and so they cannot ask questions like "Who are *they?*" or "What do you mean by *everybody?*" Look at the revised versions of the statements you just read:

I wanted to register today, but the clerks in the Registrar's Office wouldn't let me.

Two of the students in my sociology class say Ms. Torres is a tough teacher.

The candidate says he will not increase taxes, but few voters believe him.

Forcing yourself to be more specific may also force you to be more accurate. The "everybody" who tells you to enroll in a certain teacher's class may turn out to be two fellow students. And if you truly wanted to prove that "nobody" believes what a candidate says, you'd have to ask every voter—an impossible task.

EXERCISE 6   REPLACING VAGUE PRONOUNS

Replace the italicized pronouns with more specific expressions.

1. *Things* were only getting worse, so Curtis decided to move out of his parents' house.

    _____

2. Sheila followed several leads from the help wanted ads and attended an interview arranged by her school's career counselor, hoping to find *something* before graduation.

    _____

3. Dr. Madison did a brain scan on the patient but didn't find *anything*.

    _____

4. My trash container sat by the curb all day, but *they* didn't pick it up.

    _____

5. The family walked into the dining room where the table was set for Thanksgiving. *Everything* looked delicious.

    _____

Making Verbs Specific

Verbs bring life and movement to writing. Vague, poorly chosen verbs add nothing to your writing, or worse yet, drag it down. Well-chosen verbs leap off the page, adding power and energy to your writing. Choosing effective verbs means rejecting the easy choice and looking for powerful verbs that express your meaning exactly.

A *thesaurus*, or dictionary of synonyms, helps you choose the best word for the situation. But shades of meaning vary, so don't just choose a synonym at random. If you are not sure of a word's exact meaning, check your dictionary.

Examples

✗   Exhausted after studying for the exam, I *went* to bed at midnight.

✔   Exhausted after studying for the exam, I *stumbled* to bed at midnight.

✗   At 3:00 P.M. on the last day of school, the doors *were opened* and students *came* from the building, yelling and shouting.

✔   At 3:00 P.M. on the last day of school, the doors *burst* open and students *streamed* from the building, yelling and shouting.

EXERCISE 7   USING SPECIFIC VERBS

Cross out the italicized verb in each sentence and replace it with a verb that more effectively conveys the sense of the sentence.

1. Angrily, Beatrice *retrieved* the envelope from the table.

    _____

2. Smoothly, the sailboat *moved* across the water.

    _____

3. When the cable snapped, the elevator *descended* fifteen stories.

   _____

4. Albright's glove *contacted* his opponent's jaw, sending the man reeling toward the edge of the ring.

   _____

5. A small bird *was* on the highest branch of the cherry tree.

   _____

6. The garbage truck *moved* down the street, spewing noxious fumes.

   _____

7. The crowd *reacted* as fireworks appeared in the inky night sky.

   _____

8. When asked if he wanted to speak before he was sentenced, the defendant *commented*, "Please believe me! I do not know who committed this horrible crime, but I swear that I am innocent."

   _____

9. Five thousand fans *filled* the small concert hall, screaming and shouting their approval.

   _____

10. The angry customer said that a loose shopping cart had *harmed* her new car.

    _____

Exercise 8   Making Verbs Specific

Cross out the italicized verb in each sentence and replace it with a verb that more effectively conveys the sense of the sentence.

1. The ball seemed to take flight, *going* over the outfield and into the stands.

   _____

2. The squirrel grabbed the acorn and quickly *went* up the tree trunk.

   _____

3. The roller coaster made a slow ascent, then *moved* toward the ground as its passengers screamed delightedly.

   _____

4. Suddenly, Tom *came* into the room, yelling, "Quick! Somebody call an ambulance!"

   _____

5. As Andrea flipped the light switch, dozens of cockroaches *moved* across the wall and into the cracks near the baseboard.

_____

6. Lightning *was seen* and thunder rolled.

_____

7. The basketball *went* into the street just as a garbage truck rattled around the corner.

_____

8. As he stormed out of his boss's office, Phil *commented*, "And you know what you can do with your lousy job!"

_____

9. Annoyed at the interruption from a young fan, the athlete hastily *signed* his name on the program and abruptly turned away.

_____

10. When the phone rang at 3:00 A.M., Channing sleepily *reached* for the receiver.

_____

Making Sentences Specific

Sentences with specific language are sentences with power. As you write, strive for forceful verbs and vivid phrases. As you revise, look for opportunities to make vague language more specific. Look at the following examples to see how much stronger a sentence becomes when specific words replace vague words.

Examples

Vague Word Choice

✗ Eager shoppers *entered the toy store* when the *popular toy* came in.

Specific Word Choice

✔ Eager shoppers *mobbed Toy World* when the *Avengers of Doom action figures* came in.

Vague Word Choice

✗ When my mother comes to visit, she brings *all kinds of stuff* with her.

Specific Word Choice

✔ When my mother comes to visit, she brings *four suitcases, a shopping bag filled with homemade goodies, and her miniature poodle, Pierre.*

Vague Word Choice

✗ When Martin looked in his refrigerator, he found *there was not much to eat.*

Specific Word Choice

✔ When Martin looked in his refrigerator, he found *only a half-empty jar of pickles and the two-week-old remains of a takeout dinner from Junior's Barbecue.*

Vague Word Choice

✗ Sylvester could not concentrate on the test. *The noise around him* grated on his nerves.

Specific Word Choice

✔ Sylvester could not concentrate on the test. *The popping of gum in the back of the room, a burst of laughter from outside the building, and even the breathing of the student beside him* grated on his nerves.

EXERCISE 9   MAKING SENTENCES SPECIFIC

Rewrite the sentences so that they contain more specific detail. Feel free to use more than one sentence if you wish.

1. The newscaster reported that *a terrible thing* had happened in *a large city.*

   _____

2. The clock was shaped like *an animal* and painted *in bright colors.*

   _____

3. Lynn put a package from *a store* in the back seat because her trunk had *something* in it.

   _____

4. On their way to *their destination,* Asha and her husband stopped at *a little place by the roadside.*

   _____

5. *Bad weather* kept Mark from *doing what he had planned.*

   _____

6. When Percy saw *what had happened to his car* he *reacted strongly.*

   _____

7. *A noise* startled the *animal.*

_____

8. The mailbox held *several unimportant pieces of mail* and *one important piece of mail.*

_____

9. On our street, *they* have organized a neighborhood watch because of *various crimes that have taken place.*

_____

10. *In certain situations,* Jack gets *a bad feeling.*

_____

EXERCISE 10   MAKING SENTENCES SPECIFC

Rewrite the following paragraph, replacing the underlined vague terms with specific details.

When I decided to clean out the small storage closet in our garage, I was amazed at how much junk it contained. First, I cleared and sorted <u>items</u> I had meant to recycle later. Then, I tackled a pile of <u>various garden tools</u> that were <u>dirty</u>. After <u>dealing with</u> the gardening tools, I worked on the shelves. The top shelf was <u>filled</u> with <u>items</u> I had used when I painted the interior of the house last spring. I threw <u>some stuff</u> into a trash bag and kept the rest. Beneath the <u>assorted junk</u> I was clearing away, the middle shelf contained a surprise. A <u>sizeable insect</u> suddenly came out, startling me into dropping and breaking <u>something fragile</u>. When I had swept away <u>what had broken</u>, I rearranged the tools and <u>things</u> on the bottom shelf. Then I threw away <u>one broken item</u> and three empty <u>containers</u>. When I was finally through, I wondered how one small storage closet could have contained so much junk.

_____

_____

_____

_____

_____

_____

_____

_____

_____

_____

_____

_____

_____

_____

_____

EXERCISE 11   ANALYZING PARAGRAPHS FOR SUPPORT

One of the following paragraphs is well supported with specific details and examples, while the other is poorly supported with vague, general sentences. Read each paragraph, then answer the questions at the end of the exercise.

Paragraph A

In my experience, college professors are the worst-dressed people in the world. If there were an award for "worst-dressed professor," my history professor, Dr. Bloom, would be a leading candidate. He is the ultimate fashion victim. When I saw him walk into the classroom on the first day, I could not believe the clothes he was wearing. I thought that maybe he had just been in a hurry that morning, but on the second day of class, his clothing was just as bad. I cannot imagine where he finds that awful clothing. Then there is Professor Hunter, who teaches art. She wears the strangest clothes, even for an art teacher, who might be expected to have unusual taste. It is as if she is living in a different decade. It's a sure thing she hasn't looked at a fashion magazine lately. But I think my personal choice for the worst-dressed professor award is Mr. Nelson, my English teacher. Like clockwork, the same loud pants, jackets, and shirts appear in strict rotation, each for a different day of the week. When I go into his classroom, I make sure I sit in the back. I am not sure I could stand all those bright colors if I were sitting in the front row. I have great respect for my professors' knowledge, but most of them deserve an "F" in fashion.

Paragraph B

   In my experience, college professors are the worst-dressed people in the world. If there were an award for "worst-dressed professor," my history professor, Dr. Bloom, would be a leading candidate. When I saw him walk into the classroom on the first day in a green checked shirt, red bow tie and shapeless brown sweater vest, I thought perhaps he was just having a bad day. But each day in Dr. Bloom's class is a parade of mismatched rag-bag fashions: rumpled jackets, baggy pants, and shirts in checks, plaids, and polka dots. Professor Hunter, who teaches art, looks like a folk singer from the seventies with her straight hair and ankle-length dresses. She likes delicate rainbow colors and long strands of beads, an odd combination with her heavy white athletic shoes. But I think my personal choice for the worst-dressed professor award is Mr. Nelson, my English teacher, whose taste is not just bad, but annoyingly predictable. On Mondays, he wears a yellow and green checked polyester jacket with lime-green pants. On Tuesday, it's a polyester jacket in robin's-egg blue with a pair of mustard-colored pants. The polyester parade continues through Friday, when he wakes the class up with a pair of bright red pants worn with a pink shirt. I have great respect for my professors' knowledge, but most of them deserve an "F" in fashion.

Questions ?

Fill in the blanks of each question below.

1. Paragraph _____ is less specific.
2. Paragraph _____ is more specific. Three specific details from the paragraph are _____, _____ _____ , and _____.

PROGRESSIVE WRITING ASSIGNMENT

Progressive Writing Assignment: Providing Supporting Details and Examples

If your instructor has assigned the Progressive Writing Assignment, you have already completed your prewriting and your topic sentence. In this chapter, you will provide support for your paragraph.

Topics and Tips for Providing Supporting Details and Examples

The Topics

> Topic 1: Discuss the results of taking a specific piece of advice from a friend or family member.
>
> Topic 2: Discuss your decision to attend college.
>
> Topic 3: Discuss your greatest fear.
>
> Topic 4: Discuss types of stress experienced by college students.

Tips for Providing Supporting Details and Examples

- Make sure that your language is specific. Have you used words that create pictures by appealing to the reader's sense of sight, hearing, touch, taste, and smell? The following sentences illustrate how specific language might be used to support Topic 3, "Discuss your greatest fear."

  ✔ If I were homeless, I would have no shelter from the hot sun or the cold rain. On chilly nights, I would lie awake, listening to my stomach growl and feeling the damp chill creep into my bones.

- Check to see that you have supported your paragraphs with specific examples. If you are writing on Topic 1, "Discuss the results of taking a specific piece of advice from a friend or family member," an example might be a *specific example* that describes what happened on a particular occasion.

  ✔ Thinking of my father's advice, I walked right into my boss's office and said, "Ms. Carmichael, the mix-up with the order yesterday was my fault." She looked at me and said, "Yes, I know that, but I really appreciate hearing it from you."

CHAPTER 5

Writing Paragraphs:
Unity and Coherence

Into the loom go many threads
That soon come out a whole,
Into your writing, many words,
Which you alone control.

Only you can weave those words
With skill and perseverance,
Creating paragraphs that have
Unity and coherence.

Characteristics of an Effective Paragraph

Review the following characteristics of an effective paragraph. You have already learned how to give your paragraph direction with an effective topic sentence and how to support that topic sentence with details and examples.

This chapter looks at the two final characteristics of an effective paragraph, unity and coherence.

1. **Direction** means that the paragraph has a strong topic sentence that states the main idea and sets the course that the paragraph will follow.
2. **Support** means that the paragraph contains specific and detailed discussion of the idea stated in the topic sentence.
3. **Unity** means that the paragraph makes one main point and sticks to that point.
4. **Coherence** means that the ideas in the paragraph are logically connected and easy to follow.

Unity: Sticking to the Point

Every topic sentence offers a promise of **unity** to the reader, a promise that you will discuss the point advanced in that sentence and no other. If your topic sentence is "My friend Ellen is the messiest person I have ever known," then you will discuss the specific ways in which she is messy. You will not mention the few times you have known her to be neat; you will not discuss the other qualities that make her so good to have as a friend. You will discuss only the piles of clothes stacked on every piece of furniture in her bedroom, the assortment of books, bills, and banana peels on her desk, and the mounds of fast-food wrappers in the back seat of her car. Your paragraph will have unity because it sticks to its topic and to the specific point you make about that topic.

EXERCISE 1   FINDING PROBLEMS IN UNITY

A list of possible supporting points follows each of the topic sentences in the exercise. In each group, circle the letter of the point that interferes with the unity of the paragraph.

1. Topic sentence: Some restaurant customers make trivial complaints in the hope of getting a free meal.
    a. Some customers gripe when service is a bit slow.
    b. Many complain if they have to make a trip to the emergency room because of food poisoning.
    c. Other customers grumble if the coffee is not piping hot or the iced tea is not cold enough.

2. Topic sentence: Fear of serious injury makes many parents hesitate to encourage their children to play football.
   a. Many parents fear that the child may break a bone in a football game.
   b. They fear their child might sustain head injuries during a game.
   c. Some parents fear their child will start to do poorly in academics.
3. Topic sentence: One way that I try to keep in shape is through a proper diet.
   a. I get plenty of exercise.
   b. I eat very few sweets or sugary treats.
   c. I stay away from too many fats.
4. Topic sentence: If I had to give up one modern convenience, I would get rid of my telephone.
   a. Getting rid of my phone would eliminate interruptions from salespeople.
   b. My telephone is a vital link to emergency services.
   c. Without a phone, I would waste less time chatting.
5. Topic sentence: My neighbor's yard is an eyesore.
   a. In his front yard, he has an old Chevrolet up on blocks.
   b. At the side of his house is a beautiful old oak tree.
   c. Because he never mows his lawn, tall grass and weeds surround his house.

EXERCISE 2   FINDING PROBLEMS IN UNITY

A list of possible supporting points follows each of the topic sentences below. In each group, circle the letter of the point that interferes with the unity of the paragraph.

1. Topic sentence: Some crimes go unreported because crime victims believe they are not worth reporting.
   a. petty theft
   b. kidnapping
   c. graffiti
2. Topic sentence: Fear that they will do poorly in the classroom makes many adults hesitant to return to school.
   a. anxiety about taking tests
   b. fear of not understanding the ideas presented
   c. fear that their families will not accept their decision to return to school
3. Topic sentence: One way that I try to keep in shape is through exercise.
   a. lift weights
   b. eat nutritious foods
   c. attend aerobics classes

4. Topic sentence: Writing on a computer has helped me improve my papers.
    a. modern computer lab
    b. ease of revising on computer
    c. spelling check
5. Topic sentence: My neighbor's dog is an annoyance.
    a. "Heinz 57" mutt
    b. barks at night
    c. jumps fence and digs up my flowers

Reinforcing Unity: The Summary Sentence

One way to reinforce paragraph unity is to end the paragraph with a summary sentence that echoes the topic sentence. The summary sentence does not repeat the topic sentence; rather, it reinforces it. If the function of a topic sentence is to tell the reader where the paragraph is going, the function of a summary sentence is to tell where the paragraph has been, thus reinforcing the unity of the paragraph. A summary sentence also signals the end of the paragraph and provides a sense of closure.

Example

Topic Sentence

✔ The most valuable lesson I have learned from my parents is to be independent.

Summary Sentence

✔ I will always be grateful that my parents taught me to rely on myself and not on others.

Example

Topic Sentence

✔ A few minor changes could make our campus more welcoming to students with disabilities.

Summary Sentence

✔ These easy and inexpensive changes would ensure that all students feel safe and welcome on our campus.

EXERCISE 3 ANALYZING PARAGRAPH UNITY

In each of the following paragraphs, underline the topic and double-underline the specific point that is made about that topic. Then find the two sentences that interfere with the unity of the paragraph. If you have trouble, go back and look at the topic sentence to see the specific point that is made about the topic. Then read again to see which sentences do not support that specific point. Finally, underline the summary sentence of each paragraph.

Paragraph 1

[1]I enjoy spring because it is a season when nature comes alive. [2]Each tree sports a halo of tiny, delicate leaf buds of the palest green. [3]Soon the leaves mature and unfurl, trumpeting a brilliant green message to the world. [4]Flowers nudge their way through a new growth of grass, pushing up to find the sun. [5]Then they open into a rainbow of springtime colors. [6]Each evening, a symphony of sound serenades the listener from shallow ponds where frogs call solemn invitations to prospective mates. [7]Toward morning, as the frogs subside, birds begin their racket, their chatter reverberating from tree to tree. [8]In the ballparks, the crack of the bat and the umpire's cry of "Yer out!" echo again as baseball season opens. [9]Lights blaze, the stands fill, and the odors of hotdogs, popcorn, and beer blend on the evening breeze. [10]It is spring, and nature awakens the world to new possibilities.

Numbers of the sentences that interfere with the unity of the paragraph:____8____, ____9____

Paragraph 2

[1]The graduation ceremony at our college is dignified but dull. [2]In a large hall filled with well-dressed parents, relatives, and friends of the graduates, faculty and students file in, dressed in hot, heavy academic robes. [3]The ceremony follows a prescribed routine. [4]First, prospective graduates sing the alma mater, desperately searching their programs for the unfamiliar words. [5]The dean of the college, clad in a flowing robe, welcomes the assembled crowd with appropriate decorum. [6]The graduation speaker, usually a state legislator or a distinguished graduate, delivers a lengthy discourse as members of the audience yawn, read their programs, or pretend to listen. [7]Then, the anticipated moment arrives and the graduates begin to stir excitedly, waving at parents, who quickly ready cameras and video equipment. [8]In spite

of the dean's plea to hold applause until all diplomas have been distributed, whoops and cheers ring out from the audience as eager graduates file across the stage. [9]Finally, the majestic notes of "Pomp and Circumstance" rise in the air and the graduates march out, heads high with the dignity of their newly conferred degrees. [10]The ceremony, with its air of dull formality, is over for another year.

Numbers of the sentences that interfere with the unity of the paragraph: _____7_____ , _____8_____

EXERCISE 4 ANALYZING PARAGRAPH UNITY

In each of the following paragraphs, underline the topic and double-underline the specific point that is made about that topic. Then find the two sentences that hurt the unity of the paragraph. If you have trouble, go back and look at the topic sentence to see the specific point that is made about the topic. Then read again to see which sentences do not support that specific point. Finally, underline the summary sentence of each paragraph.

Paragraph 1

[1]I enjoy autumn because it is nature's season of color and movement. [2]The temperature falls and the wind picks up, sweeping across country roads and city streets and serving notice that nature's show is about to begin. [3]The summer green of the trees gives way to a fall tapestry of red, orange, gold, and brown. [4]People flock to the mountains to see the autumn splendor before the winter comes. [5]Many people, however, have already taken a summer vacation at the beach before the children head back to school. [6]Finally, as the grasses turn yellow and fields shade into brown, the leaves begin to fall. [7]They float to the ground, where the wind tosses them, forming a multicolored carpet that crunches underfoot as the leaves turn brown. [8]Almost as fast as parents can rake the leaves into big piles, children are ready to leap into the middle of them and scatter them into a colorful carpet once again. [9]Fall is also a season for Halloween, when children go door to door in scary costumes to collect treats. [10]In fall, nature puts on a spectacular show before the bleakness of winter comes on.

Numbers of the sentences that hurt the unity of the paragraph: _____ , _____

Paragraph 2

¹Last night, the women's softball game at our college was attended by a small but enthusiastic group of supporters. ²Below me, in the first row of the bleachers, two small boys yelled loudly and waved signs saying "Go, Mom!" whenever their mother came up to bat. ³Four young men sitting together to my left shouted encouraging comments to the players and stood and clapped whenever the team scored. ⁴More interested in gossip than in softball, three women sitting to the far left in the stands ignored the game completely. ⁵When Number 34 came up to bat, a woman sitting in a wheelchair beside the bleachers turned to bystanders and said proudly, "That's my daughter." ⁶A cluster of students seated near the field clapped rhythmically and cheered, "Go, team, go!" ⁷It is a shame that our men's athletic teams have cheerleaders, but our women's teams do not. ⁸Entering the ninth inning, our team was winning by five runs, but the fans stayed and cheered as enthusiastically as if the score were tied. ⁹As the team left the field, the enthusiastic cheers of the small crowd told the players that their winning efforts had been appreciated.

Numbers of the sentences that hurt the unity of the paragraph: _____, _____

Coherence: Holding the Paragraph Together

If your writing does not have coherence, then the sentences in your paragraph are like a pile of loose bricks: there is little connection between them. Coherence is the mortar you use to make your paragraph a brick wall, with solid and strong connections between ideas. To achieve coherence, first make sure your ideas are logically related and well thought out. Then use coherence tools to cement the connections between those ideas in the most effective way possible. Two common and easy-to-use coherence tools are *transitional expressions* and *repetition*.

Transitional Expressions

As a writer, you must not only express an idea clearly, you must keep your reader oriented in time and space and aware of relationships between ideas. *Transitional expressions* help you juggle these multiple tasks without detracting from the ideas you express. Ideally, these words and phrases do their job in the background, as guideposts that show the path of your logic and the movement of your ideas through time and space. Below is a list of transitional words and expressions, organized by their function within the sentence.

Some Common Transitional Words and Expressions

* Transitions of Time

after	during	later	now	suddenly	when
as	first	meanwhile	often	temporarily	while
before	immediately	next	previously	then	yet

* Transitions of Space

above	beside	down	next to	toward
around	between	in	on	under
behind	by	near	over	

* Transitions of Addition

also	finally	furthermore	in addition	next
another	first			

* Transitions of Importance

as important	essential	major	primary
equally important	just as important	most important	significant

* Transitions of Contrast

although	even though	in contrast	instead	on the other hand
but	however	in spite of	nevertheless	yet

---

* Transitions of Cause and Effect

a consequence of	because	for	so	thus
as a result	consequently	since	therefore	

---

* Transitions of Illustration or Example

for example	for instance	including	such as

EXERCISE 5   USING TRANSITIONAL EXPRESSIONS

In the following paragraph, provide the indicated type of transition in each blank.

[1]Nothing had gone right lately, so _____*before* (time signal) the doorbell rang, Sam had a feeling it was not the Prize Patrol with a million-dollar check. [2] _____*How* (contrast signal), he did not expect quite as much trouble as he got. [3]Two police officers were standing _____*by* (space signal) his porch. [4]"Mr. Williams, we have information that your dog may have bitten a child who lives _____*down* (space signal) the street," said the tall officer. "It couldn't have been Killer," said Sam, [5]"_____*bec* (cause-effect signal) he never goes outside except on a leash." [6]"Please bring the dog out _____*now* (time signal)," said the officer. "I'm afraid we'll have to take him to the pound." Sam knew that his dog had not bitten anyone, [7] _____*Alt* (contrast signal) he saw no alternative but to hand over his dog. Would he ever see Killer again? [8] _____*Inm* (time signal) he brought Killer out on a leash, the officers had their hands near their guns, as if fearful of being attacked. [9] _____*But* (contrast signal), when they saw Killer, the officers began to laugh. "That's not the dog we're looking for," said the tall officer, bending to pet the tiny, trembling Chihuahua on the head. "We are looking for a large, fierce dog." [10] _____*Inm* (time signal), to Sam's relief, the two officers apologized for bothering him and left.

1. _____   5. _____   8. _____

2. _____   6. _____   9. _____

3. _____   7. _____   10. _____

4. _____

EXERCISE 6   USING TRANSITIONAL EXPRESSIONS

In the following paragraph, provide the indicated type of transition in each blank.

        1 _When_ (time) the Fresh-Food Supermart was robbed, Shawna had the bad luck to be the only cashier on duty. The robber came in about 7:00 A.M., 2_____ (time) the store opened. She noticed him right away 3_____ (cause-effect) his ball cap was pulled low over his eyes and he wore a jacket 4_____ (contrast) the morning was warm. He loitered for a while 5_____ (space) the door; 6_____ (time) he walked up to her register. She must have suspected him 7_____ (cause-effect) she suddenly remembered Mr. Monroe, the store manager, saying: "If you are ever robbed, remember that your life is worth more than whatever is in that cash drawer. Stay cool and hand over the money." 8_____ (time) the robber leaned 9_____ (space) her and mumbled, "I have a gun. Put the money in a bag." Remembering Mr. Monroe's words, Shawna quickly withdrew the money from the register. 10_____ (time) she reached for a bag, she was surprised at the words that automatically fell from her lips: "Paper or plastic?" Much 11_____ (time) Mr. Monroe teased that not only had she remembered his instructions, she had 12_____ (addition) remembered to offer her unwelcome "customer" a choice.

1. _____	5. _____	9. _____
2. _____	6. _____	10. _____
3. _____	7. _____	11. _____
4. _____	8. _____	12. _____

Using Transitions Effectively

Used skillfully, transitional expressions bring coherence to your writing, but moderation is the key. Using these words unnecessarily or artificially is worse than not using them at all.

Hints for Using Transitional Expressions and Examples

- Less is more. Skillfully weaving a few transitional expressions into a paragraph is better than forcing in as many as possible.

- For variety, place transitions somewhere other than the beginning of a sentence. Instead of "However, Arturo refused to place the pink plastic flamingo on his lawn," try "Arturo, however, refused to place the pink plastic flamingo on his lawn."

- Examples are sometimes more effective when they are not preceded by *for example* or *for instance*. If you feel uncomfortable putting an example in without announcement, try using *for example* in your rough draft and editing it out later.

- When you feel that a particular example needs to be announced, try placing the announcement somewhere other than at the beginning of a sentence. Instead of, "For instance, pasta is filling and low in calories," try "Pasta, for instance, is filling and low in calories."

EXERCISE 7 ANALYZING USE OF TRANSITIONS

Look at the two paragraphs that follow. Underline the transitional expressions in each. In which paragraph are transitional expressions used more skillfully? Can you pinpoint some of the reasons?

Paragraph 1

The third week of a student's first year in college is often a dangerous one. Like the "seven-year itch" that supposedly makes people give up on romantic relationships, the "three-week shock syndrome" sometimes signals the end of a student's academic career. After the excitement of the first week or two of classes begins to wear off, reality starts to set in. There is more than just the excitement of meeting new people and buying textbooks in a well-stocked bookstore. Those books, with their crisp pages and new smell, must be opened and read, marked and highlighted. The smiling professors who leaned on their lecterns and cracked jokes on the first day of class have turned into serious-faced people who talk faster than their students can write and whose lectures are sometimes boring. Worst of all is the work. Reading assignments, writing assignments, library assignments, and computer lab assignments pile up, waiting to be completed. Who has time to remember it all, much less do it all? Students who make it past the third week of classes usually find that they can adjust, that they can keep up. But some, faced with the shock that college means work, never stay long enough to find out whether they can succeed or not.

Paragraph 2

First of all, the third week of a student's first year in college is often a dangerous one. For example, the "seven-year itch" supposedly makes people give up on romantic relationships, and the "three-week shock syndrome" often signals the end of a student's academic career. In addition, the excitement of the first week or two of classes begins to wear off, and reality starts to set in. More important, there is more than just the excitement of meeting new people and buying textbooks in a well-stocked bookstore. In contrast, those books, with their crisp pages and new smell, must be opened and read, marked and highlighted. Furthermore, the smiling professors who leaned on their lecterns and cracked jokes on the first day of class have turned into serious-faced people who talk faster than their students can write and whose lectures are sometimes boring. Just as important, worst of all is the work. To enumerate, there are reading assignments, writing assignments, library assignments, and computer lab assignments. Further, who has time to remember it all, much less do it all? Nevertheless, students who make it past the third week of classes usually find that they can adjust, that they can keep up. In conclusion, some, faced with the shock that college means work, never stay long enough to find out whether they can succeed or not.

The paragraph in which transitions are used more successfully is paragraph _____.

Some reasons are _____

_____

_____

EXERCISE 8 ANALYZING USE OF TRANSITIONS

Look at the two paragraphs that follow. Underline the transitional expressions in each. In which paragraph are transitional expressions used more skillfully? Can you pinpoint some of the reasons?

Paragraph 1

One characteristic of successful students is that they know how to study. They know, for instance, that the time to begin studying is not the night before the test but much earlier. The first time they read a section of the textbook, successful students begin their study. They highlight or underline important sections and jot down key terms. When taking notes in class, they use a similar technique, jotting down the most important ideas and later transcribing their notes into a format that will be easy to study. Unsuccessful students, on the other hand, often postpone highlighting the text and organizing their notes until the night before the test, when time is short. Successful study, then, partly depends on beginning well before the date of the test.

Paragraph 2

First, successful students know how to study. First of all, they know that the time to begin studying is not the night before the test but much earlier. For example, successful students usually begin their study the first time they read a section of the textbook. In addition, they highlight or underline important sections and jot down key terms. Next, when taking notes in class, they jot down the most important ideas. Furthermore, they transcribe their notes into a format that will be easy to study from later. However, unsuccessful students postpone highlighting the text and organizing their notes until the night before the test. Therefore, successful study partly depends on beginning well before the date of the test.

The paragraph in which transitions are used more successfully is paragraph _____.

Some reasons are _____

_____

_____

Repetition

Repetition of Key Words and Phrases

Often, repetition is seen as a negative quality in writing. However, *repetition of key words and phrases* is a method of tying your ideas together and achieving coherence. While no one would advise endless hammering of unimportant words or ideas, repetition of key words and ideas helps to bring your point home strongly.

EXERCISE 9   EXAMINING REPETITION OF IMPORTANT TERMS

The following paragraph is about business telephone manners. Underline the repetitions of the key words *business*, *telephone* (or *phone*), and *manners*.

At a time when voice mail, answering machines, and computerized telephone answering systems have all but replaced the business telephone call, good telephone manners remain essential. Because the caller on the other end of the phone cannot read lips or minds, it is important for anyone who answers a business telephone to speak clearly, giving his name and the name of the department or company. If it is necessary to ask the caller to hold, it is never good manners to say "Hold, please" and leave the person wondering when, if ever, the phone will be picked up again. Good telephone manners require an explanation, such as "Ms. Smith, our manager, will be happy to help you with that. Would you mind holding for a minute while I get her?" Above all, business telephone manners require giving the caller the idea that her business is appreciated and that the phone call has been a pleasure, not a chore. For example, if the caller says, "Thank you," then the proper reply is not "Yeah, right, no problem." A reply such as "Thank you, Ms. Crabtree. We appreciate your business," demonstrates good telephone manners and excellent business sense. In an impersonal age, adding a personal touch to business telephone calls is not just good manners. It's good business.

Repetition through Pronouns

Pronouns aid coherence by allowing you to refer to someone or something without tedious repetition. Below is a partial list of pronouns often used to substitute for nouns. (For more information about using pronouns, see Chapters 18 and 19.)

Common Pronouns

Subject pronouns:	I, we, you, he, she, it, they, who
Object pronouns:	me, us, you, him, her, it, them, whom
Possessive pronouns:	my, mine, our, ours, your, yours, his, her, hers, its, their, theirs, whose
Indefinite pronouns:	one, anyone, everyone, nobody, some, somebody

In the following sentences, it's easy to see how much more smoothly the words seem to flow when pronouns link sentences and ideas together.

Example

✗ *The dog* woke up, stretched out *the dog's* legs, and yawned hugely. Then, as if realizing that *the dog* was supposed to be guarding *the dog's* yard, *the dog* shambled over to the gate and gave a halfhearted bark.

Revision

✓ *The dog* woke up, stretched out *his* legs, and yawned hugely. Then, as if realizing that *he* was supposed to be guarding *his* yard, *he* shambled over to the gate and gave a halfhearted bark.

EXERCISE 10   USING PRONOUNS TO AID COHERENCE

Use pronouns to replace the underlined words. Choose from the preceding list of common pronouns or use any appropriate pronoun.

1. Whenever Lindsay left <u>Lindsay's</u> new bicycle in the driveway, her mother worried that <u>Lindsay's new bicycle</u> would be stolen.

   _____   _____

2. When Michael tried to hand the toll booth attendant a dollar, the wind whipped <u>the dollar</u> out of his hand and sent <u>the dollar</u> sailing into the oncoming lanes of traffic.

   _____   _____

3. When personal computers first came out, Mr. Willett said that <u>personal computers</u> were just another fad, but now he has decided that he needs <u>a personal computer</u>.

   _____   _____

4. Because the pizza arrived cold and late, the delivery person did not charge us for <u>the pizza</u>. We decided that a cold, free pizza tasted even better than a hot, fifteen-dollar <u>pizza</u>.

   _____   _____

5. Timothy looked at the huge parking lot and wondered how he would ever find <u>Timothy's</u> car. He walked down aisle after aisle before he found <u>Timothy's car</u>.

   _____   _____

PROGRESSIVE WRITING ASSIGNMENT

Progressive Writing Assignment: Unity and Coherence

If your instructor has assigned the Progressive Writing Assignment, you have already completed your prewriting, a topic sentence, and supporting details. In this chapter, you will make sure your paragraph has unity and coherence.

Topics and Tips

The Topics

> Topic 1: Discuss the results of taking a specific piece of advice from a friend or family member.
>
> Topic 2: Discuss your decision to attend college.
>
> Topic 3: Discuss your greatest fear.
>
> Topic 4: Discuss types of stress experienced by college students.

Tips for Unity and Coherence

STAYING ON TRACK: TIPS FOR UNITY

- Check each paragraph to make sure that every sentence supports the topic sentence.
- Include a summary sentence at the end of the paragraph to reinforce the topic sentence.
  - ✔ No matter what else they learn on campus, most college students also learn to live with stress.
  - ✔ Becoming a nurse will be the fulfillment of a lifelong dream and the beginning of a long and rewarding career.

TRANSITIONS: TIPS FOR COHERENCE

- Read your paragraph aloud to make sure it flows logically.
- Check to make sure transitions between supporting ideas are smooth and that transitional expressions are used where needed.

  - ✔ Academic stress *also* affects most college students.
  - ✔ *However,* I have found ways of coping with my fear of public speaking.

CHAPTER 6

Revising, Proofreading, and Formatting

A ragged shrub can be revised
To form a topiary
In almost any shape you want—
Dog, tiger, or canary.

To get your words whipped
into shape,
You'll also need revision
To make sure that your writing
Is just what you envision.

To many writers, revising, proofreading, and formatting are afterthoughts, hastily completed just before the paper is turned in. But these final steps in the writing process help you present your ideas in the best possible way. Revising helps you capture your ideas more clearly and accurately, and proofreading and formatting help give them the polish they need before they are ready for an audience.

Revising

If you have ever watched your golden ideas clatter onto the page like a load of rough gravel, you understand the need for revision. Revising helps you do justice to your ideas, to give them some of their original polish.

There are also more practical reasons for revision, reasons that have their roots in the difference between writing and conversation. Conversation is constantly under revision. When your listener says, "What do you mean?" and you explain, you are revising. When your listener disagrees and you reinforce your argument or concede a point, you are revising. In a conversation, revision is a response to the listener. But writing does not offer the same opportunity for response. Your reader cannot ask questions. So you have to *anticipate* a reader's objections and meet them before they arise. That means that you need to spot possible misunderstandings and clarify them before the reader sees the finished work. Revising is a process of stepping back and looking at your work with the eyes of a reader.

The word *revise* combines the Latin root meaning *to see* with the prefix meaning *again.* In its most literal sense, *to revise* means *to see again.* "Seeing again" is the essence of good revision. The difficult part is distancing yourself far enough from the work to see it with new eyes. When the work is fresh from your pen or word processor, you often see what you *meant* to say rather than what is actually on the page.

To see your work again, you need to create a space, a mental distance, between yourself and the work. Time is your best ally. Lay the writing aside for at least a twenty-four-hour period. When you return to it, words that aren't precise, sentences that aren't clear, and explanations that don't explain enough are easier to spot.

If you do not have twenty-four hours to lay the work aside, it may help to have someone else look at it. Ask your reader to focus on content and to ask questions about any point that does not seem clear. The written word carries no facial expression, no gesture, and no tone of voice, so it is more open to misinterpretation than is face-to-face communication. Discussing work with a reader can help close the gap between what you *think* you said and what your reader actually sees.

In addition to letting a work "cool" before revising and enlisting the help of a reader, you can also check your paragraph point by point to make sure that it fulfills the purpose you had in mind. There is nothing mysterious about this procedure. It works like the diagnostic test a mechanic might perform to evaluate a car, checking all major systems to make sure they are working as they should. The following revision checklist helps you to go through a paragraph, part by part, to make sure each part is doing the job you intend it to do.

Checklist for Revision

The Topic Sentence

✔ Does the paragraph have a topic sentence that clearly states the main idea of the entire paragraph?

✔ Is the topic sentence the first or second sentence in the paragraph?

The Supporting Sentences

✔ Does each sentence of the paragraph support the topic sentence?

✔ Do your examples and explanations provide specific detail to support the topic sentence?

✔ Is each point you raise adequately explained and supported?

The Ending

✔ Is the last sentence satisfying and final-sounding?

✔ Does the last sentence serve as a summary or closing sentence for the entire paragraph?

Checking Coherence

✔ Is the order of ideas clear and logical?

✔ Are transitional words used effectively?

EXERCISE 1 ANALYZING TWO VERSIONS OF AN ESSAY

Read the two versions of the paragraph, "Some Purposes of Urban Legends." Using the preceding Checklist for Revision as your guide, decide which version is the revision and which is the rough draft.

Version 1

Some Purposes of Urban Legends

[1]Some urban legends, such as the story of a man caught speeding by a high-tech surveillance system, are meant to amuse. [2]The man was mailed a photo of his car's license plate, a radar reading of his speed, and a ticket for $120. [3]He mailed back a photo of a check. [4]The police responded with a photo of a pair of handcuffs. [5]The motorist quickly relented and sent a check. [6]Urban legends are meant to sound a warning. [7]Urban legends that tell of escaped murderers haunting lovers' lanes, of babies left alone for "just a moment" with tragic consequences, or of predators stalking women down lonely roads fit this category. [8]I myself cannot imagine a parent being careless with his or her child. [9]There is so much that can happen to a defenseless baby in seconds. [10]These legends remind us, as we go about our lives, to be careful. [11]A final type of urban legend, the "David and Goliath" story, shows how an average person can fight big business or government and win. [12]One example is the story of a woman who asked a waitress in a department store's tearoom for the store's chocolate chip cookie recipe. [13]She was told she would be charged "two-fifty," and she agreed to what she thought was a $2.50 charge on her credit card. [14]Later, she received a charge card bill for $250. [15]This legend, which still haunts the Internet, reminds its readers that even ordinary people have some measure of power. [16]Urban legends, although mostly untrue, serve a purpose as they tell of funny incidents, tragedy, or an ordinary person's revenge.

Version 2

Some Purposes of Urban Legends

[1]Urban legends, the modern equivalent of ancient folktales, serve a variety of purposes. [2]Some urban legends, such as the story of a man caught speeding by a high-tech surveillance system, are meant to amuse. [3]The man was mailed a photo of his car's license plate, a radar reading of his speed, and a ticket for $120. [4]He mailed back a photo of a check. [5]When the police responded with a photo of a pair of handcuffs, the motorist quickly relented and sent a check. [6]Another type of urban legend is meant to sound a warning. [7]In one story of warning, a couple goes to a lover's lane in spite of a news broadcast telling of an escaped murderer called "Hook Hand." [8]When they hear a noise outside the car, they become frightened and start

to leave. [9]The car seems to be stuck, but finally they pull away and drive home. [10]As they get out of the car in the young woman's driveway they notice something caught on the bumper: a hook hand. [11]A final type of urban legend, the "David and Goliath" story, shows how an average person can fight big business or government and win. [12]An example is the story of a woman who asked a waitress in a department store's tearoom for the store's chocolate chip cookie recipe. [13]She was told she would be charged "two-fifty" and she agreed to what she thought was a $2.50 charge on her credit card. [12]Later, she received a charge card bill for $250. [14]When the department store refused to remove the charge, the woman's revenge was swift. [15]She posted the recipe on the Internet for the world to enjoy, along with a letter of explanation. [16]This legend, which still haunts the Internet, reminds its readers that even ordinary people have some measure of power. [17]Urban legends, although mostly untrue, serve a purpose as they tell of funny incidents, tragedy, or an ordinary person's revenge.

The revised version of the paragraph is version _____.

EXERCISE 2   ANALYZING AN UNREVISED ESSAY

Go back to the unrevised version of "Some Purposes of Urban Legends" and fill in the blanks to answer the following questions.

1. A topic sentence should appear before sentence _____ in the unrevised version.

2. A transitional word or expression is needed as the writer moves to a new point in sentence _____.

3. Two sentences that do not support the topic sentences are sentence _____ and sentence _____.

4. More support is needed to fully make the writer's point after sentence _____.

Proofreading

Think about the last time you saw a misspelling in a newspaper. The minute you saw it, your thoughts moved away from the story itself and focused on the error. Similarly, errors in your writing take a reader's focus away from your ideas and put emphasis on grammar, spelling, or punctuation. Naturally, you want the ideas to stand in the foreground while grammar, spelling, and punctuation remain in the background. Proofreading, then, is an essential last step in your writing. Though proofreading is usually a chore, it is a necessary chore.

After you have completed the final revision of your work, proofread it at least twice, once from the top down and once from the bottom up. If you have a special problem area, such as comma splices or subject-verb agreement, you should do at least one extra proofreading focusing on those skills.

Proofreading is the job that is never done. No matter how thorough you are, some little error always escapes your notice. Then, just as you are turning in your beautifully written or word-processed manuscript, the error pops out at you as if it were written in neon. Therefore, the more thorough your approach to proofreading, the better.

The Top-Down Technique

On the first proofreading, scan from the top of the page down. Check to make sure the connections between ideas are smooth and solid and that sentences and paragraphs flow smoothly into one another. Check for parallel structure, clear pronoun reference, and appropriate transitional expressions. After correcting any problems you find in the top-down proofreading, move to the second type of proofreading, the bottom-up proofreading.

The Bottom-Up Technique

The bottom-up proofreading technique is more labor-intensive and more focused than top-down proofreading. When you read from the bottom up, you are no longer reading your essay as a single piece of writing but as disconnected sentences that do *not* flow into one another. Since your focus is on a single sentence, you can look at it closely, as if it is a sentence in a grammar exercise. Read it carefully, correct any errors you find, and then move back to the next sentence.

The Targeting Technique

If you have a "favorite error"—one that seems to plague you more than any other—try an additional proofreading to target that error. Following are some common errors and shortcuts to finding those errors. As you become more experienced, you will find yourself devising your own strategies to target your problem areas.

Subject-verb agreement. Check each subject-verb sequence. Look for present-tense verb forms and make sure they agree with their subjects.

Comma splices and run-ons. Target long sentences; they are more likely to be run-ons. Target commas and see if there is a sentence on both sides of the comma; if so, you have a comma splice.

Other comma errors. Target each comma and question its reason for being there. If you aren't sure why it is there, maybe it doesn't belong.

Pronoun agreement. Look for the plural pronouns *they* and *their*, and make sure that they have a plural, not a singular, antecedent.

Sentence fragments. Using the bottom-up technique, read each sentence to see if it could stand on its own.

Proofreading the Word-Processed Paragraph

Spelling and grammar checkers can be helpful in proofreading, but they are no substitute for knowledge and judgment. A spelling or grammar checker can find possible errors and suggest possible solutions. However, it is up to you to decide what, if anything, is wrong and how to fix it.

Even when you use spelling and grammar checkers, you should do at least two separate proofreadings. The following sentence, in which all words are spelled correctly, may illustrate the need:

✔ Weather or knot ewe use a spelling checker, you knead too proofread.

Whether to proofread onscreen or print out a hard copy to proofread is a personal choice. Some writers find it easier to scroll up and down on the computer screen, viewing the paragraph in small segments. Others swear that they cannot see their errors until they hold the printed copy in their hands. Find out what works best for you and proceed accordingly.

GROUP EXERCISE 1   Proofreading a Paragraph
Confident? Go solo!

Each of the twenty sentences in the following paragraph contains an error. Form a small proofreading team with two or three of your classmates. Pooling your knowledge, see how many errors you can identify and correct.

An Urban Legend

[1]Urban legends are stories that are often told but is seldom true. [2]One urban legend involves a young college woman traveling home for the Thanksgiving holiday's. [3]As she leaves, the dorm's custodian warned her to take precautions against the Road Killer, who is known to prey on women driving alone. [4]On the road, she stops before dark to get gas, however; she can't get the pump to work. [5]She drives off, planing to stop somewhere else. [6]But as she drive's, she begins to feel more and more apprehensive. [7]It is now fully dark, so she decide to stop at a full-service station. [8]So that she won't have to get out of the car again. [9]It seems like hrs. before she finds a station with a sign that says, "We Pump." [10]She hands the attendant her credit card, she notices he is looking at her and at her car with a strange expression. [11]As he walks toward his booth to check her credit, she feels majorly creeped out. [12]The attendant comes back and said a representative of the credit card company wants to talk to her on the phone. [13]She fears a trick but, the attendant is insistent. [14]One gets out of the car. [15]And walks toward the attendant's booth. [16]He follows closely, goes in behind her slams the door, and locks it. [17]Just as she is about to scream, he says, "I've called the police, and they're on there way. There is a man crouched in the back seat of your car." [18]Urban legends like this one are all most never true. [19]People, find them interesting. [20]Because they represent events that could happen.

Corrections

1.	_____	9.	_____
2.	_____	10.	_____
3.	_____	11.	_____
4.	_____	12.	_____
5.	_____	13.	_____
6.	_____	14.	_____
7.	_____	15.	_____
8.	_____	16.	_____

17. _____   19. _____

18. _____   20. _____

Formatting

You have heard it all your life: First impressions count. The document you hand to your instructor, the resumé you hand to a prospective employer, or the letter you send to the editor of a newspaper has the ability to present a positive first impression or a negative one. When an instructor sees a carefully formatted paper with no smudges, crossovers, or dog-eared edges, the instructor expects that paper to be a good one, written as carefully as it was prepared. On the other hand, a hastily scrawled document smudged with eraser marks or heavily laden with Wite-Out suggests that the writer did not take the time to create a good impression—or to write a good paper.

Manuscript format is so important that entire books have been written about it. An instructor who asks you to use MLA style, APA style, or Chicago style is referring to styles outlined in books published by the Modern Language Association, the American Psychological Association, and the University of Chicago.

If you are given instructions for formatting a document, follow those instructions carefully. If you have no specific instructions, use the guidelines in the following section. They will help you to format a document effectively, whether that document is written in class or out of class, by hand or on a word processor.

Handwritten Documents

Paragraphs and Essays

For handwritten paragraphs and essays, use lined white 8½ × 11-inch paper and blue or black ink. Write on one side of the paper only, and leave wide margins.

In the upper right-hand corner of the page, put your name and the date. If you wish, include your instructor's name and the name of the class for which you are preparing the assignment. Center your title, if any, on the first line of the paper, but do not underline the title or put it in quotation marks. Indent each paragraph five spaces, or about three-quarters of an inch. In a handwritten document, do not skip lines unless your instructor specifically requests it. If you make an error, draw a single line through the error and rewrite your correction above the crossed-out error. Put a single paper clip, not a staple, in the upper left corner to join the pages.

Essay Tests

When you take an essay test, you may be required to use a "blue book" or to write on the test itself. If you are allowed to use your own paper, use lined paper and write on one side only.

Answers to questions on essay tests should be written in blue or black ink. Since time is too limited for a rough draft, take a moment to organize your thoughts, and then answer the question. Indent each paragraph five spaces (three-quarters of an inch to one inch). State your main idea first; then add specific supporting details and examples.

If you misspell a word or make a mistake, cross through it with a single line. Be sure to write clearly and legibly, and if your handwriting is difficult to read, try printing instead.

Word-Processed Documents

Setting up the Word-Processing Software

Choose a font and a font size that are easily readable, such as Times New Roman in a 12-point size. Do not use a bold or italic font.

Margins should be one inch all around. One-inch margins are the default on most word processors, so you probably will not have to set margins. Set the word processor to double-space the text. Leave the right edge ragged rather than justifying it. (To justify means to line up in a straight edge, like a newspaper column. Most word processors have settings that allow you to justify, but these settings are not commonly used for academic work.)

Formatting the Document

Put your name and the date in the upper right corner of the page. Other information, such as the name of your instructor or the class for which you are preparing the assignment, is optional. Center the title and indent each paragraph as shown in the sample that follows. A title page is not necessary unless your instructor asks for one.

Derek Smith

April 1, 2004

Format Reform

I am ashamed to say that I used to be a format abuser. I used strange fonts such as Adolescence and Space Toaster. I tried to make my papers look longer by using two-inch margins with 14-point font. At my lowest point, I turned in a report on lime-green paper printed in 15-point Star Trek font. A caring instructor saw that I had a problem and helped me to turn my formatting around. Now, I know how to format a document perfectly.

The first step in formatting a document is setting up the word processor. Margins should be set at one inch all around—left, right, top, and bottom. Fonts should be easily

Printing and Presenting Your Document

When the document has been revised and proofread, print it on good-quality 8½ × 11 white paper. To hold the pages together, place a single paper clip in the upper left corner. Do not staple your document or put it in a report cover.

PROGRESSIVE WRITING ASSIGNMENT

Progressive Writing Assignment: Revising, Proofreading, and Formatting

If your instructor has assigned the Progressive Writing Assignment, you are almost finished. All that remains is to revise the paragraph, proofread it carefully, and put it in the proper format.

Topics and Tips

The Topics

Topic 1: Discuss the results of taking a specific piece of advice from a friend or family member.

Topic 2: Discuss your decision to attend college.

Topic 3: Discuss your greatest fear.

Topic 4: Discuss types of stress experienced by college students.

Tips for Revising, Proofreading, and Formatting

- Ask someone else to look at your paragraph and tell you if any point is not clear or if any idea needs further explanation.

- Evaluate your paragraph using the "Checklist for Revision" in this chapter.

- Use your word processor's spelling and grammar checkers, but don't forget to proofread the document at least three times yourself.

- Check the formatting of your paragraph against your instructor's instructions or against the guidelines in this chapter. Improper formatting can be distracting to a reader, but proper formatting allows your paragraph to shine.

CHAPTER 10

Writing an Essay

·ADMIT ONE·

T   This ticket entitles those who have
I   mastered the essay to move freely
C   within the academic world, to express
K   themselves in a way that professors will
E   respect, and to modify the essay format
T   to fit any type of academic writing.

·ADMIT ONE·

Y ou are about to meet a form of writing that offers a ticket to just about anywhere in the academic world. When you master the fundamentals of the essay, you master a form of writing that can be used to express an opinion, analyze a poem, or compare two methods of government. Shrunk down a bit, it can be used to answer a question on an essay test or an employment application. Expanded a bit, it can be used to write a research paper, a term paper, or even a master's thesis. Even this textbook is, in many ways, an expansion of the essay format.

Parts of an Essay

Once you learn to write an essay, you can modify the essay form and length to suit your purpose for writing. Here's how an essay looks: First comes an introduction that catches the reader's attention, provides background, introduces the subject, and states the thesis, or the main idea of the essay.

Then come the body paragraphs. Each one discusses one aspect of your thesis. The topic sentence of each paragraph tells which thesis point the paragraph will develop.

The essay ends with a conclusion that sums up the points you have made and lets your reader know that you have ended the essay.

A diagram of a five-paragraph essay follows. Study it to get a mental map of the essay, then use it for planning and checking your own essays.

Essay Diagram

Introduction

- The first sentence attracts the reader's attention.
- The introduction provides background and introduces the subject.
- The last sentence states the thesis (main idea) and may list the points of development.

First Body Paragraph

- The topic sentence states the first thesis point that you will develop.
- Support sentences give specific examples, information, and explanation of the topic sentence.
- A summary sentence (optional) sums up the entire paragraph.

Second Body Paragraph

- The topic sentence states the next thesis point that you will develop.

- Support sentences give specific examples, information, and explanation of the topic sentence.
- A summary sentence (optional) sums up the entire paragraph.

Third Body Paragraph

- The topic sentence states the third thesis point that you will develop.
- Support sentences give specific examples, information, and explanation of the topic sentence.
- A summary sentence (optional) sums up the entire paragraph.

Conclusion

- The first sentence of the conclusion is a broad, thesis-level statement. It may restate the thesis.
- The last sentence of the conclusion is satisfying and final-sounding.

Sample Essay

Like Father, Like Son

attention-getting opening — "Like father, like son," my aunt always said. Then her eyes would slide over to my mother in a secretive way, and I knew even as a child that it was not a compliment. Now that I have a child of my own, it is important to me to prove my aunt's words wrong. As a

thesis statement — parent, I plan to be different from my own father in all of the ways that count.

topic sentence 1 — The first difference that my aunt—and my child—will see in me is that I will lead a more sober life than my father did. During all my growing-up years, my father abused alcohol and drugs. Since he

support — and my mother were not together, I never saw the worst of it. But even on our rare visitation days, he could not take me to a ball game or a mall without stopping by a convenience store for a six-pack. Maybe because of that example—or maybe because I was young and stupid—I followed in my father's footsteps for a while. But now that I am older and have a son, my wild days are over. I realize the importance of setting a good example and of being a role model to him. Drugs and alcohol will never be a part of the

summary sentence — image of me that my son Brandon carries through life.

(continued)

topic sentence 2 —— Another difference will be in my financial support of my child.

support —— My father drifted from job to job and had periods of unemployment, so his financial support was undependable. To make ends meet, my mother had to work two jobs, one in the mornings on a hotel janitorial staff and the other waiting tables on a part-time basis. Even then, times were often tough. Financial support is part of being a father. It is the reason that I work, and the reason I am

summary sentence —— enrolled in school. Brandon's mother will never have to work an extra job because I am not meeting my obligations.

topic sentence 3 —— Unlike my father, I am going to be there for my child. My father's

support —— visits were as unpredictable as his support checks. He was not there when I was six and had my tonsils taken out, and he was not there for my high school graduation. I will be there for Brandon. Brandon's mother and I have chosen to live separately, but both of us agree that I should have an active role in his life. When he was a baby, I held him and fed him and changed his diapers. Now, I am the one who takes him to T-ball practice and attends all his games.

summary sentence —— He can count on me to be there during the important moments in his life.

I have never been a perfect person, and I won't be a perfect

thesis restatement —— father. But I am determined to do better than my father did. I will be a good role model and support my son financially and emotionally.

closing thought —— One day, someone may look at us and say, "Like father, like son." When that happens, I want Brandon to feel proud.

Meeting the Challenge of Essay Writing

How do you get from an idea or assignment to a polished, fully developed essay? It is sometimes difficult to make the transition from paragraph-length compositions to essays. The length and the format of your assignments have changed. But the basic principles you have been following have not changed. The writing process is still the same: you still prewrite, plan, draft, revise, and proofread.

Similarly, the characteristics of an effective paragraph also apply to the essay. **Direction, unity, coherence,** and **support** are part of the makeup of effective paragraphs *and* essays. Review those characteristics on page 169, and see how these qualities of effective writing apply to the essay.

Characteristics of an Effective Essay

1. **Direction** means that the essay has a strong thesis sentence that states the main idea and sets the course that the essay will follow.

2. **Unity** means that the essay makes one main point and sticks to that point. Each body paragraph may discuss a different thesis point, but the essay never strays from the idea expressed in the thesis.

3. **Coherence** means that the essay is logically connected and easy to follow.

4. **Support** means that the essay contains specific and detailed discussion of the idea stated in the topic sentence.

Writing the Essay

Because the essay is so much longer than the paragraphs you have been writing, it may appear to be not so much a writing exercise as a major construction project. Like any major project, the construction of an essay is accomplished word by word, sentence by sentence, paragraph by paragraph. The next few sections of the chapter deal with the major parts of the essay and with how those parts fit together to form a coherent whole.

Providing Direction: Writing the Thesis Statement

Your **thesis statement** is the most important sentence in your essay. It states the main idea of your essay, often states or implies your attitude or opinion about the subject, and gives your essay **direction**. In an essay, the thesis statement is the controlling force behind every sentence and every word. It is a promise to your reader that you will discuss the idea mentioned in the thesis statement and no other.

Types of Thesis Statements

When constructing your thesis statement, you have a choice. You may write a **thesis with points** that lists the points the essay will cover or a **thesis without points** that does not list the points of development.

The Thesis with Points

A thesis with points presents the main idea and the points of development, listed in the order in which you will discuss them in the essay. The thesis with points has a long tradition in college writing. Listing your thesis points provides a road map that lets the reader see where the essay is headed.

Examples of a Thesis with Points

             point 1   point 2

Playing with my children, shopping with my mother and sister, and

                      point 3

spending time with my husband are my weekend pleasures.

                                        point 1

Older students may attend college to prepare for a new career, to

            point 2   point 3

advance in their present career, or to satisfy a hunger for learning.

point 1   point 2   point 3

Action, an exciting plot, and strong characters are essential ingredients

for any movie.

EXERCISE 1   **COMPLETING THESIS STATEMENTS**

Complete the following thesis statements.

1. Our camping trip was a disaster. We were pelted by rain, bitten by _____, and _____ by _____.

2. Writing an essay requires good ideas, _____, and _____ _____.

3. _____, _____, and _____ are my mother's best qualities.

4. These days, the best candidate for the job is usually the one _____ _____, _____, and _____.

5. Some of the things people fear about getting old are _____, _____, and _____.

The Thesis without Points Listed

A thesis without points listed presents the central idea of the essay without enumerating the points of development. Without the "road map" that listing your points provides, it is even more important that your essay flow logically and smoothly. Therefore, topic sentences require careful planning so that they are clearly connected to the thesis. When you plan a thesis without points, plan each topic sentence, too, to ensure that you stay on track. Not listing thesis points does not mean that you do not plan them; it simply means that you do not list them.

Examples of a Thesis without Points Listed

Thesis: My weekend pleasures revolve around my family.

Topic sentence 1: On Friday evenings, my husband and I often enjoy a movie.

Topic sentence 2: On Saturdays, I take the children shopping or swimming.

Topic sentence 3: Every Sunday, we visit my parents or my husband's parents.

Thesis: Starting an exercise program has made me a healthier person.

Topic sentence 1: For one thing, exercise has improved my aerobic capacity.

Topic sentence 2: I also feel stronger since I began exercising.

Topic sentence 3: Thanks to my exercise program, I have also dropped a few unwanted pounds.

Thesis: Losing my parents at the age of eighteen was the hardest thing I have ever gone through.

Topic sentence 1: The accident was so sudden and my parents were gone so quickly that I was numb for weeks.

Topic sentence 2: My parents' death left me with a tremendous amount of responsibility.

Topic sentence 3: It is still difficult seeing the milestones ahead that my parents will never share with me.

EXERCISE 2   WRITING THESIS STATEMENTS

For each of the following topics, write a thesis statement without points.

1. What was the best (or worst) day of your life?

    _____

2. Should drivers and their passengers be required to wear seat belts?

    _____

3. Is there ever any justification for cheating?

    _____

4. If you could spend a week visiting any place in the world, where would you go?

_____

5. What popular activity do you consider overrated? Why?

_____

Getting Started: Introducing the Essay

It is said that you will never have a second chance to make a first impression. Because first impressions are so important, it pays to put extra effort into your introduction. However, an introduction is more than just a way to make a good impression. It does several jobs that no other part of the essay could do quite so effectively.

Purposes of an Introduction

1. **An introduction draws your reader into the essay.** The first sentence of your introduction should be irresistible. It won't always turn out that way, but aim high anyway.

2. **An introduction presents the general topic of your essay.** When you ease into the thesis by bringing up your general topic first, your reader has time to turn her thoughts away from whatever is on her mind—the price of gas or what to eat for lunch—and to get in the mood to listen to what you have to say.

3. **An introduction provides necessary background.** Background information is not always necessary. But if it is, the introduction is a good place for it. Background information tucked into the introduction gives the necessary details to set up the rest of the essay.

4. **The introduction presents your essay's thesis.** The most important job of an introductory paragraph is to present your essay's thesis. Every sentence in the introduction should follow a path of logic that leads directly to your thesis, which will be the last sentence of your introduction. Once you have stated the thesis, stop. Your body paragraphs will flow naturally from a thesis that comes at the end of the introduction.

Writing the Introductory Paragraph

Introductions that draw a reader in don't just happen; they are carefully crafted. Three common types of introduction follow. Try them all, using the examples as models.

The Broad-to-Narrow Introduction

The *broad-to-narrow introduction* is a classic style of introduction. Sometimes called the *inverted triangle introduction*, it funnels your reader from a statement of your topic to the narrowest point in the introduction: your thesis.

Example

Driving is a great American pastime. Roads and highways swarm with drivers going back and forth from work, school, shopping, or recreation. And with so many drivers on the road, there are bound to be a few who should never have been trusted with that little plastic card called a license. The worst drivers on the road are those who tailgate, those who weave in and out of traffic, and those who drive drunk.

The Narrow-to-Broad Introduction

Instead of beginning with a statement of your general topic, the *narrow-to-broad introduction* begins at a point that is smaller than your thesis—often just a detail—and expands toward that thesis. With this method, you can create an unusual and intriguing opening.

Example

I see the tires first, grimed with the dirt of a long journey. Then I catch a glimpse of a face in the window of the long, boxy vehicle. The RV passes, giving me a last look at the bikes hooked to the back and "The Wanderer" painted above the rear window. I just don't get it. Why would anyone want an RV? An RV is a poor choice for vacationing because of its cost, size, and the chores that come along with it.

The Contrast Introduction

Gold placed on black velvet in a jeweler's window takes on extra luster against the contrasting background. In a *contrast introduction,* your ideas can shine through the drama of contrast. Starting with a contrasting idea is an easy and effective technique to use. Make sure that your introduction contains a change-of-direction signal such as *but* or *however* so that the two contrasting elements are clearly set apart.

Example

Modern life often means that people work long hours to buy possessions that they don't have time to enjoy. Sometimes, it means that children have too many toys and not enough of their parents' time. But many people have decided to leave the rat race. Instead of striving for more, these families live on less in exchange for working fewer hours or sometimes quitting their jobs entirely and working for themselves. A simpler lifestyle can reduce stress, teach self-reliance, and encourage family unity.

The Body Paragraphs: Unity

Once you begin writing the body of your essay, you are in familiar territory once again. You already know how to write a topic sentence and support a paragraph. In writing the three body paragraphs of a five-paragraph essay, you are simply doing that familiar task three times. In an essay, however, each of the three body paragraphs is directly related to the thesis statement. Specifically, each body paragraph discusses one aspect of the thesis statement. This arrangement gives an essay **unity**. Look at the thesis from an earlier sample essay:

> **Thesis:** As a parent, I plan to be different from my own father in all of the ways that count.

From reading the thesis, it is clear that the writer plans to discuss *ways his parenting style will be different from his father's*. Each body paragraph, then, will discuss one way in which the writer will be different from his own father.

Now look at the topic sentences from the sample essay and notice how each relates directly to the thesis (*being different from his father*) while at the same time discussing a distinct and separate point of that thesis:

> *Topic sentence 1:* The first difference that my aunt—and my child—will see in me is that I will lead a more sober life than my father did.

> *Topic sentence 2:* Another difference will be in my financial support of my child.

> *Topic sentence 3:* Unlike my father, I am going to be there for my child.

A thesis statement gives your essay direction. The topic sentences must follow that direction or the unity of the essay will be compromised.

EXERCISE 3   ELIMINATING FAULTY TOPIC SENTENCES

Each of the following thesis statements is followed by three topic sentences. Circle the letter of the topic sentence that does *not* support the thesis statement.

1. Football is my favorite sport.
   a. When I was in high school, I was on the football team three out of four years.
   b. During football season, I am glued to my television set to watch the games.
   c. Attendance at professional football games has risen in recent years, demonstrating the sport's popularity.

2. Like dogs themselves, there are several kinds of dog owners.
   a. Like the wolves they are descended from, dogs are pack animals and need to be part of a social structure.
   b. Some dog owners simply want a companion around the house or apartment.
   c. Another type of dog owner wants the protection that a dog can provide.

3. The city's new indoor skating park will have several positive effects.
   a. Skaters and skateboarders will have a place to call their own.
   b. Pedestrians will no longer be endangered by fast-moving skaters on downtown streets.
   c. Skating can be dangerous, so skaters and skateboarders should always wear safety equipment.

4. Our college should consider scheduling classes around a "Wonderful Wednesday" or a "Fabulous Friday," a day during the week when no classes meet.
   a. A weekly day off would give students time to go to the library and work on class projects.
   b. The idea has been rejected by the school's administration because students might not use the day productively.
   c. The day would also give professors a chance to catch up on grading and have conferences with students.

5. Looking at movies of the 1950s and movies of today, it is easy to see how their differences reflect social changes over the years.
   a. Romantic comedies of the 1950s almost always ended in marriage, but today's movies reflect a different social trend.
   b. Special effects in 1950s movies were unsophisticated, but today's advanced techniques produce impressive effects.
   c. Minorities and women were often stereotyped in 1950s movies, but today's films have fewer stereotyped characters.

The Body Paragraphs: Support

Once you have written the thesis and topic sentences, you have an outline composed of the main idea and major subpoints of the essay. All that remains is to flesh out the body paragraphs with strong, vivid, detailed support, just as you would in any paragraph. Review the principles of support by completing the exercise below.

EXERCISE 4   RECOGNIZING SPECIFIC SUPPORT

The introduction on recreational vehicles is extended here with three sets of body paragraphs. In the blank to the left of each paragraph, mark *S* if the paragraph contains specific support and *V* if the paragraph contains vague support.

Body Paragraph 1a

_____ First of all, an RV is extremely expensive. As anyone who has ever visited an RV dealer or an RV show can testify, the initial outlay for a new RV is considerable. In addition, there are numerous other expenses associated with RV ownership. Some of those expenses relate to traveling, while others relate to maintenance. For the cost involved in owning and maintaining an RV, a person might be able to enjoy a luxury vacation at the finest hotel.

Body Paragraph 1b

_____ First of all, an RV is extremely expensive. A new RV can cost $100,000 or more, as much as some houses. Add to that the cost of gas, maintenance, hookup at RV parks, storage, and repairs, and an RV becomes even more expensive. If a person put $100,000 in the bank at 5 percent interest instead of buying an RV, he would get $5,000 in interest each year, enough to take a vacation or two every year and still keep his $100,000.

Body Paragraph 2a

_____ Second, an RV is just too large. Its size makes it difficult to maneuver and gives it a greater stopping distance, thus requiring greater driving skill. It can't be parked just anywhere, nor can its driver just whip into a drive-through for a hamburger when the travelers get hungry. Its size also makes storage a problem during the months when it is not being used. My neighbors' RV is too large to fit into their garage, so they had to build a separate storage barn in their backyard just to keep their RV out of the weather. That's fine for people who have the money and the space to build a storage facility, but people who live in condominiums or who have small lots have to make other arrangements. An RV's size makes it more of a liability than an asset.

Body Paragraph 2b

_____ Second, an RV is just too large. The size of an RV is enormous, dwarfing every car on the road. Size has several disadvantages. Many of the maneuvers that drivers of smaller vehicles take for granted cannot be performed by an RV because of its size. Further, there is the consideration of RV storage, which must take size into account. An RV's size makes it more of a liability than an asset.

Body Paragraph 3a

_____ Finally, an RV is just too much work. People who travel in RVs have to clean, cook, make beds, and empty toilets. If they run out of food, they have to shop. If I have to take all that work on vacation with me, I might as well stay at home. When I go on vacation, I want to eat in restaurants and have my food brought to me perfectly prepared. I do not want to stand over a hot stove and know that I have to wash dishes after I eat. In the morning, I want to leave my bed unmade and my towels in the tub, walk on the beach, and come back to my room to find everything in perfect order. In an RV, I would have to do all the work myself.

Body Paragraph 3b

_____ Finally, an RV is just too much work. People who travel in RVs have to do all the work normally associated with a maintaining a house. In many cases, there are other associated tasks that relate to travel. Why would a person take all of those household chores on vacation? It seems to me that the purpose of a vacation is to leave everyday chores behind. In a hotel these tasks are accomplished by the hotel staff, so that the traveler has little to do. That seems like the ideal situation for any traveler. That way, when the traveler returns home, he is rested and refreshed, not worn out from trying to accomplish all the tasks associated with traveling in an RV.

The Body Paragraphs: Coherence

An essay requires not only coherence *within* paragraphs, but coherence *between* paragraphs. That is, movement from one paragraph to the next should seem graceful, natural, and seamless.

Coherence within paragraphs is provided by transitional words, use of pronouns, and use of repetition. (To review these principles, glance back at the section on coherence in Chapter 5.) Look below for tips for making graceful transitions between paragraphs.

Tips for Smooth Transitions

1. In the first body paragraph, you do not necessarily need a transitional word. If you want to use one to indicate that this paragraph is making the first of several points, the choices are easy: *first of all, one reason* (*factor, cause,* or similar term), or *first.*

2. The second body paragraph gives you more choices. You can use a phrase like *a second reason* or a word such as *next, another,* or *also.* For variety, try slipping the word or phrase in the middle of your topic sentence instead of using it at the beginning: "Job security is *another* reason I have chosen a career in the medical field."

3. The third body paragraph gives you all of the transitional options of the second body paragraph and a few others as well. Since the third body paragraph is your last, you can use expressions like *finally* or *the last reason.* If you are using emphatic order (order of importance), you might want to try *most important, the major factor, best,* or *worst.*

4. Transitions of time and place are preferable in narrative or descriptive essays and can be used in any essay organized around time or place. Transitions of time might include phrases such as *after I had finished my classes for the day, the next morning,* or *a few weeks later.* Transitions of place might include phrases such as *just down the hall, across the room,* or *on the other side of town.* (A more complete listing is found in Chapter 5.)

5. Avoid anything that would confuse your reader or make it seem as though you are just mechanically plugging in transitions instead of trying to write an artful essay. A reader would be confused, for instance, if you used a phrase such as *in conclusion* to begin your last body paragraph. The last body paragraph contains your last major point, but it is not your conclusion. (In fact, *in conclusion* is not even a recommended opening for conclusions.)

    Any transitional sequence that uses counting throughout—*first, second, third; my first reason, my second reason, my third reason*—gives your reader the impression that you are using transitions mechanically and unthinkingly rather than choosing them for best effect. If you use numbers, combine them with other transitional expressions for best effect: *the first reason, another factor,* and *the final cause.*

A Graceful Exit: The Conclusion

The etiquette of concluding an essay, like that of ending a telephone conversation, is simple: Keep the goodbye short and don't introduce any new information that keeps the other person hanging on too long.

After the specific and detailed support of the body paragraphs, the first sentence or two of your conclusion takes the reader back to a broad, thesis-level view of the topic. Often, this takes the form of a thesis restatement.

Then comes the closing statement, harder to write but vital because it is the last impression your reader takes away from the essay. The key requirement of a closing statement is that it should *sound* like a closing statement. It should sound as final as the slam of a door.

Sample Conclusion 1: A Summary Conclusion

The summary conclusion sums up the main points and ends with a sentence that provides a ring of finality.

Example

Recreational vehicles are too costly, too big, and too labor intensive. When I go on vacation, I'll drive my own car, stay at a reasonably priced motel, and let someone else do all the work.

Sample Conclusion 2: A Recommendation

A recommendation conclusion suggests a solution to a problem raised in the essay. A logical way to end an essay that discusses a problem is to offer a solution or suggest that one is on the horizon.

Example

In spite of a few problems, our school library is a valuable resource for all students. Extending weekend and evening hours, keeping the computer room open whenever the library is open, and setting aside a special group study area for students who need to converse will go a long way toward easing the frustrations many students experience when they visit the library.

Sample Conclusion 3: A Prediction

A look toward the future is another good way of ending an essay. The example below ends an essay discussing the advantages of online music stores with a summary and a prediction.

Example

Online music stores have a wide selection of merchandise, offer convenience, and allow customers to listen before they buy. With all of those advantages, it won't be long before a majority of people begin turning away from conventional music shops and taking their business online.

Wordsmith's Corner: Sample Essays

Below are two essays. One explores "inner space"—the writer's search for who she is—while the other discusses exploration of outer space. Read each essay and answer the questions that follow.

Essay 1

In the essay, Autumn discusses her lifelong search for her heritage.

A Mixed-up Kid

I opened the wedding invitation and read, "As we form a new union, we draw on the strength of our heritage and the unity of our family. Celebrate with us." A wave of longing and downright envy swept over me. I do not envy Kim her marriage. I envy her strong sense of who she is and where she comes from. It is a feeling I have never known. All my life, I have been searching for who I am.

When I look at the two people who adopted me twenty years ago, I feel lucky, secure, and loved, but I see nothing of where I came from. My mom's red hair and freckles tell of her Irish heritage, but say nothing of mine. She sets our Thanksgiving table with her great-grandmother's crystal and linen, and tells me to look forward, not back. She just doesn't understand. My dad, who has Scottish and Cherokee ancestry, understands a bit more. When I was younger, he would stretch his arm out, comparing his fawn-colored skin to mine. "That's a pretty close match," he'd say.

"You might have a little Cherokee in you somewhere." Hearing him say that always made me feel connected and secure.

When I look in the mirror, I see no clear clues to my heritage. I see light caramel skin, coarse, wavy hair, and brown eyes. My face is wide, with a small, flat nose and delicate lips. I am short—just 5'2"—with a sturdy build. When I was in the sixth grade, a new girl at school asked me what race I was. I told her that my parents had told me my background was mixed, but I was adopted and not sure what the mixture was. "I'm a mixed-up kid, too," she said. I thought that was the perfect way of expressing how I felt—a mixed-up kid.

When I look to society to find out who I am, I get no answers. My adoption records are sealed, and my mom and dad know nothing about my birth parents. Was I given up by a teenage mother who loved me but couldn't keep me? Was I thrown in a dumpster by an uncaring parent or left on a doorstep by a desperate one? I may never know. Because I know so little about my background, I have tried to seek a mirror in many different social groups, and I have friends of all races. Yet there is still a part of me that feels like an outsider in any group because I am not sure where I come from.

For the most part, I am a happy person who feels fortunate in her family and friends. Mostly, I follow my mother's advice to look forward and not back. But when I look around me, hoping to see a reflection of who I am, all I see is a mixed-up kid.

Questions ?

1. Underline the thesis statement. Is it a thesis with points listed or without points listed?

_____

2. Underline the topic sentence of each body paragraph.

Essay 2

Harley, the writer of this essay, discusses the value of the U.S. space program.

The Final Frontier

On the day that I was born, Neil Armstrong, the first person on the moon, took "one small step for man, one giant leap for mankind." I guess that is why I have always taken an interest in our space program. The space program, unlike many government programs, has something to give to every American.

The space program links every American to the mysteries that lie beyond Earth's atmosphere. Human beings have always looked to the heavens with a sense of wonder. Only in the last century have we actually been able to explore our moon and other planets. The Mars <u>Pathfinder</u> mission in 1997 gave us a closer look at the red planet with a mobile rover that took soil samples and pictures from all angles, even showing us a Martian sunset. The <u>Voyager</u> traveled outward among the planets, taking photographs of red Mars, ringed Saturn, and blue Neptune. In photographing the planet Jupiter and its moons, <u>Voyager</u> discovered ice on one of the moons, and where there is water or ice, there is the possibility of some form of life. What could be more exciting than the discovery of life beyond Earth's boundaries?

Another important contribution of the space program is that it gives us heroes in a time when heroes are few. Alan Shepherd, the first American in space, had the courage to go "where no one had gone before" as Americans sat mesmerized in front of black-and-white TV sets. Neil Armstrong, the first to set foot on the moon, was my hero for many years. Sally Ride, the first woman in space, inspired people all over the United States to cheer her on with the words "Ride, Sally Ride!" And who can forget Christa McAuliffe, the first teacher in space, who died tragically in the explosion of the space shuttle <u>Challenger</u>? John Glenn, a veteran space traveler, was the first senior citizen to test the effects of space travel on an aging body. All of these people are heroes because they are pioneers, among the first to travel where our descendants may one day live.

The most important contribution of the space program is the hope it gives for the future. All around us, the earth's resources are being depleted. If we don't replenish the forests, repair the ozone layer, and repopulate endangered species, life on Earth will be in danger. The growth of the human population also raises the possibility that one day, the earth may no longer have room for everyone. The vast, cold reaches of space may hold a solution to these problems. Human beings have lived for months on the <u>Mir</u> space station, and that is just the beginning. Self-sustaining space colonies could eventually provide room for a spreading human population. People may one day find a way to populate the planets in the solar system or even to reach other solar systems through interstellar travel. In the future, space may hold the key to human survival.

Space travel has fascinated me since I was old enough to know that on my birthday, the first human set foot on the moon. I believe that the space program returns value for every penny that is spent on it. It links us to the ancient mysteries of the universe, it provides us with heroes, and it brings hope for a brighter future for every human being.

Questions

1. Underline the thesis statement. Is it a thesis with points listed or without points listed?

_____

2. Underline the topic sentence of each paragraph.

Topics for Writing Essays

Essay Assignment 1: Reflections of You

In Sample Essay 1, "A Mixed-up Kid," the writer speaks of searching for her reflection in her parents, in her own mirror, and in society. Write an essay discussing who you are in your own eyes and in the eyes of two other groups or individuals. Possibilities include your parents, friends, teachers, members of your church, and children. Or you might move in a widening circle, first discussing how you see yourself, how your close friends see you, and how casual acquaintances see you. Another possibility, particularly if your view of yourself has changed radically over the years, is an essay explaining how you saw yourself in the past, how you see yourself now, and how you hope to see yourself in the future.

Constructing Your Essay

Step 1: Prewrite using one of the methods in Chapter 2. Prewriting is even more important in longer compositions, which usually require more thought. Try **freewriting** for ten minutes about the image that you have of yourself and that various other people or groups have of you. Or try a cluster diagram, with each branch of the cluster showing a different view of the person you are. Next, review your prewriting and choose the three viewpoints you want to include in your essay. Make sure that they are separate and distinct viewpoints. If all three viewpoints show you as the same exact person, your three body paragraphs will be nearly identical in content.

Step 2: Plan, making a brief outline of the essay you plan to write. Here's where you'll decide on the order in which to present your paragraphs and get some idea of the supporting examples you want to use. After you've done a scratch outline, write out your thesis statement and your three topic sentences. You may want to change the wording later, but completing a thesis statement and topic sentences prepares you for the next step.

Step 3: Draft your essay as completely as you can. If you have trouble with the introduction, start with your thesis and proceed from there. You can always come back and write your introduction later. Complete each paragraph as if it were an individual paragraph like the ones you have been writing in class, including plenty of specific support for each topic sentence. When you have completed your draft, including the introduction and conclusion, lay it aside for a while before proceeding to the next step.

Step 4: Revise your essay. First, do a visual check. Does your essay look balanced, with the three body paragraphs approximately equal in length? Are the body paragraphs framed by an introduction and conclusion that are shorter than the body paragraphs?

Next, check your word count. If you are writing on a computer, your word processor can check the count for you. If you have written in longhand, pick three lines at random. Count the number of words in each line, add them together, and then divide by three. The result is your average number of words per line. Count the number of lines, then multiply by the average number of words per line. The result is your approximate word count. If your word count is between 400 and 550, you are in the ballpark. If the count is over 600, check to make sure that everything you are saying supports your thesis and that you are not repeating yourself. If your word count is under 400, you probably need to add more support.

Finally, check the specific parts of your essay, using the Checklist for Revision at the end of this chapter.

Once you have completed the Checklist for Revision, you might want to show your essay to a classmate. Ask your classmate to focus on content and clarity. Does he or she understand everything you say? Are examples plentiful and specific?

Once you have looked at your essay, completed the revision checklist, and perhaps gotten a second opinion, rewrite the essay.

Step 5: Proofread after you have revised your essay and are satisfied that it is the essay you want to turn in. Correct any errors in grammar or spelling.

Essay Assignment 2: What Interests You?

In Sample Essay 2, "The Final Frontier," the writer discusses a lifelong interest in the space program. What interests you, either as an onlooker or a participant? Are you a movie buff, a music lover, or a follower of a particular sport? Do you read every book and watch every TV special about a particular historical period? Are you into collecting teacups, playing the alto sax, riding motorcycles, attending garage sales, or singing in a choir or chorus?

Whatever your interest, write about it, following the steps of the writing process as outlined in Essay Assignment 1. To get started, think of the following questions:

How long have you been pursuing your interest?

Who got you started?

What is it that inspires and fascinates you about it?

Are there people associated with it that you admire?

What activities do you participate in that involve your interest?

Checklist for Revision

The Introduction

✔ Does the introduction draw the reader in?

✔ Does the introduction provide background information, if needed?

The Thesis

✔ Is the thesis the last sentence of the introduction?

✔ If the thesis does not include points of development, does it state the main idea broadly enough to include all the points you raise in your body paragraphs?

✔ If the thesis lists points, does it list three separate and distinct points?

Topic Sentences

✔ Does each topic sentence raise one separate and distinct thesis point?

✔ If the thesis lists points, are body paragraphs arranged in the same order as thesis points?

The Body

✔ Does each body paragraph provide specific detail and examples for each thesis point?

✔ Have you provided enough specific support for each thesis point?

✔ Does each sentence of each body paragraph support the topic sentence?

The Conclusion

✔ Is the first sentence of the conclusion a broad, thesis-level statement?

✔ Is the conclusion short, with no new information introduced?

✔ Is the last sentence satisfying and final-sounding?

Checking Coherence

✔ Have you used transitional words effectively within paragraphs?

✔ Have you used transitional words effectively between paragraphs?

PART 2

Grammar

Verbs and Subjects

A Journalist's Questions
Who?
What?
When?
Where?
Why?

If there were no verbs or subjects, the top two items in the list of traditional journalist's questions would be eliminated. Verbs tell *what* was done, while subjects tell *who or what* the sentence is about.

The **verb** of a sentence carries the action, if any, and directs that action to and from the other words in the sentence. Some verbs, called **linking verbs**, function as connectors for related words.

A subject is what the sentence is about. It is usually a noun or a pronoun. It is probably not the only noun or pronoun in the sentence, but it is the only one that enjoys such a direct grammatical connection to its verb. If you ask, "Who or what _____?" putting the verb in the blank, the answer to your question is always the subject of the sentence.

Action and Linking Verbs

Verbs work in two ways within a sentence. They show the action, physical or mental, of the subject of the sentence, or they link the subject with other words in the sentence.

Action Verbs

Action verbs show physical or mental action performed by a subject. Look at the action verbs below, highlighted in italic type.

Examples

✔ Beth *sat* at her desk. (physical action)

✔ She *noticed* that her clock *had stopped*. (mental action, physical action)

✔ She *wondered* how long she *had been studying*. (mental action)

PRACTICE 1   RECOGNIZING ACTION VERBS

Underline the action verb in each sentence.

1. Buzz leaped for the volleyball.
2. Pilar quickly ate her tuna salad sandwich.
3. A crop duster droned overhead.
4. The dog barked loudly at the stranger's approach.
5. Melvina returned two books to the library's drop box.

Linking Verbs

A linking verb links its subject with a word that describes or renames it. The most common linking verb in English is the verb *to be*, in all its various forms: *is, are, was, were, has been, will be,* and so on. Look at the following examples to see how the verb *to be* functions as a linking verb.

Examples

✔ The glass *is* empty.

The verb *is* links the subject, *glass,* with an adjective describing it.

✔ Li *has been* student body president for the past year.

The verb *has been* links the subject, Li, with a noun, *president,* that renames him. In other words, he could be referred to as either "Li" or "the student body president." ("Student" and "body" are adjectives.)

Other common linking verbs include the verbs *to seem, to appear, to grow,* and *to become.* Verbs of the senses, such as *to smell, to taste, to look, to sound,* and *to feel,* can be action or linking verbs depending on how they are used.

Examples

L The book *seems* interesting. (The verb links *book* with an adjective that describes it.)

L The burned potatoes *looked* terrible. (*Looked* is a linking verb. The potatoes are performing no action.)

A Terralyn *looked* at the schedule of classes. (The verb shows Terralyn's physical action.)

L The sliced turkey *smelled* bad. (The verb links *turkey* with an adjective that describes it.)

A The dog *smelled* his owner's pockets, hoping for a treat. (The verb shows the dog's physical action.)

The Linking Verb Test

To tell if a verb is a linking verb, see if you can substitute *is* or *was* in its place. If the substitution works, the verb is probably a linking verb.

Examples

? The drone of the engine *grew* louder as the plane approached the airport.

L The drone of the engine ~~grew~~ *was* louder as the plane approached the airport.

The substitution makes sense; therefore, *grew* is used here as a linking verb.

?   The friendship between Della and Miriam *grew* quickly because they shared many interests.

A   The friendship between Della and Miriam grew *was* quickly because they shared many interests.

The substitution does not makes sense; therefore, *grew* is used as an action verb.

?   After drinking four cups of coffee, Martin *felt* jittery.

L   After drinking four cups of coffee, Martin felt *was* jittery. (linking verb)

?   Casey *felt* someone tap her shoulder and turned to see who it was.

A   Casey felt *was* someone tap her shoulder and turned to see who it was. (action verb)

PRACTICE 2   **RECOGNIZING ACTION AND LINKING VERBS**

Underline the verbs in each sentence. In the blank to the left, write *A* if the verb is an action verb, *L* if it is a linking verb.

_____   **1.**   The picture on the wall is crooked.

_____   **2.**   Lu Ana smelled the milk to see if it was fresh.

_____   **3.**   This crossword puzzle looks difficult.

_____   **4.**   The squirrel scampered up the trunk of the tree.

_____   **5.**   Kim prepared her report carefully.

_____   **6.**   The company's representative asked for Zelda's account number.

_____   **7.**   The scrambled eggs tasted good.

_____   **8.**   Anna tasted the eggs cautiously.

_____   **9.**   Two young men lounged against a car in the parking lot of the fast-food place.

_____   **10.**   The mail carrier seemed cheerful.

Recognizing Verbs and Subjects

Finding the Verb

Finding the subject and verb of a sentence is easier if you look for the verb first. Following are some guidelines to help you spot the verb in a sentence.

1. **A verb may show action.**
   - ✔ Laney <u>laughed</u> aloud at the cartoon.
   - ✔ Kirsten <u>wondered</u> what was so funny.

2. **A verb may link the subject to the rest of the sentence.**
   - ✔ The inspection sticker in the elevator <u>was</u> four years old.
   - ✔ The broken glass on the floor <u>looked</u> dangerous.

3. **A verb may consist of more than one word. Some verbs include a main verb and one or more *helping verbs*.**
   - ✔ Zeke <u>has been working</u> in the campus bookstore for three months.
   - ✔ Melanie <u>had</u> not <u>planned</u> to attend a commuter college.
   - ✔ Gavin <u>might have been expecting</u> me to return his call.

4. **Some verbs are compound verbs.**
   - ✔ Nick <u>pulled</u> a muscle in his shoulder and <u>went</u> to see the doctor.
   - ✔ The loan officer <u>calculated</u> the payments and <u>handed</u> the customer a loan agreement.
   - ✔ Angelo <u>ate</u> octopus once but <u>did</u> not <u>know</u> what it was.

5. **An infinitive (*to* + verb) cannot act as a verb in a sentence.**
   - ✘ Kendall has begun <u>to accept</u> too many credit card offers.

   The phrase *to accept* is an infinitive and cannot be the main verb of the sentence. The verb in this sentence is *has begun*.
   - ✘ The advertiser's claims about the new skin cream sounded too good <u>to be</u> true.

   The phrase *to be* is an infinitive, not the verb of the sentence. The verb in this sentence is *sounded*.

6. **A verb form ending in *-ing* cannot act as a verb in a sentence unless a helping verb precedes it.**
   - ✘ The smell of baking bread drifted into the street, <u>inviting</u> passersby into the bakery.

   Inviting cannot be the verb because a helping verb does not precede it. The verb in this sentence is *drifted*.
   - ✘ The basset hound's <u>drooping</u> jowls gave him a mournful appearance.

   Drooping cannot be the verb because a helping verb does not precede it. The verb in this sentence is *gave*.
   - ✔ Elaine's mother <u>was waving</u> from the porch.

   The verb in this sentence is *was waving* (helping verb + main verb).

✔ Jeff said he <u>had</u> not <u>been sleeping</u> well for the last few months.

The verb in this sentence is *had been sleeping* (helping verb + main verb).

PRACTICE 3   RECOGNIZING VERBS

Underline the verbs in each sentence.

1. Vernon shared his hamburger with a stray dog.
2. Melanie noticed a footprint on the kitchen wall.
3. The woman's hair was long enough to brush the pockets of her jeans.
4. April did not move except to turn a page of her book now and then.
5. The employee guided a long line of grocery carts, pushing them through the parking lot toward the store.
6. The governor announced a new program to help preschool children.
7. The photograph on the calendar showed a polar bear relaxing on an ice floe.
8. Sleepily, Tony poured a cup of coffee and popped a frozen waffle into the toaster.
9. My grandmother believes that people behave more irrationally during a full moon.
10. A rumor about the company's closing had been circulating for some time.

Finding the Subject

A subject answers the question "*Who or what* _____?" To find the subject of a verb, ask the question, "Who or what _____?" The verb fills in the blank.

Who?
what?

Note: Be sure the words *who* or *what* are stated *before* the verb, or you will find the object rather than the subject.

✔ Inside Maurice's briefcase, his cell phone <u>rang</u>.

Who or what rang? The cell phone rang. *Cell phone* is the subject of the verb *rang*.

✔ The hot coffee <u>burned</u> Adrienne's tongue.

Who or what burned? The hot coffee burned. *Coffee* is the simple subject of the verb *burned*. (The words *the* and *hot* are modifiers and are part of the complete subject.)

✔ Katelyn and Marie <u><u>wanted</u></u> to ride the ferris wheel.

Who or what wanted? Katelyn and Marie wanted. *Katelyn and Marie* is the compound subject of the verb *wanted*.

✔ Carefully, Tom <u><u>measured</u></u> the olive oil and <u><u>folded</u></u> it into the pizza dough.

Who or what measured? Tom measured. Who or what folded? Tom folded. *Tom* is the subject of the compound verb *measured and folded*.

✔ Carefully, Tom <u><u>measured</u></u> the olive oil while Ruthie <u><u>kneaded</u></u> the pizza dough.

Who or what measured? Tom measured. *Tom* is the subject of the verb *measured*. *Who* or what *kneaded*? Ruthie kneaded. *Ruthie* is the subject of the verb *kneaded*.

PRACTICE 4 RECOGNIZING VERBS AND SUBJECTS

Double underline the verb in each sentence. Then find the subject by asking "Who or what _____?" Underline the subject once.

1. Marvin squeezed behind the wheel of the small sports car.
2. A candy jar sat on top of the filing cabinet.
3. The photograph showed a much thinner Bert.
4. The computer emitted a strange clunking noise.
5. Gwyn opened the door and called the dog.

Recognizing Prepositional Phrases

A subject will not be part of a <u>prepositional phrase</u>. In many sentences, prepositional phrases intervene between subject and verb.

✔ The top *of the refrigerator* was covered with dust.

When we pick out the subject of the verb by asking "What is covered with dust?" it is tempting to say, "The refrigerator is covered." But *refrigerator* cannot be the subject of the verb in this sentence. Grammatically, it already has a job: It is the object of the preposition. The subject of this sentence is *top*.

To avoid mistakes in picking out the subject of the sentence, cross out prepositional phrases before picking out subject and verb.

Below are a few tips for recognizing prepositional phrases:

- **Prepositional phrases always *begin* with a preposition.** Prepositions are often short words like *of, to, by, for,* or *from.* They are often words of location, such as *behind, beside, beneath, beyond,* or *below.* Below is a list of common prepositions.

Frequently Used Prepositions

about	beneath	in	to
above	beside	into	toward
across	between	like	under
after	beyond	near	underneath
along	by	next to	until
along with	down	of	up
around	during	off	upon
at	except	on	with
before	for	outside	within
behind	from	over	without

- **Prepositional phrases always *end* with a noun or pronoun.** The object of a preposition, always a noun or pronoun, comes at the end of a

Famous PREPOSITIONAL PHRASES

The prepositional phrases below have been used as titles for songs, television shows, movies, and books. How many do you recognize? Can you think of others?

Above Suspicion	In Living Color
Against the Wind	Of Mice and Men
Around the World in Eighty Days	On Golden Pond
At Long Last Love	On the Waterfront
At the Hop	Over the Rainbow
Behind Closed Doors	Under the Boardwalk
Behind Enemy Lines	Under the Yum Yum Tree
Beneath the Planet of the Apes	Up a Lazy River
Beyond the Sea	Up on the Roof
In Cold Blood	Up the Down Staircase

> ## *Real-World Writing: Is it okay to end a sentence with a preposition?
>
> How else would you say, "Will you pick me up?" or "I feel left out"?
>
> Sometimes, what seems to be an objection to a preposition at the end of a sentence is really an objection to an awkward or redundant construction. "Where are you at?" will bring a scowl to any English teacher's face—not because it ends in a preposition, but because it is redundant: *where* and *at* are both doing the same job—indicating location.
>
> But by all means, say "I have nothing to put this in" or "The dog wants to go out." Except in the most formal writing, ending sentences with prepositions is something almost everyone can live with.

prepositional phrase: of the *ceiling,* beside the *restaurant,* with *us,* to *Rita and Dean,* within *four months.*

• **Prepositional phrases often have a three-word structure.** Often, prepositional phrases have a three-word structure: preposition, article (*a, an,* or *the*), noun. Thus phrases like *of an airplane, under the bleachers,* and *with a frown* become easy to recognize. But prepositional phrases can also be stretched with modifiers and compound objects: Everyone made fun *of Sam's extra-distance, glow-in-the-dark, Super-Flight golf balls and his tasseled, monogrammed golf club covers.* More often, though, the three-word pattern prevails.

PRACTICE 5   ELIMINATING PREPOSITIONAL PHRASES

Cross out prepositional phrases in the each sentence. Underline subjects once and verbs twice.

1. The smell of cough drops and the sound of sneezing filled the waiting room of the doctor's office.
2. Siren blaring, the fire truck pulled into the street.
3. The cracked and uneven cement walk in front of the science building posed a danger to students and faculty walking to class.
4. The sugary taste of the cereal and the bright colors on the box were appealing to children.
5. The smell of fried chicken drifted from the kitchen, tantalizing Fran.

Regular and Irregular Verbs

Regular verbs follow a predictable pattern in the formation of their principal parts. Every verb has four principal parts: the present-tense form, the past-tense form, the past participle (used with helping verbs), and the present participle (the -*ing* verb form used with helping verbs). Regular verbs add *ed* to form their past tense and past participles. Some examples of regular verbs follow.

Regular Verb Forms   *Gerundio*

Present	Past	Past Participle	Present Participle
walk	walked	(have) walked	(are) walking
change	changed	(have) changed	(are) changing
add	added	(have) added	(are) adding
pull	pulled	(have) pulled	(are) pulling

Irregular verbs, on the other hand, follow no predictable pattern in their past and past participle forms. Sometimes a vowel changes: *sing* in the present tense becomes *sang* in the past tense and *sung* in the past participle. Sometimes an *n* or *en* will be added to form the past participle: *take* becomes *taken*, *fall* becomes *fallen*. Some verbs, such as *set*, do not change at all. Others change completely: *buy* in the present tense becomes *bought* in the past and past participle.

Below are some common irregular verbs and their principal parts. If you are unsure about a verb form, check this list or consult a dictionary for the correct form.

Principal Parts of Common Irregular Verbs

Present	Past	Past Participle	Present Participle
become	became	(have) become	(are) becoming
begin	began	(have) begun	(are) beginning
blow	blew	(have) blown	(are) blowing
break	broke	(have) broken	(are) breaking
bring	brought	(have) brought	(are) bringing
burst	burst	(have) burst	(are) bursting
buy	bought	(have) bought	(are) buying
catch	caught	(have) caught	(are) catching

Present	Past	Past Participle	Present Participle
choose	chose	(have) chosen	(are) choosing
come	came	(have) come	(are) coming
cut	cut	(have) cut	(are) cutting
do	did	(have) done	(are) doing
draw	drew	(have) drawn	(are) drawing
drink	drank	(have) drunk	(are) drinking
drive	drove	(have) driven	(are) driving
eat	ate	(have) eaten	(are) eating
fall	fell	(have) fallen	(are) falling
feel	felt	(have) felt	(are) feeling
fight	fought	(have) fought	(are) fighting
find	found	(have) found	(are) finding
fly	flew	(have) flown	(are) flying
freeze	froze	(have) frozen	(are) freezing
get	got	(have) gotten (or got)	(are) getting
give	gave	(have) given	(are) giving
go	went	(have) gone	(are) going
grow	grew	(have) grown	(are) growing
have	had	(have) had	(are) having
hear	heard	(have) heard	(are) hearing
hide	hid	(have) hidden	(are) hiding
hold	held	(have) held	(are) holding
hurt	hurt	(have) hurt	(are) hurting
keep	kept	(have) kept	(are) keeping
know	knew	(have) known	(are) knowing
lay (put)	laid	(have) laid	(are) laying
lead	led	(have) led	(are) leading
leave	left	(have) left	(are) leaving
lend	lent	(have) lent	(are) lending
lie (recline)	lay	(have) lain	(are) lying
lose	lost	(have) lost	(are) losing
put	put	(have) put	(are) putting
ride	rode	(have) ridden	(are) riding

prestar —

Present	Past	Past Participle	Present Participle
rise	rose	(have) risen	(are) rising
run	ran	(have) run	(are) running
see	saw	(have) seen	(are) seeing
set (place)	set	(have) set	(are) setting
sing	sang	(have) sung	(are) singing
sit (be seated)	sat	(have) sat	(are) sitting
speak	spoke	(have) spoken	(are) speaking
swim	swam	(have) swum	(are) swimming
take	took	(have) taken	(are) taking
tear	tore	(have) torn	(are) tearing
throw	threw	(have) thrown	(are) throwing
write	wrote	(have) written	(are) writing
be, am, are, is	was, were	(have) been	(are) being

PRACTICE 6   USING IRREGULAR VERBS

Fill in the blank with the correct form of the verb shown to the left of each question. For help, consult the list of irregular verbs above.

(become)   **1.** Tamiki has _become_ an avid baseball fan.

(break)   **2.** Before putting the eggs in his grocery cart, Ed opened the carton to make sure none were _broken_.

(drink)   **3.** Someone has _drunk_ all the orange juice.

(eat)   **4.** Did you _eat_ breakfast this morning?

(go)   **5.** The secretary said Mr. Cavanaugh had _gone_ for the day.

(lead)   **6.** The kindergarten teacher _lay_ the children down the hall in single file.

(lend)   **7.** A classmate _lay_ me a pen, but I forgot to return it.

(run)   **8.** The cashier _ran_ to catch the customer who had forgotten his keys.

(see)   **9.** When David's parents _saw_ his grade report, they told him they were proud.

(swim)   **10.** When Jennifer had _swum_ fifteen laps, she stopped to rest.

Puzzling Pairs

Some irregular verbs are easily confused with other words. The following section will help you make the right choice between *loan* and *lend, lie* and *lay,* and *sit* and *set.*

Lend and *Loan*

Prestar

Lend is a verb meaning "to allow someone to borrow," as in "*Lend* me ten dollars until payday," or "She *lent* her book to another student." *Loan* is a noun meaning "something borrowed," as in "He went to the bank for a mortgage *loan.*" *prestamo*

---

* Real-World Writing: Lend? Loan? Who Cares?

People who care about English also care about the distinction between *lend* and *loan.* Though the use of *loan* as a verb is widespread, it is not considered acceptable by careful writers and speakers of English.

Therefore, it's best to avoid such constructions as "Loan me a quarter for the telephone," or "He loaned me his car."

Examples

✗   I hoped my neighbor would *loan* me his lawnmower.

✔   I hoped my neighbor would *lend* me his lawnmower.

✗   Shakespeare wrote, "Friends, Romans, countrymen, *loan* me your ears."

✔   Shakespeare wrote, "Friends, Romans, countrymen, *lend* me your ears."

✔   Without a good credit record, it's hard to get a *loan.*

PRACTICE 7   USING *LEND* AND *LOAN*

Underline the correct word in each sentence.

1.   Calvin wanted a car, but knew he could not afford payments on a (lend, loan).
2.   We can get the job finished quickly if Andrew (lends, loans) a hand.
3.   Before Josh went to camp, his mother warned him not to (lend, loan) his toothbrush or comb.
4.   "Before you can get a (lend, loan) from a bank," said Portia, "you have to prove you don't need the money."
5.   Would you mind (lending, loaning) me a dollar?

Lay and *Lie*

Lay and *lie* are often confused, partly because their forms overlap. The present-tense form of *lay* and the past-tense form of *lie* are both the same: *lay*. Look at the chart below to see the different forms of each verb.

Present	Past	Past Participle	Present Participle
lay (put)	laid	(have) laid	(are) laying
lie (recline)	lay	(have) lain	(are) lying

- The verb *lay* means "to put or place." It always takes an object: that is, there will always be an answer to the question, "Lay what?"

Examples

Whenever I need help, Manuel lays his work aside to assist me.

put
verb　　object

Carol laid her purse on the table and went to answer the phone.

verb　　object

Spiros has laid the brick for his patio.

verb　　　object

The company is laying the groundwork for further expansion.

verb　　　　object

- The verb *lie* means "to recline." It does not take an object.

Examples

When Morgan had the flu, she lay in bed for almost two days.

recline
verb

The town lay in a little valley surrounded by hills.

verb　*recline*

Grady's back was aching because he had lain too long in one position.

verb

The dog has been lying on the sofa again; his fur is all over the cushions.

verb

PRACTICE 8　USING *LAY* AND *LIE*

put　　*recline*

Underline the correct verb forms in the paragraph below.

When Jack came home from work, he found his wife [1](laying, lying) unconscious on the kitchen floor. He [2](laid, lay) his briefcase on the table and quickly dialed 911, wondering how long she had been [3](laying, lying) there. He listened numbly as the operator said, "Don't move her, just let her [4](lay, lie) there until the ambulance arrives. [5](Lay, lie) the phone down and check her breathing, but don't hang up." When the ambulance arrived, the paramedics [6](lay, laid) Arlene on a stretcher and put her in the ambulance. At the hospital, Jack paced the small waiting room, [7](laying, lying) in wait for the doctor and news of Arlene. Dr. Rodriguez finally emerged from the treatment room and told Jack that his wife had a mild concussion. "We'd like to observe her and make sure she [8](lays, lies) quietly for a day or two," the doctor said. Later, Jack brought his overnight bag and [9](lay, laid) it on the spare bed in Arlene's hospital room. "Stay with her if you like," said the nurse, "but it's not necessary. She will be fine." "I'll stay," said Jack. "I have [10](laid, lain) beside that woman every night for thirty-two years, and I see no reason to stop now."

Sit and Set

The verb *sit* means "to take a seat" or "to be located." It does not take an object.

verb
The class members <u>sit</u> in a circle to discuss what they have read.

verb
The dog <u>sat</u> on the porch, waiting for her owner to return.

verb   verb
We <u>had</u> just <u>sat</u> down to dinner when the telephone rang.

Set means to "put" or "place." The verb *set* always takes an object; that is, you will always find an answer to the question, "Set what?"

verb   object
Please <u>set</u> the <u>pizza</u> on the kitchen counter.

verb   object
The company <u>has set</u> minimum sales <u>goals</u> for its staff.

verb   verb   object
The instructor <u>has</u> not <u>set</u> a <u>due date</u> for the research paper.

PRACTICE 9   USING *SIT* AND *SET*

Underline the correct verb form in each sentence.

1. "I can't (sit, set) any longer in this uncomfortable chair," said Leo.
2. Carrie and Josh are engaged but have not (sat, set) a date for their wedding.
3. Two old men were (sitting, setting) at a small table playing checkers.

4. Michael says that he was never able to meet his goals until he (sat, set) them down in writing.

5. "I used to have a crock pot," said Camille, "But I never used it. It just (set, sat) on a shelf."

Review Exercises

Complete the Review Exercises to see how well you learned the skills addressed in this chapter. As you work through the exercises, go back through the chapter to review any of the rules you do not understand completely.

REVIEW EXERCISE 1   FINDING SUBJECTS AND VERBS

Cross out prepositional phrases in each sentence. Then underline the subject once and the verb twice.

1. In many theaters, advertisements for local businesses are shown before the movie.

2. More rain is forecast throughout next week.

3. Because of an unusually high number of accidents at the intersection of Kay Street and Brennan Avenue, the city installed a traffic light.

4. The bulletin board was covered with memos, reminders, and photographs.

5. The math quiz had not been announced in advance.

6. Across the top of Nan's computer monitor sat a row of small stuffed animals.

7. The noise of a lawnmower could be heard in the distance.

8. Warren accidentally spilled coffee on his computer keyboard.

9. By five o'clock, the office was deserted.

10. Junk mail and a few bills were stuffed into Kevin's mailbox.

REVIEW EXERCISE 2   FINDING SUBJECTS AND VERBS

Cross out prepositional phrases in each sentence. Then underline the subject once and the verb twice.

1. The cover of the book had been torn by accident.

2. Some of the store's customers complained about the potholes in the parking lot.

3. Wearing a yellow raincoat and carrying a red umbrella, the child walked toward the bus stop.

4. Every student at the college has an email address.

5. Bananas are tasty and high in potassium.

6. Abraham Lincoln was carrying two pairs of glasses and a penknife on the night of his death.

7. On his way to work, George stopped for gas.

8. A pen had leaked into Randy's pocket, leaving a blue ink stain on his shirt.

9. The plastic bag in the bottom of the refrigerator contained bean sprouts in the final stages of decomposition.

10. The sign advertised sweaters at 50 percent off.

REVIEW EXERCISE 3   PUZZLING PAIRS

Choose the correct form of *lend* or *loan, lay* or *lie,* and *sit* or *set.*

1. The sign in the veterinarian's office said, "(Sit!, Set!) Stay! The doctor will be with you in a moment."

2. Despite the risk of sunburn or skin cancer, many people spend their vacations (laying, lying) in the sun.

3. Fernando (lent, loaned) a set of socket wrenches to his brother.

4. Linda has promised to (lend, loan) a hand when I try to repair the washer.

5. Discarded cans, fast food wrappers, and cigarette butts (lay, laid) alongside the road.

6. "I need to be doing something," said Jacquelyn. "I can't just (lay, lie) around the house."

7. His mother's calm in the face of the thunderstorm (lay, laid) Timmy's fears to rest.

8. "I have great news!" Kelly told her mother. "Are you (sitting, setting) down?"

9. "Would you (loan, lend) me a dollar until tomorrow?" Craig asked.

10. "My roommate leaves her stuff (laying, lying) all over the place," said Ebony.

REVIEW EXERCISE 4   USING IRREGULAR VERBS

Fill in the blank with the correct form of the verb shown to the left of each question. For help, consult the list of irregular verbs in this chapter.

(lie)   1. Several motorists stopped to help gather the boxes that _____ scattered around the overturned truck.

(burst)   2. After the meal, James leaned back in his chair and said, "I feel like I am about

to _____."

(fly)   3. Have you ever _____ before?" the flight attendant asked?

(put)   4. Alison asked her daughter if she had _____ away her toys.

(hurt)   5. "I think I _____ my ankle, coach," said Ben.

(begin)   6. The student apologized for entering after class had _____.

(leave)   7. "Has Mr. Simmons already _____?" asked Mandy.

(buy)   8. Kali _____ four boxes of Girl Scout cookies this year.

(fight)   9. For as long as they could remember, the couple had _____ over money.

(throw)   10. The student said he had _____ away the rough draft of his paper.

REVIEW EXERCISE 5   USING IRREGULAR VERBS

Fill in the blank with the correct form of the verb shown to the left of each question. For help, consult the list of irregular verbs in this chapter.

(bring)   1. The councilwoman said that the year had _____ many changes to the town of Newton.

(rise)   2. The morning was so cloudy and dark that it seemed as if the sun had not

_____.

(ride)   3. Amiko said that she had never _____ a subway.

(see)   4. Paco did not come with us because he had already _____ the movie.

(drink)   5. Who _____ all the orange juice?

(lay)   6. For warmth, the cat _____ on top of the television.

(break)   7. Harold was fired because he had _____ the company's rules.

(go)   8. "I would never have _____ to the party if I had known Amanda would be there," said Tom.

(lose)   9. Sherrod has _____ his computer password again.

(drive)   10. Carol and Monty were bleary-eyed on their first day of vacation because they

had _____ all night.

CHAPTER 13

Subject-Verb Agreement

*Plural paired with singular
Can't seem to get along,
And singular with plural
Just doesn't quite belong.*

*But singular and singular
Will need no referee,
And plural paired with plural
Is in perfect harmony.*

*In grammatical relations
You'll achieve tranquility
By using combinations
That never disagree.*

Fortunately, the rules for agreement between subjects and verbs are much simpler than the rules for human relationships. All of the rules for subject-verb agreement presented in this chapter have the same idea behind them: **A singular subject requires a singular verb, and a plural subject requires a plural verb.**

The Basic Pattern

Most subject-verb agreement problems occur in the present tense. Look at the conjugation of the present-tense verb *speak*. You can see exactly where trouble is likely to occur if you ask the question, "Where does the verb change its form?"

	Singular	**Plural**
First person	I speak	we speak
Second person	you speak	you speak
Third person	he, she, it speaks	they speak

As you see, the verb changes its form in the third person by adding an *s* to the singular form. As a result, the third-person verb has two forms, a singular form and a plural form. The third-person singular verb ends in *s;* the third-person plural verb does not. Most problems with subject-verb agreement in the present tense occur in the third person.

PRACTICE 1   CONJUGATING A VERB

All regular verbs follow the pattern above. Using the previous sample as a model, fill in the forms of the verb *look* in the spaces below.

	Singular	**Plural**
First person	I _____	we _____
Second person	you _____	you _____
Third person	he, she, it _____	they _____

Did you remember to put the *s* on the third-person singular form? Notice that the pattern of third-person verbs is exactly the opposite of the pattern seen in nouns. When you look at the noun *dog,* you know that it is singular and that the plural form is *dogs.* But verbs in the third person, present tense, work in exactly the opposite way. The third-person singular form of the verb ends in *s,* not the plural form. When you see the verb *walks,* you know it is singular because it ends in *s.*

Examples

A third-person singular subject and verb usually follow this pattern:

The *dog walks.* (The singular noun does not end in *s;* the singular verb does end in *s.*)

A third-person plural subject and verb usually follow this pattern:

The *dogs walk.* (The plural noun ends in *s;* the plural verb does not end in *s.*)

Todo el mundo cree

---

* Memory Jogger

If you have trouble with third-person verbs, remember the following verse.

The Singular S

When verbs are in the present tense,
You never need to guess.
The singular third-person verb
Always ends in *s.*

PRACTICE 2   CONJUGATING VERBS

On your own paper, fill in the first-, second-, and third-person forms of the regular verbs *install, shop, play, insist,* and *enjoy.* Remember to add the *s* to the third-person singular form.

	Singular	**Plural**
First person	I _____	we _____
Second person	you _____	you _____
Third person	he, she, it _____	they _____

Verbs Ending in *-es*

Now look at the regular verb *impress* in the present tense. Here, when the verb already ends in *s,* the third-person singular form also changes, adding an *es.*

	Singular	**Plural**
First person	I impress	we impress
Second person	you impress	you impress
Third person	he, she, it impress**es**	they impress

Using Third Person

Third person is sometimes confusing. One reason is that it is the only person where the verb form changes. The biggest reason, however, is that third person includes much more than just the pronouns *he, she, it,* and *they.* Third-person singular also includes any noun or pronoun that can be replaced by *he, she,* or *it. Janis, Mr. Brown, otter, desk, toddler, someone, convenience store clerk, one,* and *George Washington* are all third-person singular. Thus each requires a present-tense verb ending in *s* or *es.*

Any noun or pronoun that can be replaced by *they* is third-person plural. *The Smiths, both, gas and groceries, poodles, sport utility vehicles,* and *many* are words that could be replaced by *they.* Thus all are third-person plural and require a present-tense plural verb, the form that does not add *s* or *es.*

The Verb *to be*

Now look at the most common irregular verb, the verb *to be.*

	Singular	Plural
First person	I am	we are
Second person	you are	you are
Third person	he, she, it is	they are

Notice that the pattern still holds: the third-person singular form of the verb always ends in *s* or *es.*

A Fundamental Rule

Knowing the pattern that present-tense verbs follow should make it a bit easier to apply the fundamental rule of subject-verb agreement:

A singular subject requires a singular verb, and a plural subject requires a plural verb.

Examples

    S   V
Angela phones home every day to check on her dog Hector. (singular subject, singular verb)

    S   V
Halloween is celebrated across the United States. (singular subject, singular verb)

      S   V
Many students have some difficulty adjusting to college life. (plural subject, plural verb)

    S   V
Strawberries give Clifford hives. (plural subject, plural verb)

PRACTICE 3   MAKING SUBJECTS AND VERBS AGREE

Underline the correct verb form in each sentence.

1. Like most people, Norma (resists, resist) trying new things.
2. Michael (impress, impresses) everyone with his determination and hard work.
3. The candy jar (holds, hold) only paper clips and spare change since Cecile decided to eat more nutritiously.
4. Two cups of coffee (is, are) barely enough to keep Roberto alert during his eight o'clock class.
5. Wolves (lives, live) in closely knit social groups, just as humans do.

Problems in Subject-Verb Agreement

Prepositional Phrase between Subject and Verb

When a prepositional phrase comes between subject and verb, it is easy to make mistakes in subject-verb agreement. Crossing out prepositional phrases will help you avoid errors and will help you to remember this important rule:

The subject of a verb is never found in a prepositional phrase.

Example 1

Consider the following problem in subject-verb agreement:

The members of the chorus (rehearses, rehearse) in the auditorium every Tuesday.

Which verb is correct? If you try to find the subject without crossing out prepositional phrases, you might ask the question, "Who or what rehearses or rehearse?" It seems logical to say, "The *chorus* rehearses, so *chorus* is the subject of the sentence and *rehearses* is the verb." However, *chorus* cannot be the subject of the sentence because it already has a job: it is the object of a preposition, and *the subject of a sentence is never found in a prepositional phrase.*

Incorrect Solution

✗   The members of the <u>chorus</u> <u>rehearses</u> in the auditorium every Tuesday.

Correct Solution: Cross Out Prepositional Phrases to Find the Subject

✔   The <u>members</u> of the chorus (rehearse) in the auditorium every Tuesday.

Example 2

The <u>bumper stickers</u> on Nat's car <u>reveal</u> his changing political attitudes over the years.

The verb agrees with its subject, *stickers,* not with the object of the preposition.

PRACTICE 4   MAKING SUBJECTS AND VERBS AGREE

In the sentences below, cross out prepositional phrases to find the subject of the sentence. Then underline the subject and double-underline the correct verb.

1. Several signs in front of the store (warns, warn) that cars parked in the fire lane will be towed.
2. The popularity of some brands of athletic shoes (makes, make) some people willing to pay high prices.
3. The driving beat of the music in the fitness center (helps, help) people exercise longer.
4. Writing in her journal every day (is, are) difficult for Susan.
5. The free samples of food in the supermarket on Saturday (attracts, attract) many shoppers.

Indefinite Pronouns as Subjects

Problems in subject-verb agreement are also likely to occur when the subject is an indefinite pronoun, a pronoun that does not refer to a specific person or thing. The following indefinite pronouns are always singular and require singular verbs.

each	everybody	anyone	anything
either	somebody	everyone	everything
neither	nobody	someone	something
anybody	one	no one	nothing

Always Singular

> *** Memory Jogger**
>
> Remember the singular indefinite pronouns more easily by grouping them:
>
> Each, either, neither
> All the bodies (anybody, everybody, nobody, somebody)
> All the ones (anyone, everyone, one, no one, someone)
> All the things (anything, everything, nothing, something)

Examples

subject verb

Janna answered the telephone, but <u>no one</u> <u>was</u> on the other end.

The subject, *no one*, is singular, as is the verb, *was*.

subject   verb
<u>Each</u> of the cupcakes <u>has been decorated</u> with a jack-o'-lantern face.

The singular verb, *has been decorated,* agrees with the singular subject, *each.*
The plural object of the preposition, *cupcakes,* does not affect the verb.

PRACTICE 5   MAKING VERBS AGREE WITH INDEFINITE PRONOUNS

In each sentence, cross out prepositional phrases and underline the verb that
agrees with the indefinite pronoun subject.

1. Neither of the cars (has, have) all the features that Carl wants.
2. Everybody in the apartment complex (believes, believe) the manager is doing
    a poor job of groundskeeping.
3. Someone in one of Helen's classes (is, are) organizing a study group.
4. Everything in the store (has, have) been reduced to half price.
5. Each of the barbers (pays, pay) rental to the shop owner.

Subject Following the Verb

In most English sentences, the subject comes before the verb. However, the
subject follows the verb in these situations:

1. when the sentence begins with *here* or *there*
2. when the sentence begins with a prepositional phrase that is immedi-
    ately followed by a verb
3. when the sentence is a question

Examples

        verb   subject

There <u>are</u> several <u>oranges</u> left in the bowl.

The plural subject, *oranges*, requires the plural verb, *are*. The word *there* is not the subject of the sentence.

                  verb   subject

In front of the fireplace <u>sit</u> two comfortable <u>chairs</u>.

The prepositional phrases *in front* and *of the fireplace* are immediately followed by a verb. Since the subject is never found in a prepositional phrase, it must be somewhere *after* the verb. The plural verb, *sit,* agrees with the plural subject, *chairs.*

       verb   subject

What <u>was</u> the <u>price</u> of the small soft drink?

The singular subject, *price,* follows the singular verb, *was.*

       verb   subject

What <u>were</u> those strange <u>noises</u> that I heard outside?

The plural subject, *noises,* follows the plural verb, *were.*

PRACTICE 6   MAKING VERBS AGREE WITH SUBJECTS THAT COME AFTER VERBS

Cross out prepositional phrases in each sentence. Then underline the subject and double-underline the correct verb.

1. Nestled in the crawl space under the house (was, were) a mother cat and four fat kittens.
2. Why (does, do) Rodney have two cars when he can drive only one at a time?
3. There (is, are) a package outside Jamie's front door.
4. (Does, Do) anyone know where to get a parking permit?
5. There (wasn't, weren't) any seats available for Friday night's concert.

Compound Subjects

Compound subjects may also cause confusion in subject-verb agreement. The rules for subject-verb agreement with compound subjects are outlined in the sections that follow.

Compound Subjects Joined by *and*

Because *and* always joins at least two elements, compound subjects joined by *and* require a plural verb. Remember this rule:

Compound subjects joined by *and* require a plural verb.

Examples

       compound subject   verb
A <u>pizza</u> *and* a rented <u>video</u> <u>are</u> Kim and Anthony's way of relaxing on Friday nights.

       compound subject   verb
<u>Winning</u> modestly *and* <u>losing</u> gracefully <u>are</u> two ways of demonstrating good sportsmanship.

       compound subject
A prickly <u>cactus</u>, a <u>pot</u> of geraniums, *and* a <u>doormat</u> that says "Go

       verb
Away" <u>sit</u> on my neighbor's front porch.

       compound subject   verb
Discarded beer <u>cans</u> *and* cigarette <u>butts</u> <u>dot</u> the convenience store's parking lot.

PRACTICE 7   MAKING VERBS AGREE WITH SUBJECTS JOINED BY *AND*

Cross out prepositional phrases, then double-underline the verb that agrees with each compound subject.

1. A trip to the mall with three children and a visit to a fast-food restaurant (was, were) not Harriet's idea of relaxation.

2. A tight waistband and the numbers on his scale (tells, tell) Arthur that it's time to start a diet.

3. At the movie theater, a giant soft drink, a large bag of popcorn, and a candy bar (costs, cost) more than the price of admission.

4. Finishing on time and remembering all the material (is, are) just two of the pressures of taking tests.

5. A timer shaped like a hen and a glass jar filled with spare change (sits, sit) on top of the microwave in Natalie's kitchen.

Compound Subjects Joined by *or, either/or,* or *neither/nor*

When subjects are joined by *or, either/or,* or *neither/nor*, it is not always possible to use logic to determine whether the verb will be singular or plural.

Therefore, one rule applies to all compound subjects joined by *or, either/or,* or *neither/nor:*

> **When a compound subject is joined by *or, either/or,* or *neither/nor,* the verb agrees with the part of the subject closer to it.**

Consider the following sentence:

Seth or his brother (is, are) opening the shop on Saturday morning.

How many will open the shop? The answer is "just one": either Seth *or* his brother. Therefore, using the singular verb is logical. The singular verb *is* also agrees with *brother,* the part of the subject closer to the verb.

<u>Seth</u> *or* his <u>brother</u> <u>is</u> opening the shop on Saturday morning.

Now, let's change the sentence a bit.

Seth's brothers or his assistants (is, are) opening the shop on Saturday.

How many will open the shop? In this sentence, *more than one:* either Seth's brothers or his assistants. It makes sense, then, to use a plural verb. The plural verb *are* also agrees with *assistants,* the part of the subject closer to the verb.

Seth's <u>brothers</u> *or* his <u>assistants</u> <u>are</u> opening the shop on Saturday.

The next two sentences do not respond to logical examination.

Seth or his assistants (is, are) opening the shop on Saturday.

Seth's assistants or his brother (is, are) opening the shop on Saturday.

How many will open the shop? There is no way to tell. Simply follow the rule and make the verb agree with the part of the subject closer to it.

Seth *or* his <u>assistants</u> <u>are</u> opening the shop on Saturday.

Seth's <u>assistants</u> *or* his <u>brother</u> <u>is</u> opening the shop on Saturday.

Examples

A five-dollar donation *or* two nonperishable food <u>items</u> <u>are</u> required for admission to the concert.

Two nonperishable food items *or* a five-dollar <u>donation</u> <u>is</u> required for admission to the concert.

Either two nonperishable food items *or* a five-dollar <u>donation</u> <u><u>is</u></u> required for admission to the concert.

Neither the alarm clock *nor* her two <u>cats</u> <u><u>were</u></u> successful in getting Kendra out of bed.

MAKING VERBS AGREE WITH SUBJECTS JOINED BY OR, EITHER/OR

PRACTICE 8   OR NEITHER/NOR

Cross out prepositional phrases, then double-underline the verb that agrees with each compound subject. Some subjects are joined by *and* while others are joined by *or, either/or,* or *neither/nor.*

1. Soup or a microwaveable pizza (was, were) all that Elton had on hand for lunch.
2. Either a sweatshirt or a warm sweater (feels, feel) good on a cool day.
3. Strawberries or a sliced banana (tastes, taste) good over cereal.
4. Neither Deon nor his two brothers (talks, talk) about anything except sports.
5. Taking drugs or drinking alcohol to escape problems often (leads, lead) to even bigger problems.

Review Exercises

Complete the Review Exercises to see how well you learned the skills addressed in this chapter. As you work through the exercises, go back through the chapter to review any of the rules you do not understand completely.

REVIEW EXERCISE 1

Underline the correct verb in each sentence.

1. The room (was, were) too warm, and Larry found it difficult to stay awake.
2. Only one of the members of the jury (believe, believes) the defendant committed the crime.
3. When Emily or her brothers (needs, need) money, their father tells them to get it the old fashioned way—to earn it.
4. Each of the cashiers (has, have) a good reason for being late.
5. Long hours and her supervisor's habit of calling her in on weekends (is, are) forcing Shayna to consider quitting her job.
6. Running and weight lifting (keeps, keep) Brandon in shape and feeling good.
7. There (was, were) too many distractions in the room during the test, and Andy had a hard time concentrating.

8. Inside Marcie's lunch bag (is, are) a diet soft drink, an apple, and a gooey snack cake.

9. Why (does, do) Cathy and Dennis bother to come to class when they never do any of the assigned work?

10. The Mason jars sitting on the table (is, are) filled with homemade jam.

REVIEW EXERCISE 2

Write C in the blank to the left of the sentence if the italicized verb agrees with its subject. If the verb is incorrect, write the correct form in the blank. Two of the sentences are correct.

_____ 1. The large crowd in the doctor's waiting room *make* me think I will be here a while.

_____ 2. The noise from the washers, the dryers, and the television *makes* it hard to hold a conversation in the laundromat.

_____ 3. "One of the mechanics *are* going to call me when my car is ready," said Ann.

_____ 4. Everybody in the path of the hurricane *have* been warned to prepare for evacuation.

_____ 5. A jacket, a hat, and a pair of gloves *was* lying on the kitchen floor.

_____ 6. "Either the telephone bill or the cable bill *have* to wait till next week," said Burton.

_____ 7. The bright sunshine and the music on her car radio *were* not enough to lift Natasha's gloomy mood.

_____ 8. There *is* the keys that Nathan was looking for a few minutes ago.

_____ 9. Why *have* the professor changed the due date of the assignment?

_____ 10. Andrea says everyone *give* her strange looks whenever she wears her purple outfit.

REVIEW EXERCISE 3

Cross out the two incorrect verb forms in each item. Then write the correct forms on the lines provided.

1. Julie says she does not mind if her husband spend his Saturdays working on his old motorcycle. However, she refuse to stand around and hand him tools while he works.

   Sentence 1: _____   Sentence 2: _____

2. John's full-time job and his heavy class schedule makes it almost impossible for him to find enough time to study. "Either full-time work or full-time school are okay," he says, "but not both."

   Sentence 1: _____   Sentence 2: _____

3. The lenses in Margaret's glasses turns darker when she goes outside in the sun. The lenses were expensive, but Margaret says she come out ahead because she does not have to buy sunglasses.

   Sentence 1: _____   Sentence 2: _____

4. As she grows older, Hal's grandmother live increasingly in the past. She remembers what she wore to her high school graduation party but do not recall whether she ate breakfast or not.

   Sentence 1: _____   Sentence 2: _____

5. Above the flat, sandy beach rise a large, dome-shaped sand dune. Small bushes or tufts of grass grows from the smooth sand dune, looking like patches of hair on an otherwise bald head.

   Sentence 1: _____   Sentence 2: _____

REVIEW EXERCISE 4

In each numbered item, cross out the two verbs that do not agree with their subjects. Then write the corrected verbs on the lines provided.

1. Sonya has never met the people in the apartment next door to her, but she has already decided she don't like them. Their music, pounding from the other side of the wall at all hours, annoy her.

   Sentence 1: _____   Sentence 2: _____

2. Inside the huge grocery superstore is a bank, a dry-cleaning shop, a fast-food restaurant, and a hair salon. "A person need hiking boots to get around in that huge store," Josh complained.

   Sentence 1: _____   Sentence 2: _____

3. In the fall, the leaves on the oak tree in our front yard bursts into a beautiful blaze of red. They are not so beautiful when they fall off the tree and my brother and I has to rake them up.

   Sentence 1: _____   Sentence 2: _____

4. There are no faculty member or staff person on duty in the grammar lab on Saturday. However, Sunday through Friday, computer tutorials and help with grammar is available for students of the college.

   Sentence 1: _____   Sentence 2: _____

5. The twins' mother is angry because their membership in several of the school's clubs and activities require them to sell merchandise to raise funds.

"It is bad enough that I end up buying most of it," she says, "but even worse, each new item that I buy seem tackier and more expensive than the last."

Sentence 1: _____   Sentence 2: _____

REVIEW EXERCISE 5

Underline the ten subject-verb agreement errors in the following paragraph. Then write the corrected verbs on the lines provided.

[1]In my rural neighborhood, at the end of a long gravel driveway, sit a house that is a mystery to everyone. [2]It was built over a year ago, but neither I nor my neighbors has ever seen it. [3]A chain, heavy and made of metal, run between two thick posts at the end of the driveway. [4]Hanging from the chain and nailed to the posts is several signs: "Keep Out," "No Trespassing," "Private Property." [5]Though it is customary in our area to welcome new neighbors with a visit and a basket of fruit, nobody in the neighborhood have dared to go past those unfriendly signs. [6]Instead, everyone speculate. [7]Maybe the woods that hug the property conceal a drug manufacturing plant, or perhaps the residents is growing marijuana. [8]Or they could be members of a militia group, stockpiling guns and preparing for war with anyone who venture beyond that chain at the end of the driveway. [9]There is many possibilities, but one thing is certain. [10]Our new neighbors prefers to keep to themselves.

1. _____   6. _____

2. _____   7. _____

3. _____   8. _____

4. _____   9. _____

5. _____   10. _____

CHAPTER 14

Verb Shifts

A Shifty Excuse

"Professor, I brought my term paper with me, but when I opened my notebook, it's gone. I can't print out another copy because the file was erased by me."

The excuse above is shifty—but not just because it is unconvincing. It contains two common types of **verb shifts**. The first sentence contains an unnecessary shift from past tense to present tense, and the second contains an unnecessary shift from active voice to passive voice.

In this chapter, you will learn to correct unnecessary shifts from past to present tense and to make necessary shifts into the past perfect tense.

You will also learn to recognize active voice and passive voice and to correct unnecessary shifts between the two.

Shifts in Tense

Verb tenses give the English language its sense of time, its sense of *when* events occur. The timeline below shows six verb tenses, and the chart that follows the timeline briefly explains how each tense is used.

Verb Tense Timeline

	past I walked	present I walk	future I will walk

past ◁← - - - * - - - - - * - - - - * - - - * - - - - - - - - - - * - - - * - - - - - →◁ future

	I had walked	I have walked	I will have walked
	past perfect	present perfect	future perfect

Verb Tense Chart

◁◁◁	Furthest in the past; happened before another past action	past perfect *had* + *-ed* verb form	I *had walked* up the stairs, and I was out of breath.
◁◁	In the past; happened before now.	past *-ed* verb form	I *walked* all the way around the nature trail.
◁•	In the past but extending to the present	present perfect *have* or *has* + *-ed* verb form	I *have walked* every day for the last month. He *has walked* a mile already.
•	Happens regularly or often, or is happening now.	present base verb form or base verb + *-s*	I *walk* at least five miles a week. She *walks* quickly.
◁	Happens in the future but before another future event	future perfect *will have* + *-ed* verb form	By the time you join me on the track, I *will have walked* at least two miles.
◁◁	Happens at some time in the future	future *will* + base verb	I *will walk* with you tomorrow if we both have time.

Avoiding Unnecessary Tense Shifts

With so many ways to designate time, writers of English are bound to slip up occasionally. The most common error in verb tense is an unnecessary shift from past tense to present tense. Writers easily become so caught up in the past event they are describing that it becomes, at least temporarily, a part of "the now." Unnecessary shifts from present to past, while not quite as common, are also avoidable.

Examples

Necessary Shift:

         past   present

✔ James <u>was</u> sick yesterday, but he <u>is feeling</u> better today.

Unnecessary Shift from Past to Present:

         past   present

✗ Cameron <u>was driving</u> on Route 42 when all of a sudden a bus <u>pulls</u> out in front of her.

Unnecessary Shift Corrected:

         past   past

✔ Cameron <u>was driving</u> on Route 42 when all of a sudden a bus <u>pulled</u> out in front of her.

Unnecessary Shift from Past to Present:

         past   present   present

✗ When we <u>arrived</u> at the theater, we <u>notice</u> that the line <u>stretches</u> all the way around the building.

Unnecessary Shift Corrected:

         past   past   past

✔ When we <u>arrived</u> at the theater, we <u>noticed</u> that the line <u>stretched</u> all the way around the building.

Unnecessary Shift from Present to Past:

    present   past

✗ Jerry <u>comes</u> home every day and <u>turned on</u> the television set to watch the news.

Unnecessary Shift Corrected:

    present   present

✔ Jerry <u>comes</u> home every day and <u>turns on</u> the television set to watch the news.

PRACTICE 1   MAINTAINING CONSISTENT TENSE

Underline the correct verb in each sentence.

1. When Ralph came home, he saw that his puppy had chewed the sofa pillows and (is, was) hiding under the bed.
2. I thought Abby had quit smoking, but when I went outside for my break, there she (stands, stood), smoking a cigarette.
3. The boat towed the skier to the far end of the lake, then (turns, turned) around and headed back toward the dock.
4. Every afternoon, the children play outside until their mother (calls, called) them in for dinner.
5. The cat was sleeping on the arm of a chair, but when the doorbell rang, he (darts, darted) under the sofa.

PRACTICE 2   CORRECTING UNNECESSARY TENSE SHIFTS

In each sentence, correct the unnecessary shift from past to present.

1. Valerie fills her gas tank on Monday, but by Friday it was empty again.

    _____

2. Michael had been working all morning in the heat, and when he came in, he seems dizzy and ill.

    _____

3. Lynn woke up in the middle of the night and could not go back to sleep, so she decides to clean out the refrigerator.

    _____

4. The score was tied at the bottom of the ninth, and McGriff comes up to bat amid the cheers of the fans.

    _____

5. Sylvester thought he no longer loved Carmen until he sees her at the laundromat on a Tuesday night in April.

    _____

Active and Passive Voice

Active voice means that the grammatical subject of a sentence performs the action described by the verb, as in the following sentence:

Before the game began, Cynthia sang the national anthem.

In this sentence, *Cynthia*, the grammatical subject, performs the action described by the verb *sang*.

Rewritten in passive voice, the sentence looks like this:

Before the game began, the national anthem was sung by Cynthia.

What has changed? Simply put, the grammatical subject of the sentence is not acting, but is acted upon. The subject *anthem* performs no action, but instead is acted upon by the person who sings it. Notice, too, another hallmark of the passive voice: The verb contains a helping verb that is a form of the verb *to be*. Though an active voice verb also may have a helping verb such as *is, was, were, have been, will be,* or another form of *to be*, a passive voice verb always does. Another hallmark of the passive voice is the "by" construction (*by Cynthia*) that sometimes tells who or what acted upon the subject.

---

*Memory Jogger

In *active voice,* an action is done *by* the grammatical subject.

In *passive voice,* an action is done *to* the grammatical subject.

PRACTICE 3   EXAMINING ACTIVE AND PASSIVE VOICE

Answer the questions about each set of sentences. The first one is done for you.

Set 1

Active: The police arrested the suspected bank robbers on Thursday morning.

The subject of the verb is _____

The verb that shows the action done *by* the subject is _____.

Passive: The suspected bank robbers were arrested by the police on Thursday morning.

The subject of the verb is _____.

The verb that shows the action done *to* the subject is _____.

Set 2

Active: Samantha watered her house plants.

The subject of the verb is _____.

The verb that shows the action done *by* the subject is _____.

Passive: The house plants were watered by Samantha.

The subject of the verb is _____.

The verb that slows the action done *to* the subject is _____.

Set 3

Active: Marcus caught the ball before it could reach the plate glass window.

The subject of the verb is _____.

The verb that shows the action done *by* the subject is _____.

Passive: The ball was caught by Marcus before it could reach the plate glass window.

The subject of the verb is _____.

The verb that shows the action done *to* the subject is _____.

Set 4

Active: Claude took the mud-spattered Chevrolet to the car wash.

The subject of the verb is _____.

The verb that shows the action done *by* the subject is _____.

Passive: The mud-spattered Chevrolet was taken to the car wash by Claude.

The subject of the verb is _____.

The verb that shows the action done *to* the subject is _____.

Set 5

Active: After the restaurant closes, the employees clean the tables and vacuum the carpet.

The subject of the verb is _____.

The verb that shows the action done *by* the subject is _____.

Passive: After the restaurant closes, tables are cleaned and the carpet is vacuumed.

In this sentence, the subjects of the verbs are _____.

The verbs that show the actions done *to* the subjects are _____

and _____.

Uses of Active and Passive Voice

Active voice, with its directness and vitality, is stronger than passive and is preferred in most situations. Sometimes, however, passive voice is appropriate. For example, you would use passive voice in a sentence like

"The furniture will be delivered on Tuesday" because you don't care who delivers it, you just care that it arrives.

However, try to avoid awkward shifts between active and passive voice. Look at the following example:

✗ The professor <u>wished</u> us luck, and at exactly 8:10, the tests <u>were handed</u> out.

       _{active}   _{passive}

✔ The professor <u>wished</u> us luck, and at exactly 8:10, he <u>handed</u> out the tests.

Writing Sentences in Active and Passive Voice

To avoid unnecessary shifts between active and passive voice, you need to be able to recognize and write sentences in both voices.

Switching from Passive to Active Voice

To switch from passive voice to active voice, determine *who* or *what* acts upon the subject of the sentence, and rewrite the sentence to make that actor the subject.

Examples

Passive: The car was driven by Mario's brother.

To switch this passive voice sentence to active voice, look for the word or phrase that tells who performs the action described in the subject-verb sequence. In this sentence, look for a word or phrase that tells *who drove the car. Mario's brother* drove the car. To put the sentence into active voice, make *Mario's brother* the subject of the sentence and work from there.

Active: Mario's brother drove the car.

Sometimes, the *by* construction is omitted, and you need to mentally fill in the blank to put an actor into the sentence.

Passive: The prisoner was sentenced to life without parole.

The sentence does not say who sentenced the prisoner, but logic tells you that it must have been a judge. To rewrite the sentence in active voice, put a judge into the sentence.

Active: The judge sentenced the prisoner to life without parole.

PRACTICE 4   WRITING SENTENCES IN ACTIVE VOICE

Rewrite each of the following sentences in active voice.

1. The pizza was delivered by a man with red hair.

    _____

2. Evidence was collected by two uniformed officers.

    _____

3. The concert was attended by a small, enthusiastic crowd.

    _____

4. After eight rings, the telephone was answered by a man who sounded as though he had been sleeping.

    _____

    _____

5. At the park's entrance, hot dogs were sold by a vendor.

    _____

Switching from Active to Passive Voice

To switch from active voice to passive voice, reverse the position of the actor (the subject of the verb) and the recipient of the action (the object of the verb).

Examples

Active: The technician expertly cleaned and repaired the old lawnmower.

The actor (the subject of the verb) is *technician.* The recipient of the action is *the old lawnmower.* To convert the sentence to passive voice, switch the positions of the two.

Passive: The old lawnmower was expertly cleaned and repaired by the technician.

Here is a second example:

Active: The meteorologist predicted rain and temperatures in the seventies.

Passive: Rain and temperatures in the seventies were predicted by the meteorologist.

PRACTICE 5   **WRITING SENTENCES IN PASSIVE VOICE**

Rewrite each of the following sentences in passive voice.

1. The dog ate the rest of the leftovers.

   _____

2. Hundreds of cattle ate the contaminated feed.

   _____

3. The school board took a firm stand against the banning of books.

   _____

4. The gardening expert gave a presentation on leaf mold.

   _____

5. The sound of his mother's voice calmed and reassured the child.

   _____

Correcting Shifts in Voice

When an unnecessary shift in voice occurs within a sentence, rewrite the sentence so that it is in one voice. Active voice is usually preferred.

Examples

Unnecessary Shift:

            active   passive

✗   Before Clayton <u>took</u> the test, his notes <u>were reviewed</u> quickly.

Corrected:

            active   active

✔   Before Clayton <u>took</u> the test, he quickly <u>reviewed</u> his notes.

Unnecessary Shift:

        active   passive

✗   Camille <u>lost</u> her battered old umbrella, so a new one <u>was purchased</u>.

Corrected:

        active   active

✔   Camille <u>lost</u> her battered old umbrella, so she <u>purchased</u> a new one.

PRACTICE 6   CORRECTING SHIFTS IN VOICE

Each of the following sentences contains a shift in voice. Underline the passive-voice portion of each sentence. Then rewrite each sentence in active voice.

1. Cody's parents were firm with him, but he was spoiled by his grandparents.

   _____

2. Kelly made soup, and bread was baked by Tom and Kara.

   _____

3. Although many other job offers were received, Shenita has decided to work for Collins Corporation.

   _____

   _____

4. Because the garden was carefully tended by Sean, it thrived.

   _____

5. After the newspaper had been read by everyone in the family, Cliff put it in the recycling bin.

   _____

6. Ramon was angry when he found out that a trick had been played on him by his friends.

   _____

7. Connie wanted to monitor her food intake, so everything she ate was written down.

   _____

8. In the doctor's office, a nurse took Glenn's vital signs, and then he was examined by the doctor.

   _____

   _____

9. After Nelson wrote a cover letter, it was mailed along with his resumé.

   _____

10. As if the instructor had not given us enough work, an additional book was added to our reading list by her at midterm.

    _____

    _____

Review Exercises

Complete the Review Exercises to see how well you learned the skills addressed in this chapter. As you work through the exercises, go back through the chapter to review any of the rules you do not understand completely.

REVIEW EXERCISE 1

The italicized portions of the following sentences contain unnecessary shifts in voice or tense or verbs that need to be shifted from the past to the past-perfect tense. For each sentence, circle *a, b,* or *c* to indicate the type of problem in the sentence. Then correct the problem in each sentence.

1. In the morning, Tom left his car at the dealership. When he returned at five-thirty, the mechanics *replaced the brake pads and tuned the engine.*
   The problem in this sentence is

   a. a shift in voice

   b. a shift between past and present tense

   c. past-tense verbs that need to be further in the past (past perfect)

   _____

2. Marie's parents sat on the couch and *hold* hands as if they were teenagers.
   The problem in this sentence is

   a. a shift in voice

   b. a shift between past and present tense

   c. a past-tense verb that needs to be further in the past (past perfect)

   _____

3. In the stands, baseball fans stood for the seventh-inning stretch while *hot dogs, soft drinks, and beer were sold by vendors.*
   The problem in this sentence is

   a. a shift in voice

   b. a shift between past and present tense

   c. a past-tense verb that needs to be further in the past (past perfect)

   _____

4. In the shelter of the carport, the cats dismembered a small bird that *had been caught by them.*
   The problem in this sentence is

   a. a shift in voice

   b. a shift between past and present tense

     c. a past-tense verb that needs to be further in the past (past perfect)

     _____

5. When Adam reached his hotel room, he realized he *left* his toothbrush and toothpaste at home.
     The problem in this sentence is

     a. a shift in voice

     b. a shift between past and present tense

     c. a past tense verb that needs to be further in the past (past perfect)

     _____

Review Exercise 2

The italicized portions of the following sentences contain unnecessary shifts in voice or tense, or verbs that need to be shifted from the past to the past-perfect tense. Correct the problem in each sentence.

1. The letter said Gary was a winner if *the winning number was held by him.*

     _____

2. When I saw Anita, *she says,* "Why weren't you at the meeting yesterday?"

     _____

3. Bonita asked Alan to join our study group, but he said *he studied already.*

     _____

4. Hank shook the salesman's hand and said, "I'll let you know when *a decision has been reached by me.*"

     _____

5. In the computer store, Julia bought the new keyboard she needed, and just as she was ready to leave, she *decides* to get a mouse pad, too.

     _____

6. Since *bids were signaled by the buyers* with a nod or a slight hand movement, the auctioneer had to be alert.

     _____

7. Rowe *already finished* his report and was ready to turn it in, so he was irritated when the instructor granted the class a last-minute extension.

     _____

8. Darrell and Ellie had just fallen asleep when *the baby starts crying.*

     _____

9. Bill held his burned finger under cold running water, and then *ice was applied.*

_____

10. Kim looked at the clock and realized she *worked* for half an hour.

_____

REVIEW EXERCISE 3

The italicized portions of the following sentences contain unnecessary shifts in voice or tense, or verbs that need to be shifted from the past to the past-perfect tense. For each sentence, circle *a, b,* or *c* to indicate the type of problem in the sentence. Then correct the problem in each sentence.

1. On the first day of class, the instructor handed each student a syllabus and *says,* "Everything you need to know about the course content, exams, and assignments is in this document."
   The problem in this sentence is
   a. a shift in voice
   b. a shift between past and present tense
   c. a past-tense verb that needs to be further in the past (past perfect)

   _____

2. When Ralph arrived at home, the mail carrier *left* a note, "Package on front porch."
   The problem in this sentence is
   a. a shift in voice
   b. a shift between past and present tense
   c. a past-tense verb that needs to be further in the past (past perfect)

   _____

3. When Stephanie fed Rover, the dog *eats* an entire can of food in one gulp.
   The problem in this sentence is
   a. a shift in voice
   b. a shift between past and present tense
   c. a past-tense verb that needs to be further in the past (past perfect)

   _____

4. Ray won the race today, *and another school record was set by him.*
   The problem in this sentence is
   a. a shift in voice
   b. a shift between past and present tense
   c. a past-tense verb that needs to be further in the past (past perfect)

   _____

5. After the exam, Carolyn walked into the hall and said she was certain *she did well.*

    The problem in this sentence is

    a. a shift in voice

    b. a shift between past and present tense

    c. a past-tense verb that needs to be further in the past (past perfect)

    _____

REVIEW EXERCISE 4

Underline the voice or tense problem in each sentence. Then write the correct voice or tense on the lines provided.

1. The server asked if I tried the house dressing before.

    _____

2. The hair stylist had almost finished styling Sue's hair when the hair dryer erupts in flames.

    _____

3. The snow fell thickly and soon it covers everything in a blanket of white.

    _____

4. If the job was done by Joel, he did it right.

    _____

5. Margaret saw that she had e-mail, so she opens her mailbox.

    _____

6. When Elliott reached the bench where he planned to meet Ann, she left already.

    _____

7. Carl tried to hail a cab, but it just passes him by.

    _____

8. Justine said that we should not worry, arrangements had been made by her.

    _____

9. The lake was shrouded in mist, but one small boat is visible near the shore-line.

    _____

10. Rosie loves to paint. The oil painting on her living room wall and the water-colors in her bedroom were painted by her.

_____

_____

REVIEW EXERCISE 5

Each sentence in the paragraph contains a voice or tense problem. First, underline the problem. Then correct it by rewriting a verb in past tense or past-perfect tense or by changing a passive voice construction to active voice.

[1]At my ten-year high school class reunion last week, I saw many people I did not see in years. [2]One old classmate seen by me was Patrick, the class clown. [3]Many tricks had been played by him on the teachers at Truman High School, but now, he is a teacher himself. [4]Another former classmate I saw was Heather, who is the homecoming queen ten years ago. [5]Her bubbly personality did not change since high school. [6]She remembered everyone's name and greets them with a hug and a warm hello. [7]The person that surprised everyone was Wanda, who in high school is a computer nerd. [8]Then, she was quiet and shy, but today, a major software company is owned by her. [9]Many of the guys probably wished they paid more attention to Wanda back then. [10]The reunion was fun; I enjoy myself and can't wait to see what changes the next ten years will bring.

1. _____

2. _____

3. _____

4. _____

5. _____

6. _____

7. _____

8. _____

9. _____

10. _____

Sentence Variety

A boxful of temptation,
So many types to see;
In sentences or chocolates,
Variety's the key.

Power Tools for Writing Sentences

When you learned to write, you started by expressing one idea per sentence. But as your ideas become more complex, so should your writing. Use this chapter to strengthen your ability to write varied, interesting sentences. You can vary your sentences by using these four "power tools": Be concise, vary sentence openings, connect ideas through coordination, and connect ideas through subordination.

Power Tool 1: Be Concise

The poet Robert Browning said, "Less is more." This simple idea has been repeated in connection with everything from architecture to zoology, and it is also one of the cornerstones of good writing. In other words, use as few words as it takes to do the job well.

Examples

✗   I bought a used car. It is a Chevrolet Malibu. It is blue. It has only eighteen thousand miles on it. (five sentences, twenty-one words)

✔   I bought a blue Chevrolet Malibu with only eighteen thousand miles on it. (one sentence, thirteen words)

The second sentence in the example above represents a savings of eight words. In the omission of those eight words, has any of the substance been left out? True, the word *car* is left out in the second version, but most Americans old enough to read the word "Chevrolet" know that a Chevrolet is a car. The word *used* is also left out, but the reader knows that if the car has eighteen thousand miles on it, someone has used it.

Examples

✗   Charles was wearing a T-shirt. It was an old shirt. It was white. It had ketchup stains across the front. (four sentences, twenty words)

✔   Charles was wearing an old, white T-shirt with ketchup stains across the front. (one sentence, thirteen words)

PRACTICE 1   WRITING CONCISE SENTENCES

Combine the four ideas in each set of sentences into one concise sentence. Make sure that the sentence expresses the idea fully but uses as few words as possible.

1.   Alicia read her horoscope.

     The horoscope was in the newspaper.

     The newspaper was called *The Daily Spectator*.

     The horoscope said that Alicia's persuasive powers were strong.

     _____

     _____

2. Rashad picked up an empty soft drink can.
    The can was in the parking lot.
    The parking lot was a student parking lot.
    Rashad put the can in a trash container.

    _____

    _____

3. The window on the driver's side of the car was rolled down.
    The car belonged to Rosa.
    The window had been open during a thunderstorm.
    The seat on the driver's side of the car was wet.

    _____

    _____

4. Someone in the classroom was chewing gum.
    The same person was popping the gum.
    Some students were annoyed.
    The class was taking a test.

    _____

    _____

5. There was a calendar on the wall.
    The wall was in the machine shop.
    The calendar showed women.
    The women were wearing bathing suits.

    _____

    _____

Power Tool 2: Vary Sentence Openings

The most common sentence pattern in English is one that opens with a sub-ject followed by a verb, as in the following sentences:

$$\overset{S}{\underline{Imana}} \ \overset{V}{\underline{dashed}} \ \text{across the finish line.}$$

$$\overset{S}{\underline{Cattle}} \ \overset{V}{\underline{grazed}} \ \text{peacefully in a field of bright green.}$$

This pattern is common because it is strong and dynamic and gets the job done quickly. When you read a sentence in this pattern, you know immediately who the actors were and what they did. But too many sentences in this pattern can make for dull reading, especially if they are short sentences. So while you never want to give up writing strong sentences with the subject and verb at the beginning, occasional variation strengthens your writing. Two ways to vary your sentence openings are with prepositional phrases and verbal phrases.

Prepositional Phrases to Begin Sentences

You are probably used to ending sentences with prepositional phrases.

> A yellow light shone *from the window.*
>
> Bob went to the deli *during his lunch hour.*
>
> A candy wrapper had been dropped on the floor *near the front of the room.*

Occasionally, try beginning a sentence with a prepositional phrase:

> *From the window,* a yellow light shone.
>
> *During his lunch hour,* Bob went to the deli.
>
> *Near the front of the room,* a candy wrapper had been dropped on the floor.

PRACTICE 2   BEGINNING SENTENCES WITH PREPOSITIONAL PHRASES

Rearrange each sentence to begin with a prepositional phrase.

1.   Anna made a note of the appointment on a page of the calendar.

   _____

2.   Michael picked up a rain-soaked newspaper from the driveway.

   _____

3.   Perry heard laughter from the next room.

   _____

4.   A child was playing hopscotch in the street.

   _____

5.   Bryan seemed quiet and shy in the office.

   _____

Verbal Phrases to Begin Sentences

A verbal phrase is a word group that begins with an *-ing* verb or an *-ed/-en* verb:

> *Riding into the sunset,* the cowboy sat tall in the saddle.

> *Eating quickly,* Arturo hoped he would get back to work on time.

> *Written in haste,* the paper was barely legible.

> *Coated with flour,* the cockroach scurried across the floor of the restaurant's kitchen.

Opening Sentences with *-ing* Verbal Phrases

Sometimes, an idea expressed in two sentences can be compressed by converting one of the sentences into an *-ing* phrase. Be sure to put the *-ing* phrase as close as possible to the person or thing it describes:

> Samuel walked into the room.

> He was trying not to attract attention.

> *Trying not to attract attention,* Samuel walked into the room.

> Amelia was expecting to be laid off.

> She was shocked when she was offered a promotion.

> *Expecting to be laid off,* Amelia was shocked when she was offered a promotion.

PRACTICE 3   USING *-ING* PHRASES

In each sentence pair below, convert one of the sentences to an -ing verbal phrase to make one sentence.

1. The blue van sped past at a high rate of speed.
   It was swerving dangerously on the wet pavement.

   _____

   _____

2. Vernon was planning to cut his English class.
   He was dismayed to meet his instructor in the hall.

   _____

   _____

3. Renita was opening her mailbox.
   She was surprised to see a spider inside.

   _____

   _____

4. Allen was reaching for a piece of candy.
   He spilled the whole bag on the floor.

   _____

   _____

5. My neighbor woke me up in the middle of the night.
   She was ringing the doorbell and pounding on the door.

   _____

   _____

Opening Sentences with *-ed* Verbal Phrases

Sometimes, an idea expressed in two sentences can be compressed by converting one of the sentences into an *-ed/-en* phrase:

The grass was covered with dew.

It was impossible to mow.

Covered with dew, the grass was impossible to mow.

The television was broken beyond repair.

It was placed beside the curb for trash pickup.

Broken beyond repair, the television was placed beside the curb for trash pickup.

PRACTICE 4   USING *-ED* PHRASES

In each sentence pair, convert one of the sentences to an *-ed* verbal phrase to make one sentence.

1. The interviewer was impressed by the candidate's credentials.
    She decided to offer him a job.

    _____

    _____

2. Alonzo was inspired by the speaker's message.
    He decided to pursue his dream of becoming a veterinarian.

    _____

    _____

3. Tia promised herself she would do better on her next test.
    She was disappointed by her grade on the chapter test.

    _____

    _____

4. Jon was annoyed by the telephone's constant ringing.
    He decided to buy an answering machine.

    _____

    _____

5. The sand castle was swept from the shore.
    It was engulfed by a huge wave.

    _____

    _____

Power Tool 3: Connect Ideas through Coordination

Often, ideas expressed in short, simple sentences can be joined to make a more effective sentence. One way to join sentences is called coordination. Coordination can be done in two ways: by using a comma and a coordinating (FANBOYS) conjunction or by using a semicolon and a joining word.

Comma and FANBOYS

FANBOYS conjunctions, more commonly called *coordinating conjunctions,* are used with a comma to join two independent clauses. If you can remember the nonsense word FANBOYS, you can remember all seven coordinating conjunctions: *for, and, nor, but, or, yet, so.*

This is the pattern used when a FANBOYS conjunction is used with a comma to join two clauses. The comma goes before the FANBOYS conjunction.

<u>Independent clause</u> , and <u>independent clause</u> .

Example

John worked the math problem twice.
He came up with a different answer each time.

The two independent clauses above can be joined with a FANBOYS and a comma:

John worked the math problem twice, **but** he came up with a different answer each time.

A list of FANBOYS conjunctions appears below:

* FANBOYS Conjunctions						
for	and	nor	but	or	yet	so

PRACTICE 5 JOINING SENTENCES WITH *FANBOYS* CONJUNCTIONS

Join each sentence pair below with a comma and a FANBOYS.

1. The telephone was ringing on the secretary's desk., *yet*
   No one bothered to answer it.

   _____

2. Harlan's suitcase had a broken handle, *so*
   He decided to buy another one before his vacation.

   _____

3. The mall's parking lot was crowded, *and*
   The store was packed with shoppers.

   _____

4. Lisa did not have time to make coffee at home., *so*

    She bought a cup of flavored coffee from a machine in the convenience store.

    _____

5. Allen may go skiing on his vacation., *yet*

    He may stay home and paint his house.

    _____

Semicolon and Joining Word

Another method of coordination is using a semicolon and a joining word. As with a comma and FANBOYS conjunction, a complete sentence (or independent clause) will appear on both sides of the semicolon.

   <u>Independent clause</u> ; therefore, <u>independent clause</u> .

Example

   Anthony would like to make more money.

   He fears that working more hours would interfere with his studies.

The two separate sentences can be combined with a semicolon and a joining word.

   Anthony would like to make more money; **however,** he fears that working more hours would interfere with his studies.

The joining words also function as _transitional expressions,_ underscoring the relationship between the two clauses. A list of joining words and phrases commonly used with semicolons appears below.

Joining Words and Phrases Used with a Semicolon

accordingly	however	nevertheless
also	in addition	of course
as a result	in fact	on the other hand
besides	instead	then
finally	meanwhile	therefore
furthermore	namely	thus

PRACTICE 6   JOINING SENTENCES WITH SEMICOLONS AND TRANSITIONAL WORDS

Join each sentence pair with a semicolon, a joining word or phrase from the list on page 265, and a comma.

1. The child knew that there were no monsters in the closet. *; however,*
   He thought his mother should check anyway.

   _____

2. The instructor was ill on Tuesday. *; as a result,*
   The class was canceled.

   _____

3. The citizen firmly refused to remove the junked cars from his yard. *; in fact,*
   He argued that the city should pay him for his "art."

   _____

4. Felicia hoped that her tax refund would arrive before the weekend. *;*
   She did not get it until the following Wednesday.

   _____

5. Al had locked his keys in the car twice during the past month.
   He had an extra set made.

   _____

Power Tool 4: Connect Ideas through Subordination

Placing a **dependent word** such as *because, although, if, when,* or *after* in front of an independent clause makes it a **dependent** or **subordinate clause**, one that can no longer stand on its own as a sentence. It must be connected to another idea that is stated as a complete sentence. It will then depend on the sentence it is attached to and can no longer be separated from it. A sentence containing a dependent clause may be written in two ways: dependent clause first or dependent clause last.

Dependent Clause First

Place a comma after a dependent clause that introduces a sentence.

Example

Dan realized that he was paying over fifty dollars for cable TV.

He decided to drop his premium channels.

If a dependent clause acts as an introductory clause, a comma follows it.

When <u>dependent clause</u>, <u>independent clause</u>.

When Dan realized that he was paying over fifty dollars for cable TV, he decided to drop his premium channels.

Dependent Clause Last

Another way to connect ideas through subordination is to place an independent clause first and follow it with a dependent clause.

<u>Independent clause</u> when <u>dependent clause</u>.

Example

Traffic on the interstate was rerouted for two hours.

A tractor trailer overturned in the southbound lane.

Traffic on the interstate was rerouted for two hours **when** a tractor trailer overturned in the southbound lane.

A list of dependent words and phrases is shown below.

Commonly Used Dependent Words and Phrases

after	how	what
although	if	whatever
as	once	when
as if	since	whenever
as long as	so that	where
as soon as	that	wherever
as though	though	which
because	unless	while
before	until	who
even though		

PRACTICE 7   JOINING SENTENCES WITH DEPENDENT WORDS

Choosing from the list of dependent words on page 267, connect each sentence pair using the following pattern:

<u>Dependent clause</u> , <u>independent clause</u> .

1. My little brother turned sixteen.
   He took the test for his driver's license.

   _____

   _____

2. Quinton was not sure he was good enough to make the team.
   He decided to try out anyway.

   _____

   _____

3. Mika had lived in the same town all her life.
   She was eager to attend college in a different city.

   _____

   _____

4. The weather forecaster had predicted morning rain.
   The day dawned sunny and clear.

   _____

   _____

5. Fredo was accepted at a technical school.
   He changed his mind and decided to apply to a four-year college.

   _____

   _____

PRACTICE 8   JOINING SENTENCES WITH DEPENDENT WORDS

Choosing from the list of dependent words on page 267, connect each sentence pair using the following pattern:

<u>Independent clause</u>   when   <u>dependent clause</u> .

The first one is done for you.

1. A small house was swept away by the flood. Onlookers watched in horror.

    A small house was swept by the flood as onlookers watched in horror.
    _____

    _____

2. Sarah let out a sigh of relief.
    She saw that she had passed her midterm exam.

    _____

    _____

3. Trenton was angry.
    He had to wait almost an hour for his job interview.

    _____

    _____

4. Brandy did not finish her research project.
    She became distracted exploring the Internet.

    _____

    _____

5. The workers were confident they would finish the project on time.
    They were three weeks behind their planned schedule.

    _____

    _____

Creating Emphasis through Subordination

Dependent words also act as transitional words, showing the relationship between the ideas. Using dependent clauses helps to downplay one idea while emphasizing another. Usually, the idea expressed in the independent clause is of greater importance, while the idea in the dependent clause is of lesser importance.

Examples

Although Diana had no money in her bank account,

emphasis on the check
she wrote a check for two hundred dollars.

Although Diana wrote a check for two hundred dollars,

emphasis on empty account
she had no money in her checking account.

emphasis on the cheer
A cheer went up from the crowd as Hank Aaron strode onto the field.

emphasis on Hank Aaron
Hank Aaron strode onto the field as a cheer went up from the crowd.

PRACTICE 9   **EMPHASIZING IDEAS WITH DEPENDENT WORDS**

Choosing from the list of dependent words on page 267, connect each sentence pair. Emphasize the idea marked with a check. Do not introduce the emphasized idea with a dependent word. The first one is done for you.

1. Jonas seldom spoke up in class.
   He was obviously an intelligent person. ✔

   Although Jonas seldom spoke up in class, he was obviously an intelligent person.

   _____

2. Jordan took vitamins every day.
   She was sure her diet was nutritionally adequate. ✔

   _____

   _____

3. Lu-Chen struggled to stay awake. ✔
   She tried to read just one more chapter.

   _____

   _____

4. The cottage cheese smelled sour and unpleasant. ✔
   The expiration date was five days away.

   _____

   _____

5. Katelyn said she was too full to eat her broccoli.
   She had plenty of room for dessert. ✔

   _____

   _____

Review Exercises

Complete the Review Exercises to see how well you have learned the skills addressed in this chapter. As you work through the exercises, go back through the chapter to review any of the rules you do not understand completely.

REVIEW EXERCISE 1   WRITING CONCISE SENTENCES

In each problem, combine the four ideas into one concise sentence. Make sure that the sentence expresses the idea fully but uses as few words as possible.

1. Gordon looked at a dent.
    He looked at it unhappily.
    The dent was in the door of his car.
    His car was new.

    _____

    _____

2. A pleasant aroma drifted through the air.
    It came from the restaurant.
    The restaurant was called Myra's Kitchen.
    It was on the corner.

    _____

    _____

3. Bill saved his pocket change.
    He saved it in a jar.
    The jar had once held pickles.
    The jar sat on the table.

    _____

    _____

4. The telephone rang.
    It rang several times.
    Michaela ignored it.

She ignored it until the ringing stopped.

_____

_____

5. Tom ate a ham sandwich.
    It was on rye bread.
    He also ate an apple.
    He ate the sandwich and the apple for lunch.

    _____

    _____

REVIEW EXERCISE 2   USING PREPOSITIONAL PHRASES TO BEGIN SENTENCES

Rearrange each sentence to begin with a prepositional phrase.

1. Two children were playing catch in the middle of the street.

    _____

2. A cement truck slowly rumbled along in the lane ahead of us.

    _____

3. It was dark and deliciously cool in the movie theater.

    _____

4. Jake has lived in the same house for twenty years.

    _____

5. Claudia sounded charming and capable over the telephone.

    _____

REVIEW EXERCISE 3   USING VERBAL PHRASES TO BEGIN SENTENCES

Join each sentence pair by converting one of the sentences to an *-ed* or *-ing* verbal phrase.

1. The washing machine stopped in the middle of its cycle.
    It was clogged by lint from a cotton blanket.

    _____

    _____

2. Myesha was sitting on a bench in the park.
   She found it difficult to concentrate on the book she was reading.

   _____

   _____

3. Elena was annoyed at Roberto's self-centeredness.
   She finally decided to end their relationship.

   _____

   _____

4. Michael ran into the parking lot and leaped into his car.
   He was hoping he would not be late for the meeting.

   _____

   _____

   _____

5. Elliot was chilled by the icy wind.
   He decided to stop and get a cup of coffee.

   _____

   _____

REVIEW EXERCISE 4   CONNECTING IDEAS THROUGH COORDINATION

Connect each sentence pair using a coordination. Use a comma and a FANBOYS *or* a semicolon, a joining word, and a comma.

1. There was nothing that Tina wanted to see at the movie theater.
   She rented a video.

   _____

2. Horton realized the cashier had given him five dollars too much.
   He knew he should return it.

   _____

3. The laundromat was crowded.
   Sam decided to do his laundry some other time.

   _____

4. The job required extensive travel.
   Deloris decided not to take it.

   _____

5. The woman was trying to walk at a brisk pace.
    Her little dog kept stopping to sniff at the ground.

    _____

REVIEW EXERCISE 5   CONNECTING IDEAS THROUGH SUBORDINATION

Connect each sentence pair using a subordination. Use a dependent word (and a comma if necessary).

1. Brendan should have been writing his English paper.
    He was playing Solitaire on his computer.

    _____

    _____

2. Nancy cleaned out her refrigerator.
    She found six half-empty containers of cottage cheese.

    _____

    _____

3. Alexa headed for the last parking space in the lot.
    A battered Volkswagen rounded a corner and zipped into the space.

    _____

    _____

4. The building looked like a toy from a distance.
    It boasted twenty floors and state-of-the art environmental controls.

    _____

    _____

5. Burton hated to fly.
    He never went anywhere that his car would not take him.

    _____

    _____

CHAPTER 16

Run-on Sentences

*Two cars spun in a crazy dance
And spiraled to a stop,
Locked in a less-than-fond embrace,
Both destined for the shop.*

*And so it is with sentences
When they're too closely linked;
It's up to you to fix them
And make them each distinct.*

What Is a Run-on Sentence?

A run-on sentence is not one sentence, but two or more, run together without proper punctuation. The sentence below is a run-on.

✗ Tasha worked slowly and carefully she had trouble finishing tests on time.

By examining the sentence, you can probably figure out where the first thought ends and the second begins: between *carefully* and *she*. Grammatically, too, you can figure out why the thoughts should be separate. Each has a subject and a verb and is an independent clause, a clause that can stand alone as a sentence or that can be combined with other clauses in specific patterns.

Another type of run-on is called a comma splice because two independent clauses are spliced, or joined, with a comma.

✗ Tasha worked slowly and carefully, she had trouble finishing tests on time.

The run-on can be corrected in a variety of ways. Here are two of them.

✔ Tasha worked slowly and carefully, so she had trouble finishing tests on time.

✔ Because Tasha worked slowly and carefully, she had trouble finishing tests on time.

The first step toward writing paragraphs and essays that are free of run-on sentences is to learn to recognize run-ons and comma splices. When you see a sentence that you believe is a run-on, test it. Read the first part. Is it a sentence that could stand alone? If your answer is "yes," read the second part, asking the same question. If your answer is again "yes," the sentence is probably a run-on.

PRACTICE 1   RECOGNIZING RUN-ONS AND COMMA SPLICES

In each sentence, underline the spot where the run-on or comma splice occurs. Mark *RO* in the blank to the left of the sentence if the sentence is a run-on, *CS* if it is a comma splice.

_____ 1. Harold had one claim to fame he could wiggle his ears without moving his face.

_____ 2. The renovated theater was beautiful, the plush seats and velvet curtains recalled a more elegant era.

_____ 3. Leonard was seasick he stayed in his cabin on the first evening of the cruise.

_____ 4. "All I do is work and go to school, I feel like I'm on an endless treadmill," said Angelica.

_____ 5. Kaya stopped at a convenience store for gas she also bought a cup of coffee and a doughnut.

Correcting Run-ons

Five methods of correcting run-ons are presented in the following sections. The first three methods are simple; the final two are more complex. Learning all five methods will give you more than just ways to correct run-ons; it will give you a variety of sentence patterns and transitional words to use in your writing.

Method 1: Period and Capital Letter

Correcting a run-on with a period and capital letter is the easiest method to use. The hard part is knowing when and how often to use it. Short, single-clause sentences can emphasize ideas by setting them apart. However, too many short sentences can make your writing seem choppy and disconnected.

Pattern: <u>Independent clause</u>. <u>Independent clause</u>.

Put a period between the two sentences. Use a capital letter to begin the new sentence.

Example

✗   Leon looked glumly at the blank sheet of paper he could not think of a thing to write.

✔   Leon looked glumly at the blank sheet of paper. He could not think of a thing to write.

PRACTICE 2   CORRECTING RUN-ONS WITH A PERIOD AND CAPITAL LETTER

In each sentence, underline the spot where each run-on or comma splice occurs. Write *RO* in the blank to the left of the sentence if it is a run-on, *CS* if it is a comma splice. Then correct each sentence using a period and a capital letter.

_____ 1. Carol plans to study audiology she wants to help people with hearing problems.

_____

_____ 2. Sally and Layla have been friends for years now they plan to go into business together.

_____

_____ 3. Scientists have developed a new drug it can help grow new blood vessels.

_____ 4. The short-term memory holds only five to seven bits of information, that is one reason people need grocery lists.

_____ 5. The baby's hair had not come in, she had a faint peach fuzz all over her head.

Method 2: Comma and FANBOYS Conjunction

Coordinating conjunctions, or FANBOYS conjunctions, are among the most useful and powerful connecting words in the English language. If you can remember the nonsense word FANBOYS, you can remember the seven coordinating conjunctions: *for, and, nor, but, or, yet, so.*

Pattern: <u>Independent clause</u>, and <u>independent clause</u>.

When a FANBOYS conjunction is used with a comma to separate two clauses, the comma goes before the FANBOYS conjunction.

Example

✗ Greg had not eaten breakfast, he cooked some instant oatmeal in the microwave.

✔ Greg had not eaten breakfast, so he cooked some instant oatmeal in the microwave.

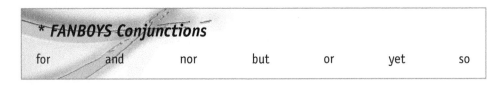

*FANBOYS Conjunctions						
for	and	nor	but	or	yet	so

PRACTICE 3   CORRECTING RUN-ONS WITH A COMMA AND *FANBOYS*

In each sentence, underline the spot where each run-on or comma splice occurs. Write *RO* in the blank to the left of the sentence if it is a run-on, *CS* if it is a comma splice. Correct each run-on or comma splice by using a comma and a FANBOYS conjunction.

_____ 1. The address label was shaped like a teacup, the sender's address was on the saucer.

_____

_____ 2. Victoria tried to tell Jim his plan would not work he did not want to hear her criticism.

_____

_____ 3. Tyler's neighbors had three new cars and a recently installed hot tub, they each worked two jobs to pay for them.

_____

_____ 4. Sabrina felt stylish in her new coat, there was a little bounce in her walk.

_____

_____ 5. A cat rested on the porch rail it scampered away as a visitor approached.

_____

Method 3: Semicolon

Using a semicolon to join clauses works best with ideas that are closely connected and need no transitional word to explain the connection between them. The semicolon, as used here, is the grammatical equivalent of a period, but the first letter of the clause after the semicolon is *not* capitalized.

Pattern: Independent clause; independent clause.

The semicolon goes between the two clauses.

Example

✗ The book had been assigned for two weeks, Emily had not read a single page.

✔ The book had been assigned for two weeks; Emily had not read a single page.

PRACTICE 4   CORRECTING RUN-ONS WITH A SEMICOLON

In each sentence, underline the spot where each run-on or comma splice occurs. Write *RO* in the blank to the left of the sentence if it is a run-on, *CS* if it is a comma splice. Then correct the sentences using a semicolon alone.

_____ **1.** The drama club held a car wash in a grocery store parking lot, cars lined up to take advantage of the low prices.

_____

_____ **2.** Bruce thought he was typing in the Internet address of a government agency he accessed a page of nude photographs instead.

_____

_____ **3.** Fashion trends exist in language, new words come into fashion as old ones go out.

_____

_____ **4.** Valerie had several errands to run, her first was to go by the dry cleaners.

_____

_____ **5.** The mailbox was filled with colorful sale flyers and catalogs Terry threw them in the trash.

_____

Method 4: Semicolon and Joining Word

A run-on sentence may also be corrected with a joining word. These joining words also function as transitional expressions, underscoring the relationship between the two clauses.

> **Pattern:** Independent clause; therefore, independent clause.

A semicolon precedes the joining word and a comma follows it. With the words *thus* and *then*, the comma is often omitted.

Example

✗   The bananas on the produce department's display were turning brown, the lettuce looked wilted.

✔   The bananas on the produce department's display were turning brown; furthermore, the lettuce looked wilted.

Joining Words Used with a Semicolon

accordingly	furthermore	nevertheless
also	however	of course
as a result	in addition	on the other hand
besides	in fact	then
finally	instead	therefore
for example	meanwhile	thus
for instance	namely	

PRACTICE 5   CORRECTING RUN-ONS WITH A SEMICOLON AND JOINING WORD

In each sentence, underline the spot where each run-on or comma splice occurs. Write *RO* in the blank to the left of the sentence if it is a run-on, *CS* if it is a comma splice. Then correct the sentence using a semicolon and an appropriate joining word.

_____ 1. The elevator did not come Mina pushed the button again.

_____

_____ 2. The deli clerk was daydreaming, he cut nearly two pounds of meat instead of one.

_____

_____ 3. Shane finally finished his phone call and returned to his soup it had gotten cold.

_____

_____ 4. Sarah noticed a telephone number written inside the cover of her psychology book, she could not remember whose number it was.

_____

_____ 5. The movie theater was dark Michelle almost sat on someone's lap.

_____

Method 5: Dependent Word

Placing a dependent word in front of an independent clause makes it a dependent clause, a clause that can no longer stand on its own as a sentence.

It now *depends* on the sentence it is attached to and can no longer be separated from it.

Two variations of the dependent word method are shown below.

Example

✗   The restaurant was dark Martha could barely read her menu.

   Pattern: Because <u>dependent clause,</u> <u>independent clause</u>.

When the dependent clause acts as an introductory clause, a comma follows it.

✔   Because the restaurant was dark, Martha could barely read her menu.

   Pattern: <u>Independent clause</u> because <u>dependent clause</u>.

When the dependent clause comes last in the sentence, no comma is used.

✔   Martha could barely read her menu because the restaurant was dark.

Commonly Used Dependent Words

after	if	whatever
although	once	when
as	since	whenever
as if	so that	where
as long as	that	wherever
as soon as	though	which
as though	unless	while
because	until	who
before	what	whoever
even though		

PRACTICE 6   CORRECTING RUN-ONS WITH A DEPENDENT WORD

In each sentence, underline the spot where each run-on or comma splice occurs. Write *RO* in the blank to the left of the sentence if it is a run-on, *CS* if it is a comma splice. Correct each sentence using a dependent word.

_____   1.   Every computer in the lab was busy, Nelson put his name on the waiting list.

Five Ways to Correct Run-on Sentences

Method 1: Period and Capital Letter

Pattern: Independent clause. Independent clause.

Method 2: Comma and FANBOYS Conjunction

Pattern: <u>Independent clause</u>, and <u>independent clause</u>.

A comma goes before the FANBOYS conjunction in this pattern.

FANBOYS Conjunctions

for   and   nor   but   or   yet   so

Method 3: Semicolon

Pattern: <u>Independent clause</u>; <u>independent clause</u>.

Method 4: Semicolon and Joining Word

Pattern: <u>Independent clause</u>; therefore, <u>independent clause</u>.

A semicolon goes before the joining word and a comma follows it. With the words *thus* and *then*, the comma is often omitted.

Joining Words Used with a Semicolon

also	however	of course
as a result	in addition	on the other hand
besides	in fact	then
finally	instead	therefore
for example	meanwhile	thus

Method 5: Dependent Word

Pattern 1: Although <u>dependent clause</u>, <u>independent clause</u>.

When a dependent word begins the sentence, a comma is used between the dependent and independent clause.

Pattern 2: <u>Independent clause</u> when <u>dependent clause</u>.

When the dependent clause ends the sentence, a dependent word separates the clauses.

Dependent Words

although	because	that	whenever
as	before	though	where
as if	if	unless	wherever
as long	once	until	which
as soon as	since	whatever	while
as though	so that	when	who

_____ 2. The truck rumbled past, Veronica gripped the steering wheel of her small car.

_____

_____ 3. Phil pumped gas into his car he noticed that the station across the street had lower prices.

_____

_____ 4. Rita's week had been long and tiring, she did not feel like going out.

_____

_____ 5. A little flag began to wave at the bottom of Joe's computer screen he knew he had email.

_____

Review Exercises

Complete the Review Exercises to see how well you have learned the skills addressed in this chapter. As you work through the exercises, go back through the chapter to review any of the rules you do not understand completely.

REVIEW EXERCISE 1

In each sentence, underline the spot where the run-on or comma splice occurs. Then correct the ten run-on sentences, using each of the five methods at least once.

1. The rain poured down in sheets Nell could barely see the road in front of her.

_____

2. The edges of the wooden desk were once square and sharp now they are rounded from wear.

_____

3. The lasagna was frozen solid, Linda knew it would take too long to reheat it.

_____

4. Jemal tried to answer the telephone he dropped the receiver on the floor.

_____

5. The delivery truck was behind schedule the hardware store employee said he did not think our order would be delivered today.

_____

6. Fred bit into a crisp toasted marshmallow, delicious white goo slid onto his tongue.

    _____

7. Representatives from businesses and industries visited campus today, students crowded around to sign up for interviews.

    _____

8. Bootsie was due for her rabies shot, the vet sent a reminder in the mail.

    _____

9. The loud pounding beat of the music in the aerobics room gave Jill a headache she wished someone would turn down the sound.

    _____

10. Brian fell asleep in front of the television he woke up at 2:00 A.M. with a crick in his neck.

    _____

REVIEW EXERCISE 2

In each sentence, underline the spot where the run-on or comma splice occurs. Then correct the ten run-on sentences, using each of the five methods at least once.

1. Channing knew it was getting late he could not seem to stop playing his computer game.

    _____

2. The children visited the museum some of them petted a boa constrictor.

    _____

3. Heather likes parties and people her husband prefers quiet evenings at home.

    _____

4. Jim bought highlighters, pens, index cards and a notebook he still had trouble motivating himself to study.

    _____

5. Vijay had his term paper stored on disk, however, he could not find the disk.

    _____

6. The lines were long the fast-food place was giving free fries to everyone.

    _____

7. The deli clerk asked how the customer wanted his bologna sliced he replied, "I want it so thin that I can read my newspaper through it."

    _____

8. Under the porch, a patch of flowers grew apparently the amount of sunlight was just right for them to thrive.

_____

9. I saw Tom just a minute ago, where is he now?

_____

10. A storm came through last night two trees were uprooted, and power lines were down.

_____

REVIEW EXERCISE 3

In the following exercise, underline the spot where each run-on or comma splice occurs. Then correct the two run-ons in each sentence group.

1. A line of cars waited at the toll booth Alec impatiently craned his neck to see what was holding up traffic. A dog had jumped out of a car window the owner was frantically trying to coax it back.

_____

_____

2. Trevor fixed himself a plate of spaghetti he piled it high on the plate. As he carried it back to the table, a meatball fell then the whole plateful slid off onto the floor.

_____

_____

3. The children complained that there was nothing to do, their mother told them they could help her with the laundry. They decided they weren't bored after all they suddenly found plenty of games to play.

_____

_____

4. Colonial Americans used brightly colored "witch balls" to prevent evil spirits from entering their homes the witch balls were made of glass. Threads within the ball were supposed to trap evil spirits, once entangled in the threads, the spirits could not fly out.

_____

_____

5. Terrell says he never watches the news any more it only depresses him. He says he does not need to hear about the meanness in the world, he would rather focus on the good.

_____

_____

REVIEW EXERCISE 4

In the following exercise, underline the spot where each run-on or comma splice occurs. Then correct the two run-ons in each sentence group.

1. Marian browsed through the video store the only selections left were children's movies. She decided to watch *The Lion King* one more time, she had always liked it.

_____

_____

2. Fran rushed through the grocery store, she wished that the man in front of her would hurry. Then she noticed that the man was walking with a cane, she was ashamed of her impatience.

_____

_____

3. The Gullah people are descendants of slaves they speak their own unique language. Their music incorporates the rhythms of clapping hands and stamping feet, their songs date back to the days of slavery.

_____

_____

4. The Tomlinsons have just one television, they own two computers. They believe that their time is better spent on the computer, watching television does not engage their minds.

_____

_____

5. At the barbecue place, Samuel ordered a quart of barbecue then he decided to add a rack of ribs to his order. He might be sorry tomorrow, at least he would eat well tonight.

_____

_____

Review Exercise 5

In the following paragraph, underline the spot where each run-on or comma splice occurs. Then correct the ten run-on sentences or comma splices, using the five methods presented in this chapter. Try to use each method at least once.

[1]David woke up and squinted at the clock, the blue numbers on its face read 8:35. [2]Immediately, he was filled with panic he had to be at work at nine. [3]He leaped out of bed then he ran quickly to his son's room. [4]"Get up, Jason, it's time for school, and Daddy's running late." he said. [5]When David saw that his son was awake, he turned on the shower as the water warmed up, he thought of all the things he had to do. [6]He would grab a shower and get dressed, then he would make sure Jason got ready for school. [7]He would make a quick call to his office to say he would be a few minutes late he and Jason could take off, eating their breakfast in the car. [8]After showering and dressing quickly, David went to check on Jason his son was still in his pajamas, eating Cheerios from the box and watching television. [9]He stopped, astonished that his son was not getting ready for school Jason looked up at him and said, "Dad, it's Saturday." [10]David laughed and flopped on the couch beside his son "Pass the Cheerios," he said.

1. _____

2. _____

3. _____

4. _____

5. _____

6. _____

7. _____

8. _____

9. _____

10. _____

Sentence Fragments

As Alice threw the looking glass,
It struck the bathroom tile
And shattered into fragments—
Bad luck for quite a while.

But how much worse the writer's luck,
Who misses when he proofs,
A dozen sentence fragments
And shows the world his goofs.

What Is a Sentence Fragment?

✗ Susan finished reading the last section of the newspaper. *And dropped it on the floor beside her chair.*

✗ *When gasoline prices rise dramatically and stay high for a long time.* Automobile companies see a rise in the sale of smaller, more fuel-efficient cars.

289

The italicized word groups are <u>sentence fragment</u>s: <u>pieces of sentences that cannot stand alone</u>. A sentence fragment is an incomplete sentence. It may be a dependent clause that cannot stand on its own, or it may lack a subject, a verb, or both. If you read a fragment by itself, without the other sentences that surround it, you will usually recognize that it does not express a complete thought. It is only a part, or fragment, of a sentence.

Dependent Clause Fragments

✗ *Because Javarez had missed the first bus.* He stood on the corner shivering and hoping that another one would come along soon.

✗ No one answered Alicia's knock. *Although someone was obviously at home.*

Each of the italicized fragments above is a <u>dependent clause fragment</u>. A dependent clause fragment always begins with a dependent word. To fix a dependent clause fragment, attach it to a complete sentence.

✔ Because Javarez had missed the first bus, he stood on the corner shivering and hoping that another one would come along soon.

✔ No one answered Alicia's knock although someone was obviously at home.

Dropping the dependent word or changing it to another type of transitional expression is an alternative to connecting the fragment to the sentence.

✔ Javarez had missed the first bus. He stood on the corner shivering and hoping that another one would come along soon.

✔ No one answered Alicia's knock. However, someone was obviously at home.

---

* Punctuation Pointer

In general, use a comma to attach a dependent clause fragment at the beginning of a sentence.

Commonly Used Dependent Words

after	before	though	whenever
although	even though	unless	which
as	how	until	while
as if	if	what	who
as long as	once	whatever	whoever
as soon as	since	when	
as though	so that	whenever	
because	that	where	

PRACTICE 1   CORRECTING DEPENDENT CLAUSE FRAGMENTS

Correct the dependent clause fragments by attaching them to an independent clause.

1. While several of her friends planned to go out of town over the long weekend. Sarah preferred to stay at home, relax, and save her money.

    _____

2. Tyrell was put off by a salesman. Who placed an arm around his shoulder and greeted him like an old friend.

    _____

3. Because Mary slept through her alarm. She missed her 10:00 A.M. class.

    _____

4. As Dan unloaded the groceries from the car. He realized that the gallon of milk he had bought was not in the trunk.

    _____

5. My grandparents say they have never considered divorce as a solution to their problems. Although Grandma says she has occasionally considered murder.

    _____

Verbal Phrase Fragments (*to, -ing,* and *-ed*)

✗ *To keep gasoline costs down.* Many people carpool to work or school.

✗ *Worrying about damage to his car.* Jonathan ran out into the hailstorm to pull it into the garage.

✗ *Curled in a protective ball in the corner of his cage.* Jo's hedgehog looked unhappy.

The examples above are verbal phrase fragments. A verbal phrase fragment begins with a verb form that is not used as a main verb. Verbal phrase fragments include *to* fragments, *-ing* fragments, and *-ed/-en* fragments.

Correct verbal phrase fragments by attaching them to a complete sentence.

✔ To keep gasoline costs down, many people carpool to work or school.

✔ Worrying about damage to his car, Jonathan ran out into the hailstorm to pull it into the garage.

✔ Curled in a protective ball in the corner of his cage, Jo's hedgehog looked unhappy.

to Fragments

Correct *to* fragments by connecting them to a sentence or by adding a subject and verb.

Examples

✗ To keep her children entertained on the long trip home. Kayla challenged them to see who could spot license plates from the largest number of states.

✔ To keep her children entertained on the long trip home, Kayla challenged them to see who could spot license plates from the largest number of states.

✗ Last Friday, Ron invited his friends over. To help him celebrate his graduation from college.

✔ Last Friday, Ron invited his friends over to help him celebrate his graduation from college.

✗ Joann practiced for hours over the weekend. To make sure everything would go well during her interview on Monday.

✔ Joann practiced for hours over the weekend. She wanted to make sure everything would go well during her interview on Monday.

> *** Punctuation Pointer**
>
> A *to* fragment attached to the beginning of a sentence is followed by a comma because it is an introductory phrase. A *to* fragment connected to the end of the sentence needs no comma.

PRACTICE 2   CORRECTING *To* FRAGMENTS

Underline and correct the *to* fragments.

1. To strengthen her back and improve her posture. Shauna began a weightlifting program.

    _____

2. The cook used a wide metal spatula. To turn the pancakes on the grill.

    _____

3. To give himself time to review for the exam. Damon set his clock a half hour early.

    _____

4. The networks schedule popular movies and special shows. To attract viewers during "sweeps week."

    _____

5. To unwind at the end of the day. Marcy took a walk and watched the sun set.

    _____

-ing Fragments

To correct an *-ing* fragment, connect it to the rest of the sentence with a comma. You may also correct it by adding a subject and a helping verb.

Examples

✗   Eating the hearty bean soup that he had made. Ed decided that he was becoming a good cook.

✔   Eating the hearty bean soup that he had made, Ed decided that he was becoming a good cook.

✗   The decorator stepped back from the paintings she had hung. Checking to make sure they were precisely aligned.

✔   The decorator stepped back from the paintings she had hung, checking to make sure they were precisely aligned.

✔   The decorator stepped back from the paintings she had hung. She was checking to make sure they were precisely aligned.

> *** Punctuation Pointer**
>
> Usually, *-ing* fragments can be connected to the rest of the sentence with a comma.

PRACTICE 3   CORRECTING *-Ing* FRAGMENTS

Underline and correct the *-ing* fragments.

1. Realizing that the high noise level could damage employees' hearing. The factory's management required workers to wear earplugs.

   _____

2. Hearing a commotion in the living room. Rita wondered whether she should check on the children.

   _____

3. Samantha quickly locked the door and left. Knowing she was probably going to be late for work.

   _____

4. Swinging their bare feet and gazing down into the green water. The two children amused themselves while their father fished from the dock.

   _____

5. The police officer raised a white-gloved hand. Stopping traffic to let a group of children cross the street.

   _____

Missing-Subject Fragments

Fragments beginning with a joining word such as *and, or, but*, or *then* followed by a verb are missing-subject fragments. The subject of the verb is usually in a previous sentence. Connect the fragment to the sentence or add a subject to begin a new sentence.

Examples

✗ The crowd grew silent when the player clutched his leg and fell. Then cheered as he was helped off the field.

✔ The crowd grew silent when the player clutched his leg and fell, then cheered as he was helped off the field.

✗ Kara mailed her telephone bill. But forgot to enclose a check.

✔ Kara mailed her telephone bill, but she forgot to enclose a check.

✔ Kara mailed her telephone bill. But she forgot to enclose a check.

PRACTICE 4   **CORRECTING MISSING-SUBJECT FRAGMENTS**

Underline and correct the missing-subject fragments.

1. Anthony started to fill out the questionnaire. Then decided that it asked too many nosy questions.

   _____

2. The snow began to stick around 10:00 in the morning. And was four inches deep by 5:00 in the afternoon.

   _____

3. Tanisha longed for a double cheeseburger with a side order of fries. But decided to have a plain chicken sandwich on whole wheat.

   _____

4. Narcissus was a mythological character who bent to look at himself in a pool of water. And fell in love with his own image.

   _____

5. Beth jumped at a strange noise that seemed to come from her living room. Then decided it was her imagination and turned back to her computer.

   _____

---

* Real-World Writing: Is it okay to start a sentence with but?

Yes and no. Grammatically, it is correct to start a sentence with *but* or any other FANBOYS conjunction. However, your instructors may discourage the practice, for two good reasons.

1. Beginning a sentence with *but* is an informal technique. It may work in personal essays but should not be used in formal compositions such as research papers. (This text, you may have noticed, takes an informal, conversational approach, addressing you directly and occasionally using a FANBOYS conjunction to begin a sentence.)

2. Using *but* to begin a sentence can be addictive. *But* is the strongest contrast signal in our language, and it's easy to overuse.

The bottom line: Use conjunctions to begin sentences only if your instructor gives the green light, and then use them sparingly.

Example and Exception Fragments

Fragments often occur when a writer adds an example or notes an exception. Example fragments often begin with *such as, including, like, for example*, or *for instance*. Exception fragments often begin with *not, except, unless, without*, or *in spite of*. To fix the fragment, connect it to the sentence with which it logically belongs. If the fragment begins with *for example* or *for instance*, it is often best to make the fragment into a separate sentence.

Examples

✗ Holly remained focused on the paper she was writing. In spite of her little brother's constant interruptions.

✔ Holly remained focused on the paper she was writing, in spite of her little brother's constant interruptions.

✗ Ed signed up for the Great American Smokeout, but he was not sure he could make it through the day. Without smoking a cigarette.

✔ Ed signed up for the Great American Smokeout, but he was not sure he could make it through the day without smoking a cigarette.

✗ Clayton says that there are many things he cooks well. For example, instant breakfasts and microwaveable dinners.

✔ Clayton says that there are many things he cooks well. For example, he does a great job with instant breakfasts and microwaveable dinners.

---

* Punctuation Pointer

Usually, you can connect fragments beginning with *such as, including, not, especially,* and *in spite of* with a comma and fragments beginning with *except, unless, without,* and *like* with no comma.

A fragment beginning with *for example* or *for instance* may be attached with a comma if it immediately follows the idea it illustrates: **The chef enjoyed cooking with beans, for example, lima beans, garbanzo beans, and kidney beans.** If the idea that the example illustrates is expressed earlier in the sentence, place the example in a new sentence: **Beans are the specialty of the house at Rizzoli's Restaurant. For example, the chef makes delicious dishes from lima beans, garbanzo beans, and kidney beans.**

PRACTICE 5 CORRECTING EXAMPLE AND EXCEPTION FRAGMENTS

Underline and correct the example and exception fragments.

1. Stacie says she never takes her children anywhere. Without bringing along water, juice, and snacks.

_____

2. Kendrick complains that his wife has a few bad habits. For example, never turning a light off when she leaves a room.

_____

3. The dentist told Sharon she did not need to floss. Unless she wanted to keep her teeth.

_____

4. During the holidays, the department store where Amy works takes extra security measures. Such as hiring store detectives who pose as shoppers.

_____

5. With a new pair of athletic shoes, a stationary bike, and a membership in a fitness center, Kyle had everything he needed. Except willpower.

_____

Prepositional Phrase Fragments

A prepositional phrase, alone or within a series, cannot function as a sentence. Correct a prepositional phrase fragment by connecting it to a sentence with which it logically belongs.

Examples

✗ Kelsey rented a small, one-bedroom apartment. In a complex that offered a pool and other recreational facilities.

✔ Kelsey rented a small, one-bedroom apartment in a complex that offered a pool and other recreational facilities.

✗ On the day of his first political science test. Lee woke up with a pounding headache and a fever of 101 degrees.

✔ On the day of his first political science test, Lee woke up with a pounding headache and a fever of 101 degrees.

> ### *Punctuation Pointer
>
> Use a comma behind an introductory prepositional phrase. No punctuation is required to connect a prepositional phrase to the end of a sentence.

PRACTICE 6   CORRECTING PREPOSITIONAL PHRASE FRAGMENTS

Underline and correct each prepositional phrase fragment.

1. In the vacant lot beside the convenience store. Someone had discarded an old recliner.

   _____

2. It was such a pleasant day that we decided to study. Under a tree beside the lake.

   _____

3. Beneath the smooth-looking, freshly painted surface. Hundreds of termites were gnawing at the wood.

   _____

4. Hassan thought he needed a new car, but he decided against it after he checked prices. In the classified ads section of the newspaper.

   _____

5. On a Greyhound bus headed toward New Jersey. Channa's woolen gloves, forgotten under the seat, traveled on without her.

   _____

Review Exercises

Complete the Review Exercises to see how well you have learned the skills addressed in this chapter. As you work through the exercises, go back through the chapter to review any of the rules you do not understand completely.

REVIEW EXERCISE 1

Underline and correct each fragment.

1. A puzzled frown creased Martin's brow. As he studied the recipe in front of him.

   _____

2. When he investigated the strange lump on his bed. Walter found the cat curled up underneath the bedspread.

_____

3. During the storm, a rotting tree toppled. And lay across the road, blocking two lanes of traffic.

_____

4. The police have set up a roadblock in front of the bridge. To catch drivers who don't have current tags or insurance.

_____

5. With its arched doorways and intricate stained glass windows. The old church was a beautiful place to hold a wedding.

_____

6. Speaking no English and with little savings. Kim's grandparents came to the United States to begin a new life.

_____

7. Eduardo and Maria built a successful business. And sent their five children to college.

_____

8. Harry says that he never reads tabloids. Except when he is standing in line at the grocery store.

_____

9. Grover sat in line at the drive-through for fifteen minutes at the hamburger place. Wondering how fast food could be so slow.

_____

10. As she looked at the clutter on top of her desk. Corinne wondered how she would ever sort it all out.

_____

REVIEW EXERCISE 2

Underline and correct each fragment.

1. After it was cleaned and pressed. Ryan's old sport coat looked like new.

_____

2. Following in her older sister's footsteps. Natalie decided she would go into the medical field, too.

_____

3. The career fair next week is open to all students. And is hosted by the college's career counseling office.

_____

4. Athough the car's bumper sticker read "Have a Nice Day." The driver's angry gesture carried a different message.

_____

5. Yellowing and nearly falling apart. The newspaper clippings were obviously very old.

_____

6. Trembling from the near-collision. Jeff pulled his car to the side of the road.

_____

7. With a dissatisfied grunt and a shake of his closely shaven head. The unhappy customer left Mack's Barber Shop.

_____

8. Because the line of cars at the gas station was so long. Anita decided to wait and buy gas another day.

_____

9. The speaker asked us to imagine what we could accomplish if we did not waste so much time on trivial activities. For example, watching television for hours on end.

_____

10. Spiros found it strange staying at his grandparents' house. Because they had no computer and no VCR.

_____

REVIEW EXERCISE 3

Underline and correct the two fragments in each numbered item.

1. When Nora and A. J. returned from their vacation. They noticed a strange, unpleasant odor in the kitchen. They tried to find the source of the smell. And discovered a package of pita bread covered in dark green mold.

_____

_____

2. Antwan bought everything he needed for his backyard cookout. Including three kinds of meat and two varieties of barbecue sauce. He had thought of everything. Except the possibility of rain.

    _____

    _____

3. Joseph spent many hours at his kitchen table. Building and painting a delicate model ship. When he was finally finished, he set it out to dry. In a place that he hoped was too high for his three-year-old to reach.

    _____

    _____

4. Whenever she was almost finished with a task. Such as reading a novel, writing a paper, or doing a set of math problems, Jennifer was anxious to get the job done. Yet always put off reading the last few pages, writing the conclusion, or finishing the last few problems.

    _____

    _____

5. Though Paul was an expert at many things, such as carpentry and music. He had trouble functioning in daily life. He sometimes seemed unable to perform the simplest tasks. Such as balancing his checkbook or remembering to fill his car with gas.

    _____

    _____

REVIEW EXERCISE 4

Underline and correct the two fragments in each numbered item.

1. Neil bought a small car a few years ago. But kept his old pickup truck, too. Neil is glad he kept the pickup. Especially when he needs to transport a piece of furniture or some other large item.

    _____

    _____

2. As the logs in the fireplace began to burn. Ebony realized she had forgotten to open the damper. When smoke started pouring into the living room. She began to cough.

    _____

    _____

3. Maria had lived in the South all her life. But had never eaten grits. When she finally tried them. She said they tasted like buttered sand.

    _____

    _____

4. Some drivers' behavior on the road would be funny. If it were not so dangerous. For example, some drivers put on makeup while driving. Or talk on a cell phone as if they are at home.

    _____

    _____

5. In his glove compartment, Will found several items he had thought were lost. Such as an old address book and the good pen his grandmother had given him when he graduated from high school. But he did not find his license and registration. To give to the police officer who was standing patiently beside his car.

    _____

    _____

REVIEW EXERCISE 5

Underline and correct the ten fragments below.

Jessie walked through the house, looking under chairs and behind sofa pillows. And trying to find her cellular phone. "When did you see it last?" her mother asked. Jessie said she had taken it with her the night before. When she went out to walk Bruce, her big Newfoundland dog. Then had thrown it into an armchair as she walked into the family room. Jessie and her mother searched every crevice of the armchair. But did not find the phone. Jessie's brother suggested that she dial the cell phone's number. Then locate the phone by its ringing. When Jessie dialed the number. She heard a faint ringing. Leaving the phone off the hook, Jessie walked into the family room. Where Bruce was lying asleep in front of the fireplace. "It's under Bruce!" she called, trying to roll the dog over. Then she realized that the sound was not coming from underneath Bruce. But from inside him. Her dog had somehow swallowed her cell phone. Immediately, she ran back to the kitchen and called the veterinarian. As soon as the vet stopped laughing. He told Jessie not to worry. "Bruce is a big dog." he said. "The cell phone should pass through his system in a day or two." Jessie was relieved. That her dog would be all right. She could get another cell phone, but Bruce was irreplaceable.

Pronoun Case

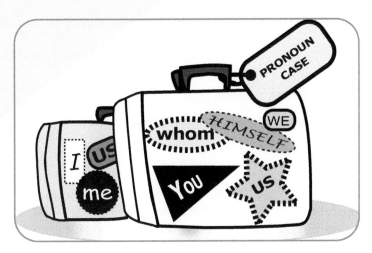

I travel with a pronoun case;
I bring myself and I.
As you and he hop in my case,
Whoever waves goodbye.

We, them, himself, herself, and who
Pile in with she and him.
Someday I'd like to travel light;
The chances seem quite slim.

And when we reach the station,
All getting on the bus,
I look for fellow travelers,
But no one's here but us.

Pronouns are words that stand in for nouns or for other pronouns. They are useful words that keep writers and speakers from tediously repeating words. The rules that govern them are complex, however, and confusion over pronoun usage is common. If you have ever hesitated over "Carlton and me" or "Carlton and I" or wondered whether to say "between you and I" or "between you and me," this chapter will help you find the answers.

Subject and Object Pronouns

Personal pronouns (*I, we, you, he, she, it, they*) refer to specific people or things. These pronouns take different forms, called cases, as they perform various jobs in a sentence. Look at the example that follows to see how the first person pronoun *I* changes form as its role in a sentence changes.

✔ When *I* went to the post office to pick up *my* mail, the clerk said there was a package for *me*.

Subject pronouns (the *subjective case*) include pronouns such as *I, we, you, he, she, it,* and *they*.

✔ *They* were up until midnight trying to put up the wallpaper.

✔ *We* tried to call you, but your line was busy all evening.

✔ The winners were Bryan and *she*.

Object pronouns (the *objective case*) are pronouns such as *me, us, you, him, her, it,* and *them*.

✔ If you are through with the book, please pass it on to *me*.

✔ The cats are waiting for Hilary to feed *them*.

✔ I looked for the flashlight but could not find *it* in the dark.

Subject Pronouns

In most instances, you probably use the subject form of the pronoun correctly without thinking about it. You probably haven't said, "Me went to the park" since you were three. However, using the subject form becomes trickier when a *compound subject* is used. Is it "Tiffany and her went to the concert" or "Tiffany and she went to the concert"? Usually, trying the sentence with the pronoun alone helps you hear the correct answer. Without "Tiffany and" the sentence becomes clear. "*She* went to the concert" is correct, not "*Her* went to the concert."

Example

? *Her and Liz* worked in the same office.

Step 1: To determine if the sentence is correct, try the pronoun alone.

✗ *Her and Liz* worked in the same office.

✗ *Her* worked in the same office.

Step 2: If the pronoun alone sounds incorrect, try changing the form.

✔ *She* worked in the same office.

✔ *She and Liz* worked in the same office. (corrected sentence)

PRACTICE 1   USING SUBJECT PRONOUNS

Underline and correct the errors in each sentence. To determine the correct pronoun form, try the pronoun alone, without the compound element.

I

1. Joel and me took the afternoon off to go fishing.

   _____ *they* _____

2. When I left for the day, Lynda and them were still working.

   _____ *he* _____

3. I heard that Monica and him made the two highest grades on the test.

   _____ *I* _____

4. You and me should work on our grammar homework together.

   _____ *he* _____

5. Have you and him known each other for very long?

   _____

Subject Pronouns after Linking Verbs

"Hello?"

"May I speak to Tanisha Jones, please?"

"This is she."

"Hello, Tanisha, this is Randall Groover from your biology class. I was wondering . . ."

This polite exchange is typical of the way many telephone conversations begin, and it illustrates a rule that many people use in telephone conversations but ignore otherwise: When a pronoun renames the subject (that is, when it is a *subject complement*) and follows the verb *to be* or any *linking verb*, that pronoun takes the subject form.

Examples

        subject   linking verb   subject complement

✔ The recipient of the award   will be   he.

✔ It is I. (not *me*)

✔ I had not seen Sheldon since grade school, so I was not sure that it was he. (not *him*)

✔ If you want to see Ms. Long, that is she in the hat and sunglasses. (not *her*)

PRACTICE 2   USING SUBJECT PRONOUNS AFTER LINKING VERBS

Underline the correct pronoun in each sentence.

1. I enjoyed Dr. Barker's English 100 class, so when I found out the teacher for English 200 would be (he, him), I signed up.
2. For many years, my closest friend was (she, her).
3. The speaker at our club's luncheon will be (he, him).
4. As he answered the phone, Leon said "Who is this?" "It is (I, me)," said Pete.
5. If there is anyone who deserves a promotion, it is (she, her).

Object Pronouns

Object pronouns are used as objects of verbs and prepositions. As with subject pronouns, problems with object pronouns commonly occur in compound constructions. These problems can usually be resolved by isolating the pronoun.

Example

? The instructor agreed to give *Tran and I* a makeup exam.

✗ The instructor agreed to give Tran and *I* a makeup exam.

✗ The instructor agreed to give *I* a makeup exam.

✔ The instructor agreed to give *me* a makeup exam.

Object Pronouns with *between*

Object pronouns always follow the preposition *between*. Thus, it is always *between you and me, between us and them, between him and her, between Larry and him.*

> *** Grammar Alert!**
>
> Pronouns are often misused with *between*. Remember to use the object form: between you and *me, him, her,* or *them.*

Examples

✗ Just between you and *I,* I think Sara is planning to quit school and work full time.

✔ Just between you and *me,* I think Sara is planning to quit school and work full time.

✗ The agreement was between Anita and *he;* I had nothing to do with it.

✔ The agreement was between Anita and *him;* I had nothing to do with it.

PRACTICE 3 USING OBJECT PRONOUNS

Underline the correct pronoun in each sentence.

1. The man behind the counter at the convenience store gave Yolanda and (I/me) directions, but we got lost anyway.

2. We aren't sure who will be elected president of the club, but the choice is between Calvin and (she/her).

3. The office barely had enough room for Leo and (he/him).

4. At the grocery store, an employee gave my husband and (I/me) a handful of coupons.

5. The table was small, but it was perfect for Tracy and (he/him).

Intensive and Reflexive Pronouns

Personal pronouns also take on forms known as *intensive* and *reflexive forms.* These pronouns are the -*self* pronouns: *myself, ourselves, yourself, himself, herself, itself,* and *themselves.*

plural.

Intensive Pronouns

Intensive pronouns are used for emphasis. They let a reader know that an action was performed by or directed toward *only* the person or thing that the pronoun refers to. It is easy to identify intensive pronouns. Since they are used strictly for emphasis, a sentence would make perfect sense and have the same meaning if the intensive pronoun were left out.

✔ The district attorney *himself* recommended that the charges be dropped.

✔ In spite of severe damage in outlying areas, the town *itself* was untouched by the tornado.

✔ Although the project was supposed to be a group effort, Sharon did every bit of the research *herself.*

Reflexive Pronouns

Reflexive pronouns show that an action was performed by someone on himself or herself (or by something on itself).

- ✔ Erica cut *herself* as she was slicing an onion.
- ✔ Brian forced *himself* to finish the job.
- ✔ The machine monitors *itself* for problems in functioning.

PRACTICE 4   RECOGNIZING INTENSIVE AND REFLEXIVE PRONOUNS

Underline the *-self* pronoun in each sentence below. Then, in the blank provided, write *I* if the pronoun is an intensive pronoun and *R* if it is a reflexive pronoun.

____I____ **1.** The president himself called to congratulate the soccer team.

____R____ **2.** Phyllis treated herself to dinner and a movie.

____I____ **3.** The building itself needs extensive repairs.

____R____ **4.** Hal bought himself a new car.

____I____ **5.** The instructor herself told Charles that the course was cancelled.

Problems with Intensive and Reflexive Pronouns

Intensive and reflexive pronouns are often used incorrectly in compound subjects or objects. Look at the examples below.

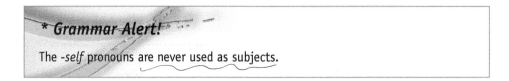

> *** Grammar Alert!**
>
> The *-self* pronouns are never used as subjects.

Example
       I

✗ *Jake and myself went to the auto parts store to pick up an oil filter.*

When you leave out the compound element, the problem is easier to spot:

✗ *Myself went to the auto parts store to pick up an oil filter.*

   I

A subject pronoun is needed to correct the sentence:

✔ *I* went to the auto parts store to pick up an oil filter.

✔ Jake and *I* went to the auto parts store to pick up an oil filter.

Example

me

✗ "Janie makes *her mother and myself* very proud," said Mr. Smith.

✗ "Janie makes *myself* very proud," said Mr. Smith.

✔ "Janie makes *her mother and me* very proud," said Mr. Smith.

---

* Grammar Alert!

Never use *hisself, theirself,* or *theirselves.* They are not words. *Himself* and *themselves* are the proper forms.

PRACTICE 5   AVOIDING ERRORS WITH *-SELF* PRONOUNS

Underline the correct pronoun in each sentence.

1. The Andersons were proud because they had built the deck (them, themselves).
2. Brad and (I, me, myself) have agreed to meet at my house at six A.M. on Sunday.
3. When Roy looked at (him, himself) in the mirror, he realized he needed to comb his hair.
4. The supervisor assigned the task to Jondrea and (me, myself).
5. "If you do the job (you, yourself), you can save nearly five hundred dollars," said the contractor.
6. "Just between you and (I, me, myself)," said Brandon, "I did not study for the test at all."
7. Sandra decided to give (she, her, herself) a break from studying, so she took a walk.
8. "Would you like to go out to lunch with Natisha and (I, me, myself)?" said Gloria.
9. "No, thanks. I made lunch for (I, me, myself) before I left home," said Morgan.
10. The governor (he, him, himself) came over to shake Miguel's hand.

Using *Who* and *Whom*

The use of *who* and *whom* poses difficulties for most people, partly because *whom* seems to be slowly disappearing from everyday speech. However, in academic writing, the distinction is still important.

While *who* and *whom* may seem intimidating, there is a shortcut to learning how to use these pronouns. It's called the *substitution method*. Once you have mastered this method, you will feel like an expert in the use of *who* and *whom*.

The Substitution Method for *Who* and *Whom*

The first step in the shortcut is a substitution. You have already seen in this chapter how natural it is—in most cases, anyway—to use the subject pronoun *he* and the object pronoun *him*. You rarely make mistakes with them because you use them all the time. Wouldn't it be nice if *who* and *whom* were as easy as *he* and *him?*

The good news is that they are—almost. *Who* is a subject pronoun, just like *he*, so we can temporarily equate the two, like this:

who (or *whoever*) = he

Whom is an object pronoun, so we can temporarily equate that with him:

whom (or *whomever*) = him

Now, look at a sentence to see how the system works.

No one knew (*who*, *whom*) had started the rumor.

Step 1: Ignore everything that comes before *who* or *whom*.

~~No one knew~~ (*who*, *whom*) had started the rumor.

Step 2: Substitute *he* for *who* and *him* for *whom*, and see which one makes sense.

✔ ~~Who~~ He had started the rumor.

~~Who Him~~ had started the rumor.

Since "He had started the rumor" makes sense, you can now rewrite the sentence with confidence, using *who* in place of *he*.

No one knew *who* had started the rumor.

PRACTICE 6   USING *WHO* AND *WHOM*

Use the substitution method to decide whether to use *who* or *whom* in the following sentences.

1. Anton was not sure (who, (whom)) to ask for advice.
2. Tawana could not remember ((who,) whom) had left the message.
3. The gems sparkled in the jeweler's case as Carlotta gazed at them, wondering ((who,) whom) could afford such expensive baubles.
4. The man ((who,) whom) donated the land for the new youth soccer field asked to remain anonymous.
5. Those of us ((who,) whom) had agreed to plan the party did not realize how much time and trouble it would take.

Who and *Whom* in Questions

Try another sentence, this time a question.

Andrea needed a ride home from school, but (who, whom) could she ask?

Step 1: Ignore everything that comes before *who* or *whom*.

~~Andrea needed a ride home from school, but~~ (who, whom) could she ask?

Step 2: Substitute *he* for *who* and *him* for *whom*, and see which one makes sense.

~~Who~~ He could she ask.

~~Who~~ Him could she ask.

Neither of these sounds natural, so the thing to do is shuffle them a bit.

She could ask *he*.

She could ask *him*.

Since "She could ask him" makes sense, you can now rewrite the sentence with confidence, using *whom*.

Andrea needed a ride home from school, but *whom* could she ask?

PRACTICE 7   *WHO* AND *WHOM* IN QUESTIONS

Use the substitution method to decide whether to use *who* or *whom* in the following sentences.

1. (Who, Whom) ordered the veggie sandwich with hot peppers?
2. Have you heard (who, whom) is going to take over as CEO of the company?
3. (Who, Whom) tracked muddy footprints all over the white carpet?
4. (Who, whom) did you say was on the phone?
5. Do you know (who, whom) Ms. Smith is interviewing for the job?

Who and *Whom* after Prepositions

Sometimes, a preposition that comes before *who* or *whom* will need to be included in your sentence for it to make sense.

Brian was not sure to (who, whom) he should deliver the package.

Step 1: Ignore everything that comes before *who* or *whom*.

~~Brian was not sure to~~ (who, whom) he should deliver the package.

Step 2: Substitute *he* for *who* and *him* for *whom*, adding the preposition that comes in front of *who* or *whom*, and see which one makes sense.

Brian should deliver the package **to** *he*.

Brian should deliver the package **to** *him*.

Since "Brian should deliver the package to him" makes sense, you can now rewrite the sentence with confidence.

✔ Brian was not sure to *whom* he should deliver the package.

PRACTICE 8   *WHO* AND *WHOM* AFTER PREPOSITIONS

Use the substitution method to decide whether to use *who* or *whom* in the following sentences.

1. The suitcase had no tag, so the airline personnel did not know to (who, whom) it belonged.
2. Jill was not able to find the person to (who, whom) the lost dog belonged.
3. To (who, whom) should I write the check?
4. The person for (who, whom) the car was ordered backed out of the deal at the last minute.
5. Most parents want to know where their children are and with (who, whom) they are associating.

PRACTICE 9   USING *WHO* AND *WHOM*

Use the substitution method to decide whether to use *who* or *whom* in the following sentences.

1. Josh shrugged one shoulder slightly and said that his ex-girlfriend Andrea could date (whoever, whomever) she chose.
2. The shy young clerk's voice cracked as he asked his customers, "(Who, Whom) is next?"
3. Jesse's cat, (who, whom) had just caught an unsuspecting bird, gently laid the still prize at Jesse's feet.
4. The angry police chief promised that his force would never rest until they caught (whoever, whomever) had killed the young officer.
5. When Malcolm told Kimberly that he wanted a woman (who, whom) could cook, she told him he should try living at home with his mother.

PRACTICE 10   USING *WHO* AND *WHOM*

Use the substitution method to decide whether to use *who* or *whom* in the following sentences.

1. The student, (who, whom) high school counselors advised not to go to college, graduated from the university with honors.
2. As the paper plane glided silently unto his desk, the teacher looked across the top of his eyeglasses and asked, "To (who, whom) does this frivolous toy belong?"
3. Everyone (who, whom) plans to graduate this spring should fill out a form in the registrar's office.

4. One study showed that many people (who, whom) win large lottery jackpots find themselves broke ten years after the win.

5. Frank admitted that he couldn't remember to (who, whom) he had given the money.

Review Exercises

Complete the Review Exercises to see how well you have learned the skills addressed in this chapter. As you work through the exercises, go back through the chapter to review any of the rules you do not understand completely.

REVIEW EXERCISE 1

Underline the correct pronoun in each sentence.

1. The coach complained that the unfavorable stories written about (he, him, himself) had led to his firing.

2. (I, Me) and my family have decided that we will try to spend more time together this year.

3. When Angie saw the quilt, she asked if Trina had made it (her, herself).

4. The winner of the scholarship was (he, him).

5. Tabitha promised (her, herself) that if she studied for one more hour, she would take the next hour off to watch her favorite program.

6. Since no one else wanted the funny-looking black and white kitten, we decided to keep it (us, ourselves).

7. Julie and (he, him) found it hard to survive on such a small paycheck.

8. Russell and (he, himself) decided that they would sand and stain the old desk over the weekend.

9. When I called Dad, he said that mother and (he, himself) were taking a vacation next month.

10. Leigh bought (her, herself) a used car with the money she earned over the summer.

REVIEW EXERCISE 2

Underline and correct the pronoun error in each sentence.

1. Rudy and me are going to take a walk if the rain has stopped.

2. Katrina said she had e-mailed both Teresa and myself about the meeting.

_____

3. "May I speak to Mr. Smith?" asked the caller. "This is him," replied Andrew.

_____

4. Bruce showed Mary and I the hand-tied fishing flies his uncle had sent him.

_____

5. Mr. Jones and her said they would not mind working late on Thursday evening.

_____

6. Merrill and myself will stay with Aunt Beatrice when we visit New York.

_____

7. Elaine wondered why the most trivial and boring jobs were always given to José and she.

_____

8. My little brother always wants me to take he and his friends to the mall on Saturdays.

_____

9. Amanda said that Morris and her had fixed the computer themselves.

_____

10. "I am glad that you and me are not fighting anymore," Al told his girlfriend.

_____

REVIEW EXERCISE 3

Underline and correct the two pronoun case errors in each sentence or sentence group.

1. Lonnie and myself went to the baseball game with Harold and he.

_____

_____

2. Please give the photographs to Anna and they, and be sure to say that they are from myself.

_____

_____

3. "Can you pick the man who robbed you from the lineup?" asked the police officer. "Officer, it was him!" said Mr. Smith, pointing to a tall red-haired man. "He pulled a gun on the night manager and I."

_____

_____

4. Nicole's mailbox was stuffed with catalogs addressed to her husband and she. "We need to buy us a bigger mailbox," said Nicole.

_____

_____

5. "Can you give Willie and I a ride?" asked Minardo. "Him and I will appreciate it."

_____

_____

REVIEW EXERCISE 4

Underline the correct pronoun in each sentence.

[1]Hiromi, a student from Japan, told me that (she, her, herself) and her family had been living in the United States for the past five years. [2]When she first came here, she knew barely enough English to make (she, her, herself) understood. [3]After taking courses in English for several years, however, (she, her, herself) and her brother are excelling in their college classwork. [4]Hiromi says that for (she, her, herself) and her family, one of the biggest differences between living in Japan and living in the United States is the amount of space. [5]"Our house here is twice as big as the one (we, us, ourselves) had in Japan, and the streets here are far less crowded," she says. [6]She told (I, me, myself) that the Japanese politeness is born out of necessity. [7]"People are so crowded together in Japan, that it would be hard for (they, them, themselves) to get along if they did not follow rules of etiquette," she said. [8]Another necessity in Japan is neatness—when people live in small spaces, (they, them, themselves) are forced to be tidy. [9]"I am not very neat (I, me, myself)," says Hiromi. [10]"Maybe living here in the United States has spoiled (I, me, myself)."

CHAPTER 19

Pronoun Agreement, Reference, and Point of View

Abbott:	I'm telling you Who is on first.
Costello:	Well, I'm asking YOU who's on first!
Abbott:	That's the man's name.
Costello:	That's who's name?
Abbott:	Yes.
Costello:	Well, go ahead and tell me.
Abbott:	Who.
Costello:	The guy on first.
Abbott:	Who!

From Abbott and Costello's
"Who's on First?"

Abbott and Costello's classic comedy routine deliberately causes confusion through use of pronouns. Sometimes, writers unintentionally cause confusion through errors in pronoun reference, agreement, and point of view. Each sentence that follow contains a pronoun error. Can you figure out why the pronouns in bold type are incorrect?

✗ The new grocery store closes on Christmas day, but **they** are open every other day of the year.

✗ Leo told Jim that **he** needed to clean up the work area.

✗ "I have looked everywhere," said Shelly, "but **you** just can't find an affordable apartment in this area."

Each of the sentences above contains a pronoun error that could confuse the reader. The first sentence contains an error in pronoun agreement. The pronoun *they* is plural, but the word it refers to is singular. The corrected sentence is shown below.

✔ The new *grocery store* closes on Christmas day, but *it* is open every other day of the year.

The second sentence contains an error in pronoun reference. The reader cannot be sure whether *he* refers to Leo or Jim.

✔ Leo told Jim, "*I* need to clean up *my* work area."

The third sentence contains an error in pronoun point of view. The speaker switches from the first person (*I* have looked) to the second person (*you* can't find).

✔ "*I* have looked everywhere," said Shelly, "but *I* just can't find an affordable apartment in this area."

Keeping your writing free of errors in pronoun agreement, reference, and point of view helps your reader move through your work smoothly and without confusion.

Pronoun Agreement

Pronoun agreement means that a pronoun agrees in number with the word it refers to. In other words, a singular pronoun can refer only to a singular noun or pronoun, and a plural pronoun can refer only to a plural noun or pronoun.

The word that a pronoun refers to is called its **antecedent**. An antecedent may be a noun such as *table* or *ideas*, a pronoun such as *everyone* or *they*, or even a compound construction such as *cars and buses* or *Ferdinand and Isabella*.

Examples

                    singular antecedent   *singular pronoun*

✔ The dog caught the <u>Frisbee</u> in midair and brought <u>it</u> back to Julie.

In the sentence above, the singular pronoun *it* refers to one word in the sentence, the singular word *Frisbee*.

                 plural antecedent   *plural pronoun*

✔ Todd gathered up the <u>bills</u> he needed to mail and took <u>them</u> to the mailbox.

Here, the plural pronoun *them* refers to the plural antecedent *bills*.

                 plural antecedent   *plural pronoun*

✔ Todd gathered up the <u>bills and letters</u> he needed to mail and took <u>them</u> to the mailbox.

Above, the plural pronoun *them* refers to the compound antecedent *bills and letters*.

Problems in Pronoun Agreement

Errors in pronoun agreement occur when a singular pronoun is used to refer to a plural word or when a plural pronoun is used to refer to a singular word.

Examples

                    singular   *plural*

✘ Mary pulled in to her bank's <u>drive-through</u>, but <u>they</u> had closed for the day.

                    singular   *singular*

✔ Mary pulled in to her bank's <u>drive-through</u>, but <u>it</u> had closed for the day.

                 plural   *singular*

✘ The teller was carrying several <u>rolls</u> of coins, but when she tripped <u>it</u> flew out of her hands and spilled onto the floor.

                 plural   *plural*

✔ The teller was carrying several <u>rolls</u> of coins, but when she tripped, <u>they</u> flew out of her hands and spilled onto the floor.

PRACTICE 1 MAKING PRONOUNS AGREE

Underline the correct pronoun in each sentence.

1. The photographs on display were so striking that people lingered for a long time to look at (it, them).
2. As snow gathered on the branches of the tree, Harold watched the limbs sag under (its, their) weight.
3. Mr. Smith banks with First City Bank because (it is, they are) locally owned.
4. Every restaurant is required to display (its, their) health inspection certificate.
5. After the hailstorm, the dented cars on the dealership's lot had price reduction stickers on (its, their) windshields.

Singular Indefinite Pronouns

The following indefinite pronouns are always singular.

each	everybody	anyone	anything
either	somebody	everyone	everything
neither	nobody	someone	something
anybody	one	no one	nothing

---

* Memory Jogger

Remember the singular indefinite pronouns more easily by grouping them:

each	either	neither
all the *bodies*	all the *ones*	all the *things*

Examples

    singular   plural

✘ Somebody called you, but they didn't leave a message.

    singular   singular

✔ Somebody called you, but he didn't leave a message.

  singular   plural

✘ Each of the team members has their own particular strength.

  singular   singular

✔ Each of the team members has her own particular strength.

PRACTICE 2   **MAKING PRONOUNS AGREE WITH INDEFINITE PRONOUN SUBJECTS**

Underline the correct pronoun in each sentence.

1.   Somebody had parked (his, their) new car so that it took up two spaces in the parking lot.

2.   Each of the treasured photographs had (its, their) own place of honor on the mantel.

3.   Each of the children brought (her, their) lunch on the field trip.

4.   Nobody in the room would admit that (he, they) had voted for the losing candidate.

5.   When the hosts of the party began to argue loudly, everyone mumbled excuses and said that (they, he) had to go.

As you probably noticed when you did the previous practice exercise, the use of singular indefinite pronouns often raises a problem. Words like *everybody, somebody, anyone,* and *everyone* often designate both males and females. Saying "Each of the team members has her own particular strength" works only if we know that all team members are female. The use of indefinite pronouns raises not only the question of pronoun agreement, but also the question of gender fairness.

Pronouns and Gender Fairness

Gender fairness means using gender-neutral terms such as *server, police officer,* and *firefighter.* It means not stereotyping professions: Gary Kubach is a *nurse,* not a *male nurse;* Sarita Gray is a *doctor,* not a *woman doctor.* Naturally, gender fairness also includes avoiding describing women solely in terms of their looks or men solely in terms of their bank accounts. Those things are fairly simple. The area of gender fairness and pronouns, however, requires more thought. Using *he or she* or *his or her* is often awkward, and constructions such as *he/she* or *(s)he* are downright ungraceful. How, then, can a writer's language be unbiased, graceful, and grammatically correct, all at the same time? There are several possible solutions.

Example

✗   *Nobody* has received *their* grades from the last term yet.

This sentence contains an error in pronoun agreement. The singular indefinite pronoun *nobody* does not agree with the plural pronoun *their.*

Below are several ways to correct pronoun agreement errors such as this one while remaining gender-fair.

Solution 1: Choose a gender and stay with it throughout a single example or paragraph. Then, in your next example or paragraph, switch to the other gender.

✗ *Nobody* has received *their* grades from the last term yet.

✔ *Nobody* has received *his* grades from the last term yet.

✔ *Nobody* has received *her* grades from the last term yet.

Solution 2: Use a "his or her" construction. Because this solution is grammatically correct but stylistically awkward, use it in situations where you will not have to repeat the construction.

✗ *Nobody* has received *their* grades from the last term yet.

✔ *Nobody* has received *his or her* grades from the last term yet.

Solution 3: Use plural rather than singular constructions.

✗ *Nobody* has received *their* grades from the last term yet.

✔ The *students* have not received *their* grades from the last term yet.

Solution 4: Solve the pronoun agreement problem by removing the pronoun.

✗ *Nobody* has received *their* grades from the last term yet.

✔ *Nobody* has received grades from the last term yet.

PRACTICE 3   MAKING PRONOUNS AGREE

Underline and correct the pronoun agreement error in each sentence, using the solutions listed above.

1. Each of the class members received a folder with their name on it.

    _____

2. The driver discovered that someone had left their camera on the tour bus.

    _____

3. Has everyone in the class decided on their major?

    _____

4. The table grew quiet as everyone began to enjoy their meal.

   _____

5. No one in the apartment building where the murder occurred wanted to give their name or talk to reporters.

   _____

6. Everybody is entitled to their own opinion.

   _____

7. Each person in the discussion group was eager to express their ideas.

   _____

8. "If one of those postal clerks puts their 'Next Window' sign up, I think I'll scream," said a woman carrying a bulky package.

   _____

9. When the driveway was poured, somebody put their handprint in the cement before it dried.

   _____

10. "I need to page someone. Would you call their name over the loudspeaker?" Anita asked the store clerk.

    _____

Pronoun Reference

If a sentence has problems with pronoun reference, then either a pronoun has no antecedent or it has more than one possible antecedent.

Pronoun Reference Problem: No Antecedent

If a pronoun has no antecedent, your reader may become confused.

Examples

✗ When Melanie went to pick up her son's birthday cake, *they* told her it wasn't ready.

Who are *they?* Replacing the pronoun *they* with a more specific word makes the sentence's meaning clear.

✔ When Melanie went to pick up her son's birthday cake, *the bakery clerk* told her it wasn't ready.

✗ Because his brother is on the basketball team, Derrick wants to be *one*, too.

What does Derrick want to be? A brother? A basketball? A team? The word that should logically be the antecedent of *one*—the word *player*—appears nowhere in the sentence. The simplest way to correct the problem is to replace the word *one* with a more specific word.

✔ Because his brother is on the basketball team, Derrick wants to be *a basketball player,* too.

PRACTICE 4 **CORRECTING PROBLEMS IN PRONOUN REFERENCE**

Underline and correct the pronoun reference problems in each sentence.

1. The instructions said the form had to be filled out in ink, but Fred had not brought one with him.

   _____

2. When Brett applied to the college, they told him he was exempt from physical education courses because he was a military veteran.

   _____

3. When she arrived at her house, Andrea called the auto mechanic and told him it was still making a funny noise.

   _____

4. Eric applied for a car loan, but they told him he would need a cosigner since he had no credit history.

   _____

5. Giselle said that from the time she first saw *The Nutcracker* as a child, she fell in love with ballet and knew she wanted to be one.

   _____

Pronoun Reference Problems with *This*

The pronoun *this* is so often used incorrectly that you should check it every time you see it in your writing.

When you see the pronoun *this* in a sentence, particularly if it begins the sentence, ask the question, "This what?" If you cannot put your finger on a noun that answers that question, then *this* probably has no antecedent.

Examples

✗ In some neighborhoods, people are afraid to go out after dark. Increased police presence in high-crime neighborhoods could help to prevent *this.*

✗   In the twenty-first century, parents are spending more time at work and children are increasingly involved in school, sports, and social activities. *This* means that families have less time to spend together.

There are two quick ways to fix the problem. The first is to place a noun that answers the question "This what?" immediately after the word *this*.

✔   In some neighborhoods, people are afraid to go out after dark. Increased police presence in high-crime neighborhoods could help to prevent *this fear.*

✔   In the twenty-first century, parents are spending more time at work and children are increasingly involved in school, sports, and social activities. *This increase in outside activity* means that families have less time to spend together.

The second solution is to take out the pronoun and replace it with an appropriate word or phrase. This solution takes a bit more time but is usually more graceful and exact.

✔   In some neighborhoods, people are afraid to go out after dark. Increased police presence in high-crime neighborhoods could help *citizens feel safer.*

✔   In the twenty-first century, parents are spending more time at work and children are increasingly involved in school, sports, and social activities. *As a result,* families have less time to spend together.

PRACTICE 5 **CORRECTING VAGUE USES OF *THIS***

Underline and correct the vague uses of *this*.

1. Edward closed his math book and put his calculator aside with a sigh. "This makes no sense to me," he said.

    _____

2. The courthouse, the oldest county building still in use and a local landmark, was burned down last year by a man who did not like the terms of his divorce. This saddened and outraged many people in the community.

    _____

3. The lack of a traffic signal at the intersection of Wilroy Road and Broad Street creates a danger to drivers and pedestrians alike. Can't something be done about this?

    _____

4. After gaining five pounds on the Chocolate Lover's Diet, Lisa tried counting calories and fat grams and exercising every day. This was more effective but not nearly as much fun.

_____

5. Joe dug his toes into the warm sand and watched the waves roll in. "This is great," he said.

_____

Pronoun Point of View

It is important to avoid unnecessary shifts in **point of view**, that is, shifts from one person to another. The chart below shows common **first-, second-, and third-person** pronouns in their singular and plural forms.

Point of View	Singular	Plural
First person (the person speaking)	I	we
Second person (the person spoken to)	you	you
Third person (the person spoken about)	he, she, it singular indefinite pronouns (everybody, anybody, etc.)	they

Examples

    1st person   2nd person

✗ I enjoy going to auctions and flea markets because <u>you</u> can find bargains and unusual items.

The sentence contains an unnecessary shift in point of view. In this sentence, *you* do not find bargains and unusual items; *I* find them.

    1st person   1st person

✔ I enjoy going to auctions and flea markets because <u>I</u> can find bargains and unusual items.

    3rd person   1st person   1st person

✗ When <u>someone</u> studies all night for a test, <u>I</u> am disappointed if <u>I</u> don't make at least a B.

    1st person   1st person   1st person

✔ When <u>I</u> study all night for a test, <u>I</u> am disappointed if <u>I</u> don't make at least a B.

3rd person   3rd person   3rd person

✔ When <u>someone</u> studies all night for a test, <u>he</u> is disappointed if <u>he</u> doesn't make at least a B.

PRACTICE 6   CORRECTING PROBLEMS IN PRONOUN POINT OF VIEW

Underline and correct the point of view problems in each sentence.

1. Dennis has decided to pursue a double major because you don't know what opportunities life will present.

   _____

2. You should always drive defensively because I see all sorts of crazy drivers on the road.

   _____

3. People enjoy the Corner Café because it's a friendly place where you can always find someone to talk to.

   _____

4. Javarez likes many types of music, but he says that when he is feeling down, you might as well listen to the blues.

   _____

5. Kayla looked out the window and shivered; you could tell it was cold just by looking at the low, gray clouds and the white-frosted ground.

   _____

Review Exercises

Complete the Review Exercises to see how well you have learned the skills addressed in this chapter. As you work through the exercises, go back through the chapter to review any of the rules you do not understand completely.

REVIEW EXERCISE 1

Underline the correct alternative in each sentence. Then in the blank to the left of the sentence, indicate whether the problem is one of *agreement* (singular with plural, plural with singular), *reference* (no clear antecedent), or *point of view* (shifts in person).

_____ 1. Claire begins her drive to work at 6:30 A.M. because (you miss, she misses) rush-hour traffic that way.

_____ 2. At his job interview, (they, the interviewer) asked Richard to write a sample memo.

_____ 3. Neither of Kim's uncles is sure that (he, they) can fly in for her wedding.

_____ 4. When Renee walked into the clothing store with her shopping bag, (they, a store employee) told her she would have to leave it at the customer service desk.

_____ 5. Each member of the women's bowling team brought (her, their) own ball and shoes to the tournament.

_____ 6. The Community Trust Bank has named Madeleine R. Bowen as (its, their) new president.

_____ 7. Rick told Mr. Flanders (that the supplies he had ordered were ready for pickup, "The supplies you ordered are ready for pickup.")

_____ 8. As he rubbed the clear liquid into his thinning hair, James said, "(They claim, The company claims) that this mixture will regrow hair in 70 percent of men. I hope I am one of the 70 percent."

_____ 9. Glen stood over the crib making strange faces and funny noises because (this, his clowning) seemed to amuse the baby.

_____ 10. Roderick had a security system installed in his home because, as a firefighter, (he has, they have) to sleep at the fire station every other week.

REVIEW EXERCISE 2

Underline and correct the pronoun reference, agreement, or point of view error in each sentence.

1. The tuna salad and the sliced turkey had been left on the counter since lunchtime, so Ian decided that the safest thing to do was to throw it away.

   _____

2. When a poll was taken, everyone in the room said that they knew someone who abused drugs or alcohol.

   _____

3. Hannah says she loves being a musician. Even when she is alone, music is your constant companion.

   _____

4. Jacob sat on a bench and watched the skateboarders. You could tell that some of them were inexperienced because they wobbled uncertainly and sometimes fell.

_____

5. Many experts advise breaking long-term goals into smaller steps. This makes the goals seem less distant and unreachable.

_____

6. Someone had left their smelly gym socks on a bench in the men's locker room.

_____

7. The shovel and the trowel rusted because Oscar had left it out in the rain.

_____

8. Tanya told Carol that she would make a good spokesperson for the group.

_____

9. "I don't know why I play the lottery," Jason said. "You have two chances of winning—slim and none."

_____

10. Each of the horses has their mane braided neatly against its neck.

_____

REVIEW EXERCISE 3

Underline and correct the two errors in pronoun agreement, reference, or point of view in each numbered item.

1. When Frank goes to the health club, they always ask him for his ID. But you don't always keep an ID in the pocket of your gym shorts.

_____

_____

2. Karalyn does not drink, so when anyone offers it to her, she says, "No, thanks." If someone tries to pressure her, she tells them that she has to drive.

_____

_____

3. Everyone said they did not think the ventriloquist was very talented. This was evident in the way his lips moved when the dummy was supposed to be talking.

_____

_____

4. Noelle refuses to take money from her parents because she thinks she should be independent once you have a job. "Everyone eventually needs to take care of themselves," she says.

_____

_____

5. Tyler told Dewayne that his car and his son's bicycle were blocking the driveway. "I'll move it right away," said Dewayne.

_____

_____

REVIEW EXERCISE 4

Underline and correct the two errors in pronoun agreement, reference, or point of view in each numbered item.

1. When the car's engine overheated, Andrew pushed it to the side of the road. He called a tow truck, but they did not come for two hours.

_____

_____

2. In my sociology class today, everyone said they had done the assigned reading. But you could tell that Professor Dunham suspected otherwise.

_____

_____

3. When Paige received her first paycheck, she thought they had made a mistake. Then she realized how much money you had to pay toward taxes, insurance, and retirement benefits.

_____

_____

4. When Dolores saw that they had brought her mail, she went eagerly to get it. But she came back with a frown on her face, asking "Why do they send me so many credit card offers?"

_____

_____

5. As Paul drove past the dumpster, he noticed that someone had left a small, shivering puppy along with their bag of trash. This made him angry; he could not understand how people could be so cruel.

_____

_____

REVIEW EXERCISE 5

Underline and correct the error in pronoun agreement, reference, or point of view in each numbered sentence.

[1]When I started college, everybody told me that registration would be difficult and time-consuming, but I did not believe them. [2]All you have to do is sign up for classes, I thought, and that can't be too difficult. [3]But registration turned out to be an all-day job that started when you walked onto the huge campus. [4]I tried asking for directions, but everybody was so new that they could not help me. [5]When I finally made it to orientation, they loaded me down with handouts and confusing information. [6]Finally, I was told to see an academic advisor in another building, but this turned out to be more difficult than I had anticipated. [7]I was herded into a big room with at least fifty other students, and it was half an hour before a harried secretary called my name and said he would see me. [8]When I had my prized class schedule in hand, I went to the business office where you had to stand in another line to pay. [9]Finally, they sent me to the bookstore to buy my books, an expensive and time-consuming process. [10]When I finally made it home, I decided that they were right: registration was a big hassle.

1. _____

2. _____

3. _____

4. _____

5. _____

6. _____

7. _____

8. _____

9. _____

10. _____

Adjectives, Adverbs, and Articles

Verbs supply the muscle
That helps a sentence go,
And prepositions are the veins
That help control its flow.

Nouns and pronouns form the bones
That make it stand upright.
Conjunctions are the sinews
That help its parts unite.

But adjectives and adverbs
Are the flesh upon the bone.
They give each sentence its own face
And make its meaning known.

335

Nouns are the bones of a sentence and verbs are the muscles that move them, but adjectives and adverbs provide the flesh and the cartilage, the color and the texture. Without adjectives and adverbs, you could convey only the basics: what happened and to whom. You could not show how and why, how many and what kind. This chapter provides a brief overview of adjectives and adverbs and reviews three useful words called *articles*.

Adjectives

Adjectives are words that give information about nouns or pronouns. They answer the questions, "What kind?" "How many?" and "Which one?" Usually, adjectives within a sentence come before the noun or pronoun they modify (*Fido nuzzled Horace's hand with his* cold, clammy *nose*) or after a verb that *links* them to the noun or pronoun (*Fido's nose was* cold *and* clammy).

Examples

A *scented* candle burned on the table.

The toffee was *smooth* and *creamy*.

Kasim looks *unhappy*.

Nick is the *smartest* person I know.

PRACTICE 1   FINDING ADJECTIVES AND THE NOUNS THEY MODIFY

Underline the two adjectives in each sentence and draw an arrow connecting each with the word it modifies.

1. The cookies were warm and delicious.
2. Holly wore a heavy coat and a pair of warm gloves.
3. The shivering dog huddled in a sheltered doorway.
4. Ben looked anxious and uncertain.
5. Comfortable benches had been placed alongside the winding pathway.

Adjective Forms: Positive, Comparative, and Superlative

Each adjective has three forms: the positive form, the comparative form, and the superlative form.

Positive

The *positive* form is the base form of the adjective. It is used when you are describing something but not comparing it to anything else.

Examples

The floor was *dirty*.

The ice cream tastes *good*.

Brenda was driving a *beautiful* car.

Comparative

The *comparative* form is used to compare two things or to compare one thing to a group of similar items.

Examples

When the two children came in, Emily was *dirtier* than Leslie.

The ice cream tastes *better* than the yogurt.

Violet thought that France was even *more beautiful* than Italy.

Donna is *more efficient* than her coworkers.

Superlative

The *superlative* form is used to compare one thing with all others in its group.

Examples

Ryan gave his grandmother a T-shirt that read, "World's *Best* Grandma."

Sam was the *least expensive* private detective we could find.

Chief was just a brown and white mutt, but to Jody, he was the *most beautiful* dog in the world.

Emily is the *most efficient* person in her office.

Adjective Forms

	Positive	**Comparative**	**Superlative**
One syllable		add *-er*	add *-est*
	cool	cooler	coolest
	smooth	smoother	smoothest

	Positive	Comparative	Superlative
Two syllables ending in y		change y to i, add -er	change y to i, add -est
	happy	happier	happiest
	tardy	tardier	tardiest
Most words of two or more syllables		use *more* or *less*	use *most* or *least*
	solemn	more solemn	most solemn
	intense	more intense	most intense
	inventive	more inventive	most inventive
	slippery	more slippery	most slippery
	important	less important	least important
Irregular adjectives	good	better	best
	bad	worse	worst

PRACTICE 2   REVIEWING ADJECTIVE FORMS

Fill in the comparative and superlative forms of each adjective. Use the Adjective Forms chart as your guide.

	Positive	Comparative	Superlative
1.	full	_____	_____
2.	crisp	_____	_____
3.	pesky	_____	_____
4.	trendy	_____	_____
5.	toxic	_____	_____
6.	pleasant	_____	_____
7.	humorous	_____	_____
8.	colorful	_____	_____
9.	good	_____	_____
10.	bad	_____	_____

> *** Grammar Alert!**
>
> Be sure to use *more* and *most* only in combination with base (positive) adjective forms, not with *-er* or *-est* forms. *More significant* is correct, but *more happier* or *most best* is not.

PRACTICE 3   USING ADJECTIVE FORMS

In each sentence below, decide whether the positive, comparative, or superlative form is needed. Then convert the adjective in parentheses to the proper form, using the Adjective Forms chart as your guide.

(careful)   **1.** Elaine is a _____ driver than her husband.

(big)   **2.** The hotel was the _____ that Chim had ever seen.

(attentive)   **3.** The children, seated in a circle, watched the storyteller with _____ faces.

(small)   **4.** Maggie carried a _____ notebook in her purse to jot down ideas and record her thoughts.

(brilliant)   **5.** Few scientists are _____ than Dr. Otto Schummer, but his work habits are erratic and his personality unconventional.

(tasty)   **6.** As the server described the items on the dessert cart, each one sounded

               _____ and more tempting than the last.

(ugly)   **7.** "Frank, I do believe that is the _____ tie I have ever seen," said his wife.

(young)   **8.** Glenn was the _____ of the three brothers.

(old)   **9.** Glenn was _____ than his sister Jackie.

(good)   **10.** Roberta has many good friends, but Ashley has been her _____ friend since grade school.

Adverbs

Adverbs give information about verbs (skated *gracefully*), adjectives (*extremely* slippery), or other adverbs (*very* badly). Often, but not always, adverbs are *ly* forms of the adjective. *Graceful* becomes *gracefully, bad* becomes *badly, quick* becomes *quickly.* The easiest way to tell an adverb from an adjective is to see what question the word answers. An adjective tells *how many, what kind,* or *which one.* An adverb tells *how, when,* or *to what degree.*

Examples

> After her run, Kerri was breathing *rapidly*. (how)
>
> Don nodded *coldly* when he passed Al in the hall. (how)
>
> The performance was *extremely well* done. (to what degree/how)
>
> The check will be sent *immediately*. (when)

PRACTICE 4   RECOGNIZING ADVERBS

Underline the adverb in each sentence.

1. The turtle slowly made its way across the sandbar.
2. Secretly, the old man had taken fifty dollars from each check he received and hidden it under his mattress.
3. Geneva artfully braided her daughter's hair and tied a small bow at the end of each braid.
4. Arthur seldom had headaches, but the loud music in the nightclub made his head pound.
5. Samantha waited anxiously for the plane to arrive.

Adverb Forms

	Positive	Comparative	Superlative
Adverbs ending in *ly*		use *more*	use *most*
	smoothly	more smoothly	most smoothly
	happily	more happily	most happily
	solemnly	more solemnly	most solemnly
	intensely	more intensely	most intensely
Irregular adverbs	well	better	best
	badly	worse	worst

---

* Memory Jogger

Adjectives tell *how many*, *what kind*, or *which one*.
Adverbs tell *how*, *when*, or *to what degree*.

PRACTICE 5   RECOGNIZING ADJECTIVES AND ADVERBS

Underline the correct word in each phrase below. Decide whether the word tells *how many, what kind, which one, how, when,* or *to what degree,* and write your response in the first blank. In the second blank, write the part of speech: *adjective* or *adverb.* The first one is done for you.

1. sang (loud, <u>loudly</u>)

    The word tells __how_____ and is an __adverb____.

2. a (beautiful, beautifully) dress

    The word tells _____ and is an _____.

3. walked (slow, slowly)

    The word tells _____ and is an _____.

4. a (slow, slowly) dance

    The word tells _____ and is an _____.

5. a (complete, completely) turnaround

    The word tells _____ and is an _____.

6. turned around (complete, completely)

    The word tells _____ and is an _____.

7. (several, severally) reasons

    The word tells _____ and is an _____.

8. (happy, happily) agreed

    The word tells _____ and is an _____.

9. (responsible, responsibly) behavior

    The word tells _____ and is an _____.

10. behaved (responsible, responsibly)

    The word tells _____ and is an _____.

PRACTICE 6   USING ADJECTIVES AND ADVERBS

Underline the correct word in each sentence.

1. Jason read the article (quick, quickly).
2. Mr. Smith made a (quick, quickly) trip to the grocery store.

3. The children had a (good, well) time at the museum.
4. "Please proceed (calm, calmly) to the exit," said the theater manager.
5. The coffee was (bare, barely) warm.
6. "Your presentation could not have gone more (smooth, smoothly)," Rick said.
7. Julia's (helpful, helpfully) attitude made everyone more cooperative.
8. The man was (angry, angrily).
9. The man was (angry, angrily) gesturing at passing cars.
10. The card wished Kevin a (speedy, speedily) recovery.

Puzzling Pairs

Certain adjective and adverb pairs are confused more often than others. The next sections explain the differences between the pairs *good* and *well*, *bad* and *badly*, and *worse* and *worst*.

Good and *Well, Bad* and *Badly*

Good and *bad* are adjectives that tell *what kind; well* and *badly* are adverbs that tell *how*.

Examples

Since she has been using the Mavis Beacon typing software, Clare has become a *good* typist. (tells *what kind* of typist)

Since she has been using the Mavis Beacon typing software, Clare has learned to type *well*. (tells *how* she types)

Todd bought *good* tires that will perform *well* even in bad weather. (tells *what kind* of tires and *how* they perform)

---

* Grammar Alert!

Well can be an adjective when it refers to health, as in "He is not a *well* man" or "I am not feeling *well*."

Ross had never been around children, and he was afraid he would
adjective
be a *bad* parent. (tells *what kind* of parent)

The dog was so timid that the animal shelter workers wondered if it had been treated *badly*. (tells *how* it may have been treated)

Helen slept *badly* after having a *bad* dream. (tells *how* she slept and *what kind* of dream)

PRACTICE 7 **USING *GOOD* AND *WELL*, *BAD* AND *BADLY***

In each sentence, choose *good* or *well, bad* or *badly*.

1. Anita has a (good, well) job that pays her (good, well).
2. Because it was (bad, badly) prepared, the souffle did not taste very (good, well).
3. Lev is not a (bad, badly) tennis player; in fact, he plays rather (good, well).
4. "(Good, Well) boy, Rex!" Mac told his dog. "Let's go to the vet so you can get (good, well)."
5. "I react (bad, badly) when I lose," said Franklin, "but I don't think that makes me a (bad, badly) person."

Worse and *Worst*

Worse and *worst* are both adjectives, but they are often confused. *Worse* is the comparative form, the form you use to compare one thing to another or one set of things to another set. *Worst* is the superlative form, used to compare one thing to all (or many) others in its class.

Examples

"I am disappointed in my grade," said Matt, "but I guess I could have done *worse*."

Matt is comparing two things: his actual grade and a hypothetical lower grade.

"This coffee tastes even *worse* with cream and sugar in it," said Kelly.

Kelly is comparing two things: the coffee before the addition of cream and sugar, and the same coffee after the flavorings were added.

Kelly made a face. "This is the *worst* cup of coffee I have ever drunk," she said.

Kelly is comparing the coffee she is drinking to all other cups of coffee she has drunk.

The *worst* meal I ever ate in a restaurant was at the No Way Café.

The meal is being compared to all others in its class.

PRACTICE 8   **USING *WORSE* AND *WORST***

Choose *worse* or *worst* in each sentence.

1. "I don't know which of them is (worse, worst)," said Kate, looking at her twin sons.
2. Not only did Adam lose the tennis match, but he probably turned in his (worse, worst) performance ever.
3. "I am your (worse, worst) nightmare," the drill sergeant snarled.
4. Nell's arthritis always gets (worse, worst) during rainy weather.
5. Meteorologists said that the hurricane was the (worse, worst) of the last century.

Articles

The articles in the English language are *a, an,* and *the.* Articles are small, easy-to-overlook words, but they are so often used that it is important to use them correctly. When a writer uses the word *pen,* for example, an article can reveal whether the writer is talking about a specific pen (the pen) or any pen (a pen).

Using *A* and *An*

The most common mistake people make with articles stems from uncertainty over when to use *a* and when to use *an.* Use *a* before a consonant sound—that is, before any word that sounds as if it begins with anything other than *a, e, i, o,* or *u.*

a bowl

a peeled onion

a youth

a useful tool (*Useful* begins with the sound of the consonant **y**—the *yoo* sound. Therefore, the article *a* is used.)

Use *an* before a vowel sound—that is, before any word that sounds as if it begins with *a, e, i, o,* or *u.*

> *an* **understanding**
>
> *an* **able-bodied person**
>
> *an* **omelet**
>
> *an* **honor** (*Honor* begins with the *ah* sound often associated with the vowels **o** and **a.** Therefore, the article *an* is used.)

PRACTICE 9   USING *A* AND *AN*

Put *a* in front of words that begin with a consonant sound. Put *an* in front of words that begin with a vowel sound.

1. _____ calendar
2. _____ eraser
3. _____ hard-boiled egg
4. _____ bottle of shampoo
5. _____ orange T-shirt
6. _____ apple pie
7. _____ honest opinion
8. _____ young man
9. _____ utility pole
10. _____ unbelievable story

11. _____ sour taste
12. _____ usable item
13. _____ unusable item
14. _____ polar bear
15. _____ irritating noise
16. _____ ambidextrous person
17. _____ can of oil
18. _____ humorous remark
19. _____ oil can
20. _____ argument

PRACTICE 10   USING *A* AND *AN*

Put *a* or *an* in the blank in each sentence.

1. Gaby bought _____ chocolate milk shake.

2. Cho went to the store for _____ half gallon of orange juice.

3. _____ orange mouse pad sat to the right of the computer keyboard.

4. Looking into his refrigerator, Esteban saw _____ egg, a bottle of store-brand grape juice and a four-day-old fast-food sandwich.

5. _____ open container of gasoline can be dangerous.

6. Since it was warm, Stacie decided to wear _____ short-sleeved shirt.

7. Peeling _____ onion always makes Shika cry.

8. The pages of the calendar were held together by _____ small plastic clip shaped like an airplane.

9. Jiro, do you have _____ opinion on the subject?

10. When _____ car pulled out in front of him, Erik blew the horn.

Review Exercises

Complete the Review Exercises to see how well you have learned the skills addressed in this chapter. As you work through the exercises, go back through the chapter to review any of the rules you do not understand completely.

REVIEW EXERCISE 1

Underline the correct article in each sentence.

1. In the newspaper, Rita saw (a, an) announcement of (a, an) new furniture store's grand opening.

2. Harvey saved the big coffee can, knowing he would find (a, an) use for it at (a, an) later date.

3. In (a, an) health magazine, Carly read (a, an) article called "The Hidden Dangers of Vitamins."

4. When she had a question about her taxes, Cheryl sent (a, an) email to her father, who was (a, an) accountant.

5. For breakfast, Pat ate (a, an) scrambled egg and drank (a, an) glass of orange juice.

REVIEW EXERCISE 2

In each sentence, decide whether the positive, comparative, or superlative form is needed. Then convert the adjective in parentheses to the proper form. Use the Adjective Forms chart in this chapter as your guide.

(bad)   1. Traffic is much _____ than it was five years ago.

(large)   2. "I want the _____ size that you have," Carl told the ice cream store clerk.

(sick)   3. When Tom woke up, he felt _____.

(small)   **4.** Although Tiffany is the older of the two children, she is the _____ of the two.

(cloudy)   **5.** The meteorologist said to expect a _____ day.

(good)   **6.** Each of the ice cream flavors seemed _____ than the last.

(good)   **7.** Anya's grade on the final test was the _____ grade she had made.

(reliable)   **8.** Mr. Morton said that Ed was the _____ employee he had ever had.

(old)   **9.** Rosetta said that her house was _____ than she was.

(roomy)   **10.** When the company moved its office into the new building, the three supervisors bickered over who should get the _____ office.

REVIEW EXERCISE 3

Underline the correct modifier in each sentence.

1. Looking at the huge stone in Mrs. Smythe-Buffington's ring, Michelle wondered if it was a (real, really) diamond.
2. The blues musician said that before a person could (real, really) sing the blues, he had to live the blues.
3. The children tried to catch the squirrels, but the squirrels were too (quick, quickly) for them.
4. "If the appointment does not suit you," said the secretary, "we can reschedule at a (more convenient, most convenient) time."
5. Hajel was ambidextrous, but the writing he did with his left hand was (neater, more neatly) than the writing he did with his right hand.
6. The professor moved through the material so (rapid, rapidly) that the class complained.
7. Brendan ran so (quick, quickly) that his little brother found it hard to keep up.
8. The school bus driver said that she was (grateful, gratefully) for weekends and holidays.
9. One advantage of oil over coal is that oil burns (cleaner, more cleanly).
10. Hal's car always looks (cleaner, more cleanly) than mine.

REVIEW EXERCISE 4

Underline the correct modifier in each sentence.

1. Duncan reads very (quick, quickly), but he is a (slow, slowly) writer.
2. Looking at the CD his daughter had (recent, recently) bought, Jim asked if there was (real, really) a band called Bunnygrunt.

3. Though the critics agree that the movie is a (good, best) one, few would call it the (better, best) movie of the year.

4. Even though she did not do (bad, badly) on the exam, Rose knew she could have done (better, more better).

5. Real estate agents say it is a good idea to buy the (smaller, smallest) house in the (more, most) expensive neighborhood you can afford.

REVIEW EXERCISE 5

Underline and correct the errors in adjectives, adverbs, and articles. Each sentence contains one error.

[1]My friends envy me because I have an healthy bank account. [2]However, they could save money easy if they would just give up some of their wasteful spending habits. [3]My friend Abby, for instance, drinks only the most fanciest bottled water. [4]She says it is pure than tap water. [5]She may be right, but bottled water is also a expensive luxury she could probably do without. [6]Another friend, Jennifer, spends a great deal of money to dress fashionable. [7]If Jennifer waited for clothing to go on sale, then she could dress good for a lower price. [8]Toni, my best friend, is always complaining about her lack of money, but when she gets her paycheck, she heads for the bookstore for the most recently novels. [9]With an library card, Toni could read the latest bestsellers for free. [10]If I have more money than my friends, it is only because I spend more careful.

1. _____

2. _____

3. _____

4. _____

5. _____

6. _____

7. _____

8. _____

9. _____

10. _____

Capital Letters

With capitals, we always try
To mind our P's and Q's,
To pay attention to the rules,
And pick up subtle clues.

Capital Letters to Begin Sentences

Capitalize the first word of a sentence or a direct quotation.

Examples

> Sarita placed her coffee cup on the windowsill.
>
> On the roof of the house lay a lime-green Frisbee.
>
> "What time does the next bus come?" Frankie asked impatiently.

Capitalization of Words Referring to Individuals

Names and the Pronoun *I*

Capitalize people's names and the pronoun *I*.

> May I have that last doughnut if you aren't going to eat it?
>
> Mr. Bittenton gave Harold an old model train set.

Family Relationships

Family Designations Used in Place of a Name

Capitalize a word that designates a family relationship if it is used in place of a name. To make sure that the word is used as a name, try substituting a name for the word. If the word is used as a name, the substitution will sound natural.

Examples

> I took Grandma out to lunch at the mall.
>
> I took Grandma Betty Smith out to lunch at the mall.

"I took Betty Smith out to lunch" sounds natural, so *Grandma* is correct.

Try your own substitution in the next sentence. If substituting a name for *Dad* sounds natural, the capitalization is correct.

> "I am taking a course," Dad said, "because if I don't use my mind, I may lose it."

Family Designations Used with Possessives and Articles

When family designations such as *father, mother,* or *great-uncle Elmo* are preceded by a possessive pronoun (*my, her, his, their*), a possessive noun (*Ted's, Penny's*), or an article (*a, an,* or *the*), they are not capitalized. For additional proof, try directly substituting a name for the family designation. It will sound awkward.

Examples

I took my grandma out to lunch at the mall.

I took my ~~grandma~~ Betty Smith out to lunch at the mall.

The phrase "my Betty Smith" sounds awkward, so *grandma* is correct.

Try substituting a name for *dad* in the next sentence, making sure to leave the pronoun *my* in the sentence. If the name does not sound natural, then the lowercase *dad* is correct.

"I am taking a course," my dad said, "because if I don't use my mind, I may lose it."

Professional Titles

Do not capitalize professional titles unless they are used immediately before a name.

Pandita Gupta is the doctor on duty in the emergency room.

The accident victims were treated by Dr. Pandita Gupta.

James Solkowski is my English professor.

I am taking American literature with Professor James Solkowski.

PRACTICE 1   CAPITALIZING WORDS REFERRING TO PEOPLE

Underline and correct the two capitalization mistakes in each sentence.

1. Uncle Ed took grandpa to the Doctor for a flu shot.

    _____

2. My Aunt always said, "Experience is the best Teacher."

    _____

3. Latrelle and jason are in professor Langley's Tuesday biology lab.

    _____

4. Nathaniel, my Cousin, is an Attorney with the firm of Vogel and Krantz.

    _____

5. Mr. peabody called his Senator to complain about taxes.

    _____

Capitalization of Words Referring to Groups

Religions, Geographic Locations, Races, and Nationalities

Capitalize words that refer to specific religions, geographic locations, races, and nationalities.

Examples

People of many races attend school with me. I have classmates who are Asian, Caucasian, African American, Latino, and Native American.

Though Bjorn is originally from Sweden, he considers himself a Los Angeleno.

Alan drives an American car, drinks German beer, and collects Mexican glassware.

Rashid was brought up Baptist, but he converted to Islam when he was twenty-six.

Organizations, Businesses, and Agencies

Capitalize specific names of organizations, businesses, and government agencies.

Examples

Harley belongs to the Meadow Community Chorus, the Spanish Club, and the Association of Nursing Students.

Perry works at the Campbell Corporation and his wife works for IBM.

After Lenore finished her accounting degree, she went to work for the Internal Revenue Service.

Do not capitalize nonspecific or generic organization names.

Examples

Clarissa is active in church and is also a member of the choir.

As an executive in a large corporation, Simone often travels.

When Claud finishes college, he wants to work for the government.

PRACTICE 2   **CAPITALIZING WORDS REFERRING TO GROUPS**

Underline and correct the two capitalization mistakes in each sentence.

1. Janet went to the Library to find information on the american red cross.

_____

2. The first methodist children's choir sold candy to benefit a charity called kids yule love.

_____

3. When he began working for ford, Dwight joined the Union.

_____

4. One of the most active clubs at the College is the association of nontraditional students.

_____

5. I heard that our Company chairperson was offered a job at the federal trade commission.

_____

Capitalization of Words Referring to Time and Place

Dates, Days, Holidays, and Seasons

Capitalize months of the year, days of the week, and names of holidays.

Examples

Thanksgiving Day is always celebrated on the last Thursday in November.

October holidays include Halloween and Columbus Day.

Do *not* capitalize the names of the four seasons.

Marvin wants to take one last summer trip before his children go back to school in the fall.

Place Names

Capitalize specific place names.

Examples

On our trip to Orlando, we visited Disney World, Sea World, Universal Studios, and Wet 'n' Wild.

We also ate at King Arthur's Feast.

When Sandra attended Glendale Community College, she worked part-time at Pizza Hut.

The robber ran out of the Kwickie Food Mart and tore down Lemon Street.

Do not capitalize *general, nonspecific* place names.

Examples

On our trip to Orlando, we visited three theme parks and a water park.

We also ate at two expensive and entertaining restaurants.

When Sandra attended college, she worked for a pizza place.

The robber ran out of the convenience store and tore down the street.

Do not capitalize compass points unless they refer to a specific geographical area.

Examples

The car traveled north on the interstate before turning east toward the city.

Having lived on the East Coast all her life, Deb found it hard to adjust to the mountainous West.

PRACTICE 3   CAPITALIZING WORDS REFERRING TO TIME AND PLACE

Underline and correct the two capitalization mistakes in each sentence.

1. Cathryn had always lived in the south, but when she was eighteen, she moved to california.

   _____

2. The bus was headed South on peachtree street.

   _____

3. People living in new mexico sometimes have trouble convincing people that they live in the united states.

_____

4. Kim's family celebrates both kwanzaa and Christmas in the Winter.

_____

5. The state of north Carolina is known for its beaches as well as its beautiful blue ridge mountains.

_____

Capitalization of Words Referring to Things and Activities

School Subjects

Do not capitalize subjects studied in school unless they are part of a *specific* course title.

Examples

Sandro is taking physics, French, and sociology this term.

Sandro is taking Physics 101, French 102, and Sociology 208 this term.

Sandro is taking Principles of Physics, Intermediate French, and Social Problems this term.

Titles

In general, capitalize titles of novels, short stories, poems, newspapers, magazines, articles, works of art, television shows, movies, songs and other musical works. There are exceptions to many rules in English, and this rule has more exceptions than most. Some newspapers and journals capitalize only the first word in the title of an article. Some writers, like e. e. cummings, do not follow the conventional rules of capitalization. When you write about an article, a poem, or any other piece of writing, preserve the title as it was published.

Otherwise, follow these rules: Capitalize the first word of a title. Do not capitalize articles (*a, an,* and *the*) or short prepositions (*to, of, from,* and similar short prepositions) unless they are the first word in a title. Capitalize all other words.

Examples

> Hisako read an article in *Sky and Telescope* called "Radio Astronomy in the 21st Century."
>
> Kelly's literature class read Anton Chekhov's play, *The Cherry Orchard*.
>
> Isabel wrote her paper on "Sorting Laundry" by Elisavietta Ritchie and "Snow White and the Seven Deadly Sins" by R. S. Gwynn.
>
> Myra tried to keep the children busy by teaching them to sing "Row, Row, Row Your Boat."

Consumer Products

For consumer products, capitalize the brand name but not the general product name.

Examples

> At the college bookstore, Roger bought a Paper Mate highlighter, a roll of Scotch tape, a Bic pen, and a Mead notebook.
>
> A Toyota broke down in front of the drive-through at Burger King.

Abbreviations

Abbreviations of organizations, corporations, and professional designations are capitalized. Some examples include NBC, AFL-CIO, FBI, NAACP, CIA, UPS, CPA, M.D., Ph.D., D.D.S. The disease AIDS is always written in all capitals.

PRACTICE 4   CAPITALIZING WORDS REFERRING TO THINGS AND ACTIVITIES

Underline and correct the two capitalization mistakes in each sentence.

1. Al pulled his toyota into the convenience store parking lot and ran over an empty Coke Bottle.

   _____

2. Mollie opened a can of alpo dog food, but when Taffy refused to eat it, she shared her mcDonald's cheeseburger with him.

   _____

3. Ann reads the miami herald or watches cbs to get the latest news.

_____

4. Since he was out of Maxwell House Coffee, Ed decided to have some Lipton Tea.

_____

5. Leshan read an article in new woman called "how I lost fifty pounds."

_____

Review Exercise

Complete the Review Exercises to see how well you have learned the skills addressed in this chapter. As you work through the exercises, go back through the chapter to review any of the rules you do not understand completely.

REVIEW EXERCISE 1

Underline and correct the two capitalization mistakes in each sentence.

1. When Mimi couldn't find what she needed at foodmax, she went to kroger.

_____

2. Alton bought a flower arrangement for his Mother to celebrate mother's day.

_____

3. When grandpa tried to cut the thanksgiving turkey, it slipped off the platter and shot across the table.

_____

4. When Randy went to his High School reunion, he borrowed a friend's lexus instead of driving his old Chevy truck.

_____

5. It was late march before Andrew received his letter of acceptance from the College.

_____

REVIEW EXERCISE 2

Underline and correct the two capitalization mistakes in each sentence.

1. Sonia wore her mickey mouse T-shirt and her nike shoes to the picnic.

_____

2. The bus pulled into the town of east point at 6:00 A.M., then headed West on Route 27.

_____

3. Before the baseball game started, the crowd at turner field stood to sing "the star-spangled banner."

_____

4. Kelsey munched on a bag of Frito's Corn Chips as she watched a rerun of *the munsters*.

_____

5. Some birds live in north america during the summer and migrate to south america in the winter.

_____

REVIEW EXERCISE 3

Underline and correct the two capitalization mistakes in each sentence.

1. Harry and his Dad went on a two-week fishing trip to Crystal Lake last Spring.

_____

2. Scientists who do aids research get a portion of their funding from the Government.

_____

3. Kim said, "a few years ago, I used to smoke Marlboro Cigarettes. Now my worst vice is Hostess Ho Hos."

_____

4. Kaya bought a half gallon of breyer's Strawberry frozen yogurt.

_____

5. Gary is from the midwest, but he has lived in south Carolina for three years.

_____

REVIEW EXERCISE 4

Underline and correct the capitalization errors in the paragraph below.

[1]A friend recently asked me, "how would you define success?" [2]The term means different things to different people, so i wasn't sure

how to answer. [3]For some people, it means a new ford explorer in the driveway. [4]Or it means a big-screen Sony Television in the den. [5]For others, it's a fat bank account at first national bank. [6]Some want a chauffeur-driven limousine stocked with bottles of Cristal Champagne. [7]To some people, success is improved health—money and possessions can't outweigh good health to a person with aids or Alzheimer's. [8]Still others aspire to fame and measure success by the number of times their faces appear on the cover of <u>People</u> or <u>time</u>. [9]Perhaps bertrand russell gave the best definition of success and its relationship to happiness. [10]He said, "success is getting what you want. Happiness is wanting what you get."

1. _____

2. _____

3. _____

4. _____

5. _____

6. _____

7. _____

8. _____

9. _____

10. _____

CHAPTER 22

Words Commonly Confused

I think that I shall never see
Someone who looks so much like me,
With the same hair and eyes and teeth,
But not the same deep underneath.

It is the same way when we write
Some words that look or sound alike
Are different in the way they're used;
These words are commonly confused.

Words Commonly Confused

a, an The article *a* is used before consonant sounds. The article *an* is used before vowel sounds. Thus you would write **a** dog, **a** rocky shoreline, **a** patch of ice, **an** icy road, **an** oblong box, **an** office. But you must base your choice on the consonant or vowel *sound*. Some words, such as those beginning with a silent *h* or with a *u* that is pronounced like *y*, require careful treatment: **an** honest person, but **a** hat; **an** uncle, but **a** used car.

✔ At the market, Trinh bought **an** eggplant, **a** large basket of crisp apples that came with **an** apple corer, and **a** few squash.

✔ The actor said that it was **an** honor to receive such **a** prestigious award.

accept, except To *accept* is to take or believe; the word *except* means *but* or *with the exception of.*

✔ The company will **accept** applications, but **except** for a few clerical positions, no jobs are available.

advice, advise *Advice* is a noun; one gives advice or asks for it. *Advise* is the verb form; one person may *advise* another.

✔ The psychic **advised** Abby to seek further **advice** at only $2.95 per minute.

affect, effect *Affect* is the verb form. It means *to cause a change or variation. Effect* is the noun form. It means *outcome or result.*

✔ Jacob's illness does not seem to **affect** his mood.

✔ Even though Janice studied hard, the **effect** on her grades was not immediate.

all right, alright *All right* is the only correct spelling. It is never all right to write *alright.*

✔ The computer was not working this morning, but it seems to be **all right** now.

a lot, alot, allot *A lot* (never *alot*) is always written as two words when you mean *much* or *many,* but it's preferable to use a word such as *much,* *many*, *several*, or a specific amount instead of *a lot*. The word *allot* means *to allow or set aside* for a special purpose: Erica allotted *fifty dollars per month to her vacation fund*.

✔ **Acceptable:** It took **a lot** of work to get the old house in livable condition.

✔ **Better:** It took **months** of work to get the old house in livable condition.

among, between   *Among* is used with three or more persons or things; *between* is used with two.

✔ At the banquet, Governor Albright was seated **between** the mayor and Senator Jones. Later, however, she walked **among** the tables, chatting with her constituents.

breath, breathe   *Breath* is the noun form: a person can take a *breath* or be out of *breath*. *Breathe* is the verb form: someone may *breathe* heavily after exercising.

✔ "I can't take a vacation," said Pierre. "I am so busy I can't even take a **breath**."

✔ "First, you need to learn how to **breathe**," said the yoga instructor.

by, buy   *By* means *beside* or *through*. *Buy* means *to purchase*.

✔ "If you go **by** the ice cream shop," said Brandon, "**buy** me a pint of strawberry."

fewer, less   Use *fewer* when writing about things you count; *less* when writing about things you measure. Specifically, if you can put a number in front of a word (five dollars), use *fewer*. If you cannot put a number in front of a word (five money), use *less*. You would write *fewer* rocks but *less* sand, *fewer* cookies but *less* flour.

✔ Anita noticed that when she used **less** fertilizer, her plants produced **fewer** tomatoes.

good, well   *Good* is an adjective that answers the question "What kind?" *Well* is an adverb that answers the question "How?" or "In what manner?" Therefore, a person writes a *good* essay. (*Good* answers the question, "What kind of essay?") But he writes it *well*. (*Well* answers the question, "How did he write it?")

✔ Carlisle has a **good** arm, but he does not pitch very **well** under pressure.

himself, ~~hisself~~   The word is always *himself,* never *hisself.*

✔ Rico was proud that he had done the repairs **himself.**

its, it's   If you mean *it is* or *it has,* use *it's* (with the apostrophe). Otherwise, use *its.*

✔ "**It's** a pleasure to drive my old Ford," said Daniel, "because **it's** been taken care of."

✔ The inchworm, bending double, then stretching full length, slowly made **its** way across the walkway.

knew, new   *Knew* is the past tense of *know; new* means *not old.*

✔ The owner of the small hardware store **knew** that he faced stiff competition from the **new** Handy Andy down the street.

know, no   *Know* means *to understand; no* means *not any* or the opposite of *yes.*

✔ "I do not **know** why there are **no** gas stations along this stretch of highway," said Joan.

loose, lose   *Loose* is the opposite of *tight; lose* is the opposite of *find.*

✔ Althea's clothes are getting **loose,** but she says she plans to **lose** more weight.

past, passed   *Past* (an adjective) means *beyond* or *before now. Past* (a noun) means *a time before now. Passed* (a verb) means *went by.*

✔ The insurance company bases its rates on a client's **past** driving record.

✔ More and more, Aunt Emma seems to talk about the **past.**

✔ Every time Tammy **passed** a fast-food place, her son yelled, "Want fries!"

peace, piece   *Peace* means *calm* or *tranquility; piece* means *a part.*

✔ Sam knew he would get no **peace** until he gave Cujo a **piece** of his hamburger.

plain, plane   *Plain* means *clear* or *simple.* A *plane* is a form of air transportation, a carpenter's tool, or a geometric surface.

✔ Joseph's **plain,** simple office belied the fact that he had a company **plane** at his disposal.

principal, principle   *Principal* means *chief* (principal reason) or *a person in charge of a school* (principal of Westmore High). A *principle* is a policy, a moral stand, or a rule.

✔ The **principal** said she hoped to encourage solid values and strong **principles** in her students.

✔ Pete's inability to get along with his coworkers was the **principal** reason he was fired.

quit, quite, quiet   *Quit* means *to stop. Quite* means *entirely* or *very,* and *quiet* means *hushed.*

✔ "I am not **quite** through with my homework," Anna told her daughter. "If you will **quit** banging on that pot and be **quiet** for just a few minutes, I will play with you when I'm through."

regardless, ~~irregardless~~   Regardless of the number of times you may have seen it, *irregardless* is not a word. The word is *regardless.*

✔ **Regardless** of the setbacks and problems that Aldo had, his term paper turned out well.

themselves, ~~themself~~, ~~theirself~~, ~~theirselves~~   The word is always *themselves.*

✔ After they did their Saturday chores, Tina and Frank decided to give **themselves** a treat and order a pizza.

then, than   *Then* is used to show time or cause and effect; *than* is used to compare.

✔ If you are going to the library tomorrow, maybe I will see you **then.**

✔ If Jerrald moves to the new apartment complex, **then** he will have a longer commute to work.

✔ The new copier takes up much less space **than** the old one did.

there, their, they're   *There* is used to mean *in that place* or to start a sentence or clause. *Their* means *belonging to them,* and *they're* means *they are.*

✔ **"They're** not for you," Kim warned as the dog nosed the bag of sandwiches.

✔ **"There** are not enough places in this mall to sit down," said Alberta.

✔ Valerie took her children to the health department for **their** school vaccinations.

through, threw   *Through* means *within, between,* or *finished. Threw* is the past tense of *throw.*

✔ After Jim was **through** with his newspaper, he **threw** it in the recycling bin and sat looking **through** the window.

two, too, to   *Two* refers to the number two; *too* means *also* or indicates an excessive amount, as in the phrase *too much.* Any other use requires *to.*

✔ Alfredo said he wanted **to** go **to** the beach **too,** but I told him we had **too** many people unless someone else agreed **to** drive so that we could take **two** cars.

weather, whether, rather   *Weather* includes natural phenomena such as temperature, rainfall, and wind velocity. *Whether* means *if* and indicates the existence of two possibilities. It is often paired with *or not. Rather* indicates a preference.

✔ The **weather** is expected to turn warm after the weekend.

✔ We aren't sure **whether** we can afford a vacation this year.

✔ Would you **rather** have ice cream or frozen yogurt?

where, were   *Where* rhymes with *air* and refers to *place. Were* rhymes with *fur* and is a past-tense form of *to be.*

✔ When Cari did not see you, she asked **where** you **were.**

Review Exercises

Complete the Review Exercises to see how well you have learned the skills addressed in this chapter. As you work through the exercises, go back through the chapter to review any of the rules you do not understand completely.

REVIEW EXERCISE 1

Refer to the explanations in this chapter to choose the correct words in each sentence. Underline the correct choice.

1. Jiro made (a, an) egg noodle soup that his guests agreed was (quite, quiet) good.
2. Leo was not sure (rather, whether) he would (rather, whether) take a biology course or an anthropology course.
3. Dorothy went (threw, through) every drawer in the kitchen because she could not remember (were, where) she had put the can opener.
4. Michael blamed (himself, hisself) for his financial troubles. He knew that he should not (buy, by) so many things on credit.
5. The twins (were, where) known around the apartment complex as "the terrible (too, to, two)."

REVIEW EXERCISE 2

Underline the correct words in each sentence.

1. After her children left for school in the morning, Monica enjoyed the (piece, peace) and (quite, quiet).
2. The singer flashed a (piece, peace) sign and said, "Everything is uptight, (alright, all right), and out of sight."
3. Lakeisha wore (a, an) caftan that was flowing and (loose, lose).
4. James could not (except, accept) Laurie's declaration that she was (through, threw) with him.
5. Aimee decided to take her conservative grandmother's (advice, advise) and print her resume on (plain, plane) white paper instead of hot pink.

REVIEW EXERCISE 3

Cross out the two word choice errors in each sentence. Then write the correct words on the line provided.

1. At the paint store, Marie found it hard to chose between the forty different shades of yellow.

   _____

2. "I used too wish I was smarter then my brother," said Joseph, "until I realized that I was."

   _____

3. "The coffee tasted very well," said Owen, "but I'm not sure weather I should have drunk it so late at night."

_____

4. Dwight and Hakim reminded theirselves that they had meant too go to the library to study.

_____

5. Carol couldn't except our invitation because she had alot of work to do.

_____

REVIEW EXERCISE 4

Cross out the two word choice errors in each sentence. Then write the correct words on the line provided.

1. Steve said that the principle reason he quit his job was that his supervisor asked him to falsify financial records. Dishonesty was against Steve's principals.

_____

2. Ellen's goldfish was floating lifelessly in it's bowl Thursday morning. She wondered weather she had overfed it the night before.

_____

3. Brian had told no one accept Courtney that he was planning to quit his job. He was surprised to find that all of his coworkers new about it.

_____

4. When a wasp landed on her magazine, Susan held her breathe. Then she quickly through the magazine over the porch railing.

_____

5. When Zack woke up screaming from his nightmare, his mother came to make sure he was alright. Then she rocked him and sang to him until he was quite.

_____

REVIEW EXERCISE 5

Cross out the ten word choice errors in the paragraph below. Then correct them on the lines provided.

[1]One of the best things about technology is that it offers a host of knew excuses for not turning in assignments on time. [2]If you have a computer and a printer, you have access to excuses that almost any professor will except. [3]Just before the class period when the assignment

is due, run breathlessly into the professor's office and say that your printer cartridge quite printing just as you were trying to print your paper. [4]Or tell the instructor that your computer's hard drive crashed and made you loose all your files. [5]Even if you do not own a computer, technology still gives you alot of excuses. [6]If you need another day on your paper, call the professor, say you are sick, and ask if it is alright for your mother (or some other person) to fax in the assignment. [7]The next day, take in your paper, apologize, and say that your mother kept getting disconnected because their was a poor line condition on the fax. [8]Another good excuse is that you tried to make a extra copy of your paper, but the copier had a paper jam as your paper went through. [9]If you fill bad about lying to your professor or think that he or she won't accept your excuse, there is another way. [10]You can take the safe, dull route and get threw with your paper in time to turn it in on the due date.

1. _____   6. _____

2. _____   7. _____

3. _____   8. _____

4. _____   9. _____

5. _____   10. _____

Word Choice

Mike is interviewing for his first postcollege job. When he is ushered into the office of the interviewer, what should he say?

a. "Yo! Got any jobs, man?"
b. "Allow me at this point in time to present and introduce myself to you."
c. "Good afternoon. I'm Mike Tan."
d. "If you're looking for the cream of the crop, it's as plain as the nose on your face that I am a cut above the rest."

If you answered *c* to the question in the box above, you have shown good judgment in word choice. But when you write, word choice is not always so clear-cut. This chapter helps you to fine-tune your judgment and to recognize categories of word choice that are generally not appropriate for college writing: slang, clichés, and wordiness.

Slang

People enjoy using slang because it is informal, up-to-the-minute, and fun. Just as a common language forms a bond among those who speak it, slang reinforces the bond within the groups that use it. Yet the very things that make slang appealing in conversation make it unsuitable for writing to a broad audience. Writing requires a common language and is usually more formal than conversation. In addition, no writer wants to use words that may be out of date if an audience reads them years later. Slang expressions such as *the bee's knees, hunky-dory,* and *groovy* may have sounded up-to-the-minute decades ago, but now they are relics of another time.

GROUP EXERCISE 1   Discussing Slang Terms

Form small groups. Try to include both sexes and as many different ages and ethnic groups as possible. Each group member should write down five slang terms and then share the list with other group members. Are some of the terms different? (The more diverse the group, the more likely that it will generate a variety of slang.) Are there any slang expressions that not all group members are familiar with? What conclusions can the group draw about the use of slang? Choose one spokesperson to report the group's findings, along with a few of the most interesting slang terms, to the class.

PRACTICE 1   AVOIDING SLANG EXPRESSIONS

Replace the italicized slang expressions in each sentence with more traditional word choices.

1. Vince was wearing a *cool* new pair of *shades* with round lenses.

   _____

   _____

2. Shara *flipped out* when she *eyeballed* the scratch on her car door.

   _____

   _____

3. Dolores went on a huge shopping spree and *maxed out* her *plastic.*

   _____

   _____

4. Instead of studying, Frank decided to *chill out* in front of the *tube* for a few hours.

_____

_____

5. Lucinda's brother is going with her to buy her car because he thinks she is so *clueless* that she would probably be *ripped off*.

_____

_____

Clichés

While slang is fresh and new, clichés are expressions used so often for so long that they have become worn out. The cliché *burn the midnight oil*, for instance, is a relic of a time when working until midnight meant lighting an oil lamp. Because they are easy to remember and widely used, clichés are often the first expressions that come to mind. It takes a deliberate effort to recognize them and eliminate them from your writing.

Look at the following list of clichés. Can you think of others?

apple of my eye	dead as a doornail	live and let live
as good as gold	easy as pie	once in a blue moon
as old as Methuselah	flat as a pancake	pretty as a picture
at the drop of a hat	in the lap of luxury	raining cats and dogs
cream of the crop	light as a feather	sick as a dog

PRACTICE 2   AVOIDING CLICHÉS

Rewrite each sentence to eliminate the two italicized clichés.

1. The job bagging groceries was as *easy as pie,* but Tom was fired because he was *slow as molasses.*

_____

_____

2. During the interview, Sally looked *as cool as a cucumber,* but inside she was *shaking like a leaf.*

_____

_____

3. Keisha says her job keeps her *as busy as a bee* and that she gets a vacation *once in a blue moon.*

   _____

   _____

4. Because Kevin has *worn so many hats* at Acme Tool and Die, he knows the company *like the back of his hand.*

   _____

   _____

5. My next-door neighbor is *as old as Methuselah,* but he seems to be *fit as a fiddle.*

   _____

   _____

Wordiness

Wordiness sometimes happens when writers do not take the time to be concise. The shortest and simplest way of expressing an idea is usually the best way.

The words and phrases below contribute to wordiness and can usually be omitted.

basically	basically performs no function in most sentences
definitely	is definitely a space-waster
in my opinion	usually weakens a sentence in my opinion
the fact is that	The fact is that facts, like opinions, can usually be stated without preamble.
totally	usually totally unnecessary
very	can very often be omitted

The phrases below are wordy and can usually be shortened and strengthened.

Wordy	Concise
at the present time	now, today
due to the fact that	because, since
for the reason that	because, since
in point of fact	in fact
in today's society	today
long in length	long

Examples

✗ I dreaded taking the course, but *in point of fact,* I needed a course in the *basic fundamentals* of English.

✔ I dreaded taking the course, but in fact, I needed a course in the fundamentals of English.

✗ *Due to the fact that at this point in time* I don't have a car, I ride the bus every day.

✔ Because I don't have a car, I ride the bus every day.

PRACTICE 3   ELIMINATING WORDINESS

Each sentence contains two italicized wordy expressions. Rewrite the sentences to eliminate wordiness.

1. I stayed awake until *1:00 A.M. in the morning* to watch the *lunar eclipse of the moon.*

   _____

   _____

2. Because of the high crime rate *in today's society,* many people are *basically* distrustful of other people.

   _____

   _____

3. *Annually each year,* an employees' picnic is held to reward the workers for the hard work they do *each and every day.*

   _____

   _____

4. *In my opinion, I think* that *financial decision-making about money matters* should be taught in high school.

   _____

   _____

5. James was *totally and completely dedicated* to *the best on-the-job performance he could deliver to his employer in the workplace.*

   _____

   _____

GROUP EXERCISE 2   Eliminating Slang, Clichés, and Wordiness Confident? Go solo!

In small groups, "translate" the sentences written here in slang, clichés, or wordy language. Then rewrite the same thought in clear, concise language.

Sentence Group 1

Slang: Leo had the pedal to the metal, but he thought his radar detector would keep him from being busted by the fuzz.

Wordiness: Leo was definitely exceeding the speed limit posted upon the signs beside the road, but he thought having a radar detector in his car to alert him to police presence would prevent the authorities from detecting or stopping him.

Your revision: _____

_____

Sentence Group 2

Slang: Catherine flipped out when she saw her main squeeze hanging out with another woman.

Cliché: When Catherine saw the apple of her eye with another woman, she hit the ceiling.

Your revision: _____

_____

Sentence Group 3

Cliché: Joanna eats like a horse, but she is still as thin as a rail.

Wordiness: Joanna eats a great deal of food of all kinds and types, but she somehow manages to maintain a thin slenderness of body that is surprising.

Your revision: _____

_____

Sentence Group 4

Slang: Jake really dug his new ride to the max.

Wordiness: Jake received a great deal of enjoyment and pleasure from his Nissan automobile, which was red in color.

Your revision: _____

_____

Sentence Group 5

Slang: I pulled out my plastic, but the clerk said I had to lay some green on him.

Wordiness: I retrieved my Visa credit card from its place within my wallet, but the store clerk in the convenience store said that the store accepted only cash money, not a Visa credit card, or for that matter, a MasterCard or American Express credit card.

Your revision: _____

_____

Review Exercises

Complete the Review Exercises to see how well you have learned the skills addressed in this chapter. As you work through the exercises, go back through the chapter to review any of the rules you do not understand completely.

REVIEW EXERCISE 1

In the blank to the left of each sentence, indicate whether the italicized expressions are slang (*S*), clichés (*C*), or wordy expressions (*W*). Then replace the italicized words to correct the problem in word choice.

_____ 1. Ben *freaked out* when he saw the parking ticket on his windshield.

_____

_____ 2. It was *raining cats and dogs* by the time Tasha got out of her political science class.

_____

_____ 3. *In point of fact,* trees prevent soil erosion, produce oxygen, and provide cooling shade.

_____

_____ 4. Because he had *prearranged plans that he had made at an earlier time to attend a conference,* the professor canceled Friday's class.

_____

_____ 5. Samantha was *born with a silver spoon in her mouth* and has lived *in the lap of luxury* all her life.

_____

_____ **6.** Professor Adams was *ticked off* because the class did so poorly on the last test.

_____ **7.** Because it was raining, the game was *postponed until a later time.*

_____ **8.** At the restaurant, we *pigged out* on hamburgers and fries, so we were too full to order dessert.

_____ **9.** Without her friends from high school, Amy was *like a fish out of water* during her first few months at college.

_____ **10.** The speaker *concluded his speech with a wrap-up that summarized his major points.*

REVIEW EXERCISE 2

Underline and correct the two word choice problems in each sentence.

1. Because Hal has a heart of gold, he agreed to take care of his sister's two rug rats while she was out of town.

2. Rollo thought he would cop some z's during class, but the professor became angry and threw him out on his ear.

3. When the strange noise persisted in continuing, Alissa put on her bedroom slippers, grabbed a flashlight, and went outdoors to examine the outside exterior of the house.

4. Since Anna has wheels, I asked her if we could ride with her, and she said she was cool with that.

5. Laurie is basically tired of Sam, but she is definitely interested in Paul.

_____

_____

REVIEW EXERCISE 3

Some slang expressions have alternate meanings that are not slang. For each sentence pair, choose the expression from the word list that best fits both sentences. Then write the slang meaning and the standard meaning of the expression in the blanks provided.

Word list: cool, bust, bug, shaft, gross

1. Sentence pair 1

    a. Jason's mother bought a gelatin mold in the shape of a human brain. She thought it was _____, but she knew Jason would love it.

    b. The store manager was sorry he had ordered a _____ of glow-in-the-dark yo-yos. In six months, he sold just 10 and had 134 left in stock.

    Slang meaning: _____

    Standard meaning: _____

2. Sentence pair 2

    a. "Don't _____ me, squirt," Al said to his little brother.

    b. Ever since a _____ crawled into his shoe one night, Bobby shakes out both shoes before putting them on in the morning.

    Slang meaning: _____

    Standard meaning: _____

3. Sentence pair 3

    a. The drug dealer peddled his wares from a bench in the park, seemingly unafraid of a police _____.

    b. On the piano, Mr. Schoenmeyer had a small _____ of Mozart.

    Slang meaning: _____

    Standard meaning: _____

4. Sentence pair 4

    a. After his divorce, Raymond's favorite song was "She Got the Gold Mine, I Got the _____."

    b. Through a high window, a single _____ of sunlight fell into the cheerless room.

    Slang meaning: _____

    Standard meaning: _____

5. Sentence pair 5

    a. The candy, called Boogers, came in a plastic nose. "_____!" said the delighted twins.

    b. When the rest of us are comfortable, Pat always shivers and says it is too _____.

    Slang meaning: _____

    Standard meaning: _____

REVIEW EXERCISE 4

Underline and correct the two word choice problems in each sentence.

1. The Chinese tea was pale green in color and deliciously fruity in taste.

_____

_____

2. Arthur was as mad as a wet hen because the car's battery was as dead as a doornail.

_____

_____

3. The dude in the gross-looking work boots is my cousin Malcolm.

_____

_____

4. Due to the fact that she had not found a job, Luanne was basically broke.

_____

_____

5. Reginald was hip to the fact that the exam would be a bummer.

_____

_____

REVIEW EXERCISE 5

Rewrite the letter below, correcting the errors in word choice in the salutation, body, and close of the letter.

[1]Yo, Professor Smith,

[2]What a major bummer it was to miss the midterm exam in your class yesterday. [3]I know that your syllabus definitely states that you basically do not give make-up exams. [4]However, I am absolutely certain beyond a shadow of a doubt that in my case you will see fit to make an exception to this policy. [5]You see, I became as sick as a dog after a late-night study session with some friends over at the Keg and Barrel.

[6]I know that we have had our differences, but aside from the unfortunate incident of the fake vomit, you have to admit that I have been as good as gold in your class. [7]I swear I am as innocent as a lamb in the matter of the stolen exam key.

[8]Let me say prior to concluding this letter that in my opinion, I think you are one of the best and most fair-minded professors on this campus. [9]I hope that you will forgive and forget, let bygones be bygones, and allow me to make up the exam.

[10]Later, teach!

Desmond Kruger

_____

_____

_____

_____

_____

_____

_____

_____

_____

_____

_____

_____

Commas

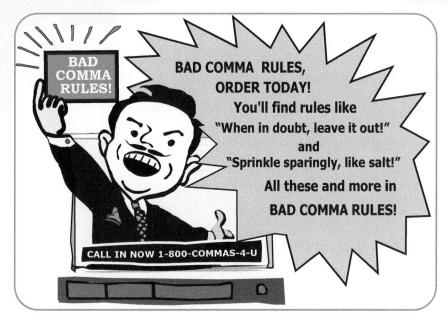

Unreliable Rules

"When in doubt, leave it out."

"Put a comma where there is a natural pause."

"Sprinkle them sparingly, like salt."

There are so many comma rules that, in desperation, people often resort to makeshift rules like the ones above. Unfortunately, these blanket statements don't always work. When it comes to commas, rules—and exceptions—abound. The rules presented in this chapter help you cope with the complexities of comma usage.

Commas to Set off Introductory Words, Phrases, and Clauses

Use commas after an introductory word, phrase, or clause.

Examples

Later, we walked on the beach and watched the sun set.

In the long run, getting an education pays.

When Ethan saw the giraffe, he laughed and clapped his hands.

In the spaces between the keys on her computer keyboard, Kim could see dust.

PRACTICE 1 USING COMMAS AFTER INTRODUCTORY ELEMENTS

Insert commas after introductory words, phrases, and clauses.

1. Painfully the man rose to his feet and walked toward us.

   _____

2. To Arlene's irritation a little sports car slipped into the parking place she had been waiting for.

   _____

3. By the time the pizza arrived it was cold.

   _____

4. Without apology or explanation Eric strolled in two hours late.

   _____

5. After Mary's coupons were deducted her grocery bill came to $34.95.

   _____

Commas to Join Items in a Series

When a series of three or more words, phrases, or clauses is connected with *and, or,* or *nor,* place a comma after each item except the last one. The final comma will come before *and, or,* or *nor.*

Examples

Ferrell said his car needed a wash, a wax job, and an oil change.

Apples, oranges, and bananas filled a wooden bowl on the kitchen counter.

Nell said she would consider herself successful if she graduated from college, opened her own business, and had a happy family.

Ellie said she knew Brett was smart because he was a good Scrabble player, he read a lot, and he had a good sense of humor.

If only two items appear in the series, no comma is used.

The old farmer said he had cut his livestock to just a few cows and three dozen pigs.

The toll collector said that there was a traffic tie-up in the tunnel and a wreck near the downtown connector.

On his new diet, Uncle Frank said he was hungry just twice a day: when he was awake and when he was asleep.

PRACTICE 2   USING COMMAS TO JOIN ITEMS IN A SERIES

Insert commas to join words, phrases, and clauses in a series of three or more. One sentence has only two items in the series and does not require a comma.

1. Jason's summer job with a lawn maintenance firm helped him learn that he hates grass dirt and heat.

   _____

   _____

2. Mom makes her special orange cookies only at Christmas because of the cost and the labor involved in making the cookies.

   _____

   _____

3. The receptionist said that Dr. Brantley was booked solid during June July and August.

_____

_____

4. The white-hatted chef pulled the souffle from the oven set it on the counter and watched as it slowly deflated.

_____

_____

5. At the opening of the ice-skating rink, skaters leaped twirled wobbled or fell, according to their level of expertise.

_____

_____

Commas to Join Independent Clauses

Use a comma with a FANBOYS conjunction (*for, and, nor, but, or, yet, so*) to join independent clauses. Recall that an independent clause has a subject and a verb and can stand alone as a complete sentence.

Examples

Evelyn needed to go to the post office, so she left the house twenty minutes early.

Thad felt an uncomfortable twinge in his right ankle, but he kept running anyway.

The temperature is expected to drop, and snow is predicted.

Do not use a comma if the FANBOYS connects a verb to a clause rather than a clause to a clause. That is, do not use a comma unless there is a complete sentence (subject *and* verb) on both sides of the FANBOYS.

subject verb   verb
Carrie put her tea in the microwave and made a tomato sandwich.

The dog stood by the door and waited for Vince to come out.

Fernando can take a new job at lower pay or stay with the old job he hates.

PRACTICE 3   USING COMMAS WITH *FANBOYS* TO JOIN INDEPENDENT CLAUSES

Place commas before FANBOYS conjunctions that join two independent clauses. One sentence contains a compound verb, not two clauses, and does not need a comma.

1. Grass and weeds grew tall around the unpainted house and shutters hung haphazardly from its windows.

    _____

2. The sun was hot but a cool breeze occasionally brought relief.

    _____

3. A police car circled the block several times but did not stop.

    _____

4. Laurie woke up early so she decided to work on her term paper.

    _____

5. Ralph thought he could fix the sink easily but it took him most of the afternoon.

    _____

Commas around Interrupters

An interrupter is a word, phrase, or clause inserted into a sentence to give more information about some element within the sentence. An interrupter is never essential to the structure of the sentence. If you took the interrupter out, the sentence would still make perfect sense.

Examples

The road, freshly paved, was no longer pitted with dangerous potholes.

The bag, crumpled and stuffed under a bench, held the remains of someone's lunch.

PRACTICE 4   USING COMMAS AROUND INTERRUPTERS

Insert commas around interrupters in the following sentences.

1. The song one of Bryan's favorites was first recorded over thirty years ago.

    _____

2. Mr. Cartwright the building's custodian retired because of poor health.

_____

3. The child sulking unhappily picked up his toys.

_____

4. The container of cottage cheese still sealed was two months past its expiration date.

_____

5. The highway long and lonely stretched through the trees and over the hill.

_____

Commas with Direct Quotations

A direct quotation is an exact repetition of the words that someone speaks or thinks. When a comma is used with a direct quotation, the comma is always placed in front of the quotation mark.

1. When a direct quotation is followed by a tag (such as _he said_), a comma goes after the quoted words and _in front of the quotation mark:_

    "I would like to go on a cruise ship someday," said Maria.

2. When a tag leads into a direct quotation, a comma goes after the tag and _in front of the quotation mark:_

    Spencer asked, "Where is the best place to buy a used car?"

3. When a sentence is written as a split quotation, commas are placed _in front of the quotation marks:_

    "If our dog had not awakened us," the woman told the reporter, "we might have died in the fire."

PRACTICE 5   USING COMMAS WITH DIRECT QUOTATIONS

Insert commas to set off direct quotations in the following sentences.

1. Tiffany asked "Which bus will take me to the library?"

_____

2. "Since I started walking every day" said Dee "I feel like a different person."

_____

3. "Can someone help me? I have locked my keys in the car" said Nando.

_____

4. "If I could choose the color of grass" said the child "I would pick purple."

_____

5. Oscar Wilde said "I can resist everything except temptation."

_____

Commas in Names and Dates

When a professional title follows a name, it is set off with commas.

The clerk's name tag read, "Betty, Associate."

Samuel Spencer, M.D., is the Holtons' family doctor.

When you write the month, day, and year, a comma goes between the day and year.

The Declaration of Independence was signed on July 4, 1776.

When you write just the month and year, no comma is used.

The Declaration of Independence was signed in July 1776.

PRACTICE 6   USING COMMAS IN NAMES AND DATES

Insert commas as needed in the following sentences. One sentence needs no comma.

1. The letter was dated September 1 1999.

_____

2. Stephanie Bascomb D.V.M. did the surgery on Sparky's paw.

_____

3. Kwame was born in May 1982.

_____

4. Burton Fellstone C.P.A. has opened an office on Grant Street.

_____

5. The sign on the door read Anne Grossman M.D.

_____

Review Exercises

Complete the Review Exercises to see how well you have learned the skills addressed in this chapter. As you work through the exercises, go back through the chapter to review any of the rules you do not understand completely.

REVIEW EXERCISE 1

Insert commas where they are needed in each sentence.

1. The theater gave away T-shirts movie tickets and coupons for soft drinks at its grand opening.

2. Predictably there was a crowd in the video store by the time Stan got there.

3. The Pet Stop a motel for animals takes care of pets while their owners are on vacation.

4. In October 1929 the stock market crashed after a long period of prosperity and excess.

5. When the pizza delivery car pulled into the driveway the children stampeded to the door.

6. Fast-food wrappers soft drink cans and empty bottles littered the picnic area.

7. The personal ad had led Lauren to expect a tall man so she was surprised when Roy approached her.

8. A lighted neon sign blaring music and laughter spilling from the open door told Alfredo that the Dew Drop Inn was still open for business.

9. "Thanks for waiting. I hope I'm not too late" Leona said breathlessly.

10. Kevin Nguyen my brother's roommate is majoring in chemistry.

REVIEW EXERCISE 2

Insert commas where they are needed in each sentence.

1. Before leaving his car in the stadium's huge parking lot Ron tied a bright orange flag to the antenna.

   _____

2. Elmont Morrison M.D. sleepily fumbled for the ringing telephone.

   _____

3. Muttering angrily under her breath Juanita retrieved her soggy newspaper from the puddle where it lay.

   _____

4. The well-dressed woman unaware of the store detective's presence slipped the silver necklace into her handbag.

   _____

5. In the basement dusty jars of Grandma's vegetables and preserves lined the shelves.

   _____

6. After the hurricane residents slowly emerged to assess the damage to houses and cars.

   _____

7. The bookstore's comfortable chairs were filled with people reading chatting or even sleeping.

   _____

8. The directory on the wall beside the elevator said that Carl Smith D.D.S. was in Suite 205.

   _____

9. Andrew saw billboards advertising motels restaurants and nightclubs.

   _____

10. With a powerful leap the cat lunged after the bird.

   _____

REVIEW EXERCISE 3

Insert commas where they are needed in each sentence. Each numbered item contains two problems that can be fixed with the addition of a comma or commas.

1. When she tried to unlock the door with her arms full of groceries Leslie dropped her keys into the bushes beside the front steps. She set the groceries

on a chair took a flashlight from her purse and hunted through the bushes for her keys.

_____

_____

2. Even though he was tired Joshua tried to stay up to watch the movie. However he soon fell asleep on the couch.

    _____

    _____

3. A stuffy head a runny nose and a sore throat told Ashley that she was coming down with a cold. She decided to stop at the drugstore on the way home for tissues cough drops and decongestant tablets.

    _____

    _____

4. Pretending to read a newspaper the detective sat outside the apartment complex for an hour and watched the door. "I never thought this would be such a boring line of work" he thought.

    _____

    _____

5. The date on the letter was April 13 1932. "This letter was written by my great-grandfather" said Michael.

    _____

    _____

REVIEW EXERCISE 4

Insert commas where they are needed in each sentence.

1. The T-shirt was old ragged and stained with paint. "It's still too good to throw away" Mia said.

    _____

    _____

2. Containers on a table beside the hot dog stand held catsup relish and even chopped onions. However there was not a drop of mustard.

    _____

    _____

3. Jeff made just one New Year's resolution but it was one he wanted to keep. He said "I want to pay off all my credit card debt."

_____

_____

4. Tacked to the bulletin board were several old receipts two greeting cards and a yellowed newspaper article. On the desk a calendar was still turned to July 2003.

_____

_____

5. Arthur wearing only his bathrobe and his underwear slipped out of the house to get his newspaper. Halfway down the driveway he realized he had accidentally locked himself out.

_____

_____

REVIEW EXERCISE 5

Insert commas where they are needed in the paragraph below. Each sentence contains one comma problem.

[1]Stephanie who used to share my apartment with me likes to hoard things. [2]When she was living with me we never had an empty closet or cabinet. [3]In the kitchen cabinet Stephanie would store all the items she had bought on sale. [4]The cabinet under the counter was jammed with bricks of coffee five-pound bags of sugar and rolls of paper towels that had been too good a bargain to resist. [5]Under the bathroom sink Stephanie stored the many boxes of toothpaste and bars of soap she had purchased at bargain prices. [6]"You'll be old enough to wear dentures before you use all that toothpaste" I told her once. [7]Stephanie however paid no attention to my teasing. [8]She said "It makes me feel secure to have enough of everything." [9]When Stephanie moved to another city she packed up all her carefully hoarded items to take with her. [10]I was sorry to see her go but I'm glad to have a little more room to store things now.

1. _____

2. _____

3. _____

4. _____

5. _____

6. _____

7. _____

8. _____

9. _____

10. _____

CHAPTER 25

Other Punctuation

In Punctuation City,
The town where I was born,
The dashes always drive fast cars
And loudly honk their horns.

Semicolons take the bus,
Parentheses, the train,
And exclamation points have got
Excitement on the brain.

These other punctuation marks
Can't wait to help us write
Sentences that make good sense
And essays that delight.

Punctuation marks other than the comma are the focus of this chapter. Some of these punctuation marks, such as the period and the question mark, are familiar. Others, such as the dash and the colon, are more exotic and less often used. This chapter reinforces the familiar marks of punctuation and introduces the less familiar.

End Punctuation: Period, Question Mark, and Exclamation Point

The period, the question mark, and the exclamation point are all forms of end punctuation; that is, they signal the end of a sentence.

The Period

The period is used to mark the end of a sentence that makes a statement.

Examples

✔ The car was less than two years old, but it already had nearly 35,000 miles on the odometer.

✔ The peacock unfurled its tail in a colorful display of blue and green.

Periods are also used to signal an appropriate abbreviation. Except for abbreviations in courtesy titles, such as *Mr.*, *Ms.*, *Dr.*, or *Rev.* used before proper names, spell out words in your paragraphs and essays. Most abbreviations should be reserved for only the most informal usage, such as your class notes or email to a friend.

Examples

✘ Marg. is going to Fla. w/her bro. in Apr. of next yr.

✔ Margaret is going to Florida with her brother in April of next year.

✔ Ms. O'Neill refuses to take Dr. Moore's advice.

The Question Mark

A question mark is used at the end of a direct question.

Examples

✔ Who borrowed my stapler?

✔ Does the tan Saturn belong to you?

No question mark is used with an indirect question.

✔ "I wonder if animals dream, too," said Jamie.

✔ Judge Gronsky asked if anyone objected to postponement of the hearing.

The Exclamation Point

Exclamation points are used to show extreme excitement or surprise and are seldom needed in college writing. Unless you are quoting someone who has just discovered that the building is on fire, there will be few opportunities to use an exclamation point. Interjections such as "Ouch!" or "Yikes!" are followed by exclamation points but are seldom needed for college writing. Use exclamation points when you quote someone who is shouting or speaking excitedly. Otherwise, let your words, not your punctuation, carry the excitement of your essay.

Examples

✗ Samantha noticed smoke streaming from under the hood of her car! She realized her engine was on fire!

✔ Samantha noticed smoke streaming from under the hood of her car. She realized her engine was on fire.

✗ She pulled to the side of the road! Now she could see flames coming from under the hood!

✔ She pulled to the side of the road. Now she could see flames coming from under the hood.

✔ She heard a bystander yell, "Get away from the car!"

PRACTICE 1   USING ABBREVIATIONS AND END PUNCTUATION

In each sentence, correct an inappropriate abbreviation or place a period after an appropriate abbreviation. Then place end punctuation (period, question mark, or exclamation point) where needed.

1. Janice asked, "Do you know why the door to the study rm. is locked"

   _____

   _____

2. I asked the dr. if she would prescribe something for my cold

   _____

   _____

3. Dr Miller told me that if she prescribed medication, my cold would be gone in two weeks. Without medication, it would take fourteen days

_____

_____

4. Aunt Rachel wants to know if you will come to her Xmas Eve breakfast

_____

_____

5. "Come back" Jason yelled, as the thief ran away with the $$ he had earned.

_____

_____

The Semicolon

Semicolon to Join Independent Clauses

A semicolon may be used with a transitional expression between independent clauses or alone between independent clauses that are closely related. (For a more detailed discussion of this use of the semicolon, see Chapter 15, "Sentence Variety," and Chapter 16, "Run-on Sentences.")

Examples

✔ The copier was out of order this morning; it seems to be working now, though.

✔ The cell phone was convenient and fun to use; however, the monthly fees were high.

Semicolon to Join Items in a List

Ordinarily, items in a list are joined by commas. However, if the items themselves contain commas, avoid confusion by using semicolons to join the items.

Examples

✔ Arlene has relatives in Richmond, Virginia; Atlanta, Georgia; and Houston, Texas.

✔ The new book on heart-healthy eating was written by James Hobson; Carletta Berry, Ph.D.; and Lazarus Salter, M.D.

PRACTICE 2   USING SEMICOLONS

Use semicolons in the following sentences to join independent clauses or items in a series.

1.   The coffee was too strong Karla felt jittery throughout the morning.

   _____

   _____

2.   Andrew says he rejects his parents' materialistic values he would rather serve others than enrich his bank account.

   _____

   _____

3.   Michael's three children were born on April 1, 1995 May 3, 1997 and July 29, 1999.

   _____

   _____

4.   Our city's tap water is of high quality in fact, it tastes better than most bottled water.

   _____

   _____

5.   At its first meeting, the club elected the following officers: Amy Gray, President Juanita Gonzales, President-elect Perry Malden, Treasurer and Kim Park, Recorder.

   _____

   _____

Colons and Dashes: Formal and Informal Punctuation

The Colon

The colon is used to introduce a list, a restatement, or a clarification. The most important thing to remember when you use a colon is that the words that come before the colon must always be a complete sentence.

1.   A colon is sometimes used to introduce a list. A complete sentence must come before the colon.

Examples

✗ On his overnight trip, Jamal carried only: a toothbrush, a change of clothes, and a good book.

✔ On his overnight trip, Jamal carried only the necessities: a toothbrush, a change of clothes, and a good book.

It is also correct—and sometimes simpler—to integrate a list into a sentence without using a colon.

✔ On his overnight trip, Jamal carried only a toothbrush, a change of clothes, and a good book.

2. A colon is used to introduce a restatement or clarification of an idea. A complete sentence must come before the colon.

Examples

✔ Ed says there are two reasons he stays broke: Visa and MasterCard.

The words *Visa and MasterCard*, preceded by a colon, restate and clarify the "two reasons" that Ed stays broke.

✔ Vera was never out of her family's reach: she carried a cellular phone and wore a pager wherever she went.

The colon introduces a clarification of the idea "never out of her family's reach."

The Dash

While the colon is a formal mark of punctuation, the dash is informal. The first two uses of a dash are exactly like those of the colon: to introduce a list, a restatement, or a clarification. A dash is also used to set off material that a writer wants to emphasize.

1. A dash introduces a list or restatement. When used in this way, a dash must be preceded by a complete sentence. A dash is typed as two hyphens, with no spaces before or after.

Examples

✔ On his overnight trip, Jamal carried only the necessities—a toothbrush, a change of clothes, and a good book.

The dash introduces a list.

✔ Ed says there are two reasons he stays broke—Visa and MasterCard.

The dash is used here to introduce a restatement and clarification of "reasons he stays broke."

2. A dash is used to set off material that the writer wants to emphasize.

✔ It was his easygoing personality—not his money—that made him popular.

A more formal way of punctuating this sentence would be to use commas to set off the interrupter: *It was his easygoing personality, not his money, that made him popular.*

✔ There was so much to do—bills to pay, errands to run, and yard work to finish—that Tom did not know where to begin.

One way of expressing the idea in the sentence more formally would be to use two sentences: *There was so much to do that Tom did not know where to begin. He had bills to pay, errands to run, and yard work to finish.*

Parentheses: Tools of Understatement

While dashes emphasize, parentheses downplay. Parentheses are used to enclose material that a reader could skip over without missing the more important ideas.

Examples

✔ Miss Clara, my elderly neighbor, says there is no better way to spend a Sunday afternoon than listening to Handel (her favorite composer) and drinking a cup of tea.

✔ Harlan told the salesman he loved driving the car. He liked the color (maroon) and he loved the interior (a rich, tan leather). But he hated the price.

PRACTICE 3   USING COLONS, DASHES, AND PARENTHESES

Rewrite each sentence as indicated, punctuating the italicized portion of the sentence with a colon, a dash (or dashes), or parentheses.

1. Analida says that staying sane on rainy weekends at home with her children requires just three things. It requires *plenty of patience, a good supply of games and songs, and a pair of heavy-duty earplugs.*

    Directions: Rewrite as one sentence, with a colon introducing the list. Remove words as needed.

    _____

2. The professor said that the price of the hardback dictionary, *just eighteen dollars,* was small, considering all the words we would get for our money.

    Directions: Rewrite so that the price of the dictionary is de-emphasized. You will need to remove the commas.

    _____

3. Allan says if his house were on fire and he could save just one possession, the choice would be easy: *his computer.*

    Directions: Rewrite so that the restatement is set off in an informal way rather than a formal way.

    _____

4. Dad's shoes (*tan loafers he has had since his college days*) are so old they are coming apart at the seams.

    Directions: Rewrite so that the parenthetical material is emphasized. Assume that the sentence can be written informally.

    _____

5. The half-gallon carton contained three flavors of ice cream: *chocolate, vanilla, and strawberry.*

    Directions: Rewrite so that the list is introduced in an informal way.

    _____

Review Exercises

Complete the Review Exercises to see how well you have learned the skills addressed in this chapter. As you work through the exercises, go back through the chapter to review any of the rules you do not understand completely.

REVIEW EXERCISE 1

Look at the punctuation printed in color in each sentence; then briefly explain the rule that justifies its use. The first one is done for you.

1. After the unexpected frost, the plants on Mrs. Kowalski's porch turned brown and died.

   A period is used to end a sentence that makes a statement.

   _____

2. Gary asked whether I had ever been to Disney World.

   _____

   _____

3. The scientist revealed his formula for success: perseverance, hard work, and a little luck.

   _____

   _____

4. The movie (which has set box-office records) contains scenes of extreme violence: two explosions, a hanging, and seventeen deaths by shooting.

   _____

   _____

5. The salesperson—who must have been in a bad mood that day—was surly and unhelpful.

   _____

   _____

6. Traffic was backed up for miles on the interstate; hundreds of cars and trucks had slowed to a crawl.

   _____

   _____

7. "Hey! Watch out for that open manhole!" the worker called to the pedestrian.

   _____

   _____

8. The company had offices in Seattle, Washington; London, England; and Tokyo, Japan.

   _____

   _____

9. The mailbox contained only two pieces of mail—a drugstore flyer and a credit card offer.

_____

_____

10. At 5:00 A.M., a garbage truck rumbled past Ed's house; Ed woke suddenly, wondering if he had remembered to take the trash to the curb.

_____

_____

REVIEW EXERCISE 2

Fill the blank(s) in each sentence with a period, question mark, exclamation point, semicolon, colon, dash (or dashes), or parentheses. On some questions, more than one answer may be possible. Be sure you can justify the answer you choose.

1. Dawn slammed on the brakes when the dog ___ a slow-moving basset hound ___ lumbered into the road.

_____

2. Steve could not remember the accident that had totaled his car and put him in the hospital, but he was sure of one thing ___ he was lucky to be alive.

_____

3. "Call 911 ___" yelled Andrea as she ran past the door.

_____

4. The lease states that any resident who has a pet ___ either a dog or a cat ___ must pay a nonrefundable pet deposit of two hundred dollars.

_____

5. "Do you mind if I cut in line ___ I have only two items," the woman said.

_____

6. The company's employees will be off on Thursday, November 27 ___ Friday, November 28 ___ Thursday, December 26 ___ and Friday, December 27.

_____

7. After Tiana loaded a new program ___ a virus scanner ___ on her computer, she felt safer downloading material from the Internet.

_____

8. "I won ___ I won ___" the red-haired woman yelled, waving her Bingo card in the air.

_____

9. The company vice president said that three things would kill a job candidate's chances ___ late arrival, poor language skills, and a sloppy appearance.

10. The woman rolled down her window and handed something ___ probably a dollar bill ___ to the man standing at the interstate exit.

REVIEW EXERCISE 3

In each sentence, add a period, question mark, exclamation point, semicolon, colon, dash (or dashes), or parentheses.

1. From the street, John could hear the persistent whoop of a car alarm

2. "Could you repeat the fourteen flavors of ice cream again" Millie asked the server.

3. The Simmonses were devastated when the house their first home together burned to the ground.

4. "Come out with your hands on your head" the police officer yelled.

5. After pulling a twelve-hour shift, Kelvin wanted only one thing sleep.

6. The headline read, "Con Artists Foiled in Aluminum Siding Scam"

7. The part for the dishwasher had to be ordered the salesperson said it would take two weeks.

8. William's parents told him he had two choices go to school or get a job.

9. "Why didn't you call me if you needed help" Natasha asked.

10. "Hey, mister, you left your wallet" the clerk called.

REVIEW EXERCISE 4

Fill in the blanks with the correct punctuation.

[1]When he twisted his knee playing softball, Jack made his own diagnosis __ just a muscle pull. [2]There was a sharp pain as he slid into second__when he tried to get up, he could not. [3]"We need help here__" the second baseman called, and his teammates came running to help him off the field. [4]"Do you want me to take you to the emergency room__" his coach asked. [5]But Jack insisted that all he needed was an ice pack and a good night's sleep__ [6]The next morning, Jack's knee was a rainbow of colors__mostly black, blue, and yellow__and was swollen to the size of a grapefruit. [7]He called a friend__his softball buddy Levon__to drive him to the doctor's office. [8]His doctor said nothing was broken but told Jack his softball days were over__at least for a while. [9]Now, Jack walks with the help of crutches__ [10]Jack won't be sliding into second for a while, but he will be at every game to support his teammates__

Apostrophes

A postrophe on a stick? It's true that when it comes to apostrophes, people are often not sure where to, well, *stick* them. In possessives, do they go before the *s*? After the *s*? This chapter will help you decide. In the meantime, be careful with that apostrophe-on-a-stick—you could put an eye out with that thing.

Apostrophes in Contractions

Contractions are informal or conversational shortenings of words: *doesn't* for *does not*, *won't* for *will not*, and *it's* for *it is* or *it has*. Contractions are used in informal writing, but are generally inappropriate for formal or scholarly writing. You will find them in some journalistic writing, in some textbooks, in works of fiction, and in informal essays. However, contractions are considered inappropriate in reports of academic research or in legal documents. Your instructor will specify the level of formality you should use in your essays and other writings.

To form a contraction, replace omitted letters with a single apostrophe. Close any spaces between words.

Examples

couldn't = could not

don't = do not

hasn't = has not

isn't = is not

won't = will not (Won't is an irregular contraction: The *i* in *will* changes to an *o*.)

wouldn't = would not

PRACTICE 1   FORMING CONTRACTIONS

Make a contraction of each expression. Be sure to place an apostrophe where letters are omitted, not in the space between the words.

1. she is   _____
2. I am   _____
3. would not   _____
4. does not   _____
5. he is   _____
6. it is   _____
7. we are   _____
8. I will   _____
9. they are   _____
10. cannot   _____

PRACTICE 2   USING CONTRACTIONS

Underline the error in each sentence. Then supply the missing apostrophe in the contraction and write the contraction in the blank provided.

_____ 1. Mariko says shes well enough to play in the hockey game next week.

_____ 2. Arthur hasnt applied for either of the jobs I told him about.

_____ 3. It isnt unusual for Tabitha to bring home dead birds and mice.

_____ 4. Its going to be hot and sunny tomorrow, just in time for our trip to the beach.

_____ 5. "After Ive found a job," said Roberta, "I have to worry about paying back my student loan."

_____ 6. "Sorry," said the teller, "but were not supposed to cash out-of-town checks."

_____ 7. "Isnt Karen planning to drop this class before midterm?" said Dean.

_____ 8. Art had no money, but he couldnt resist visiting the electronics store in the mall.

_____ 9. The children dont like couscous; they want hamburgers instead.

_____ 10. "Give me a minute," said Ella. "Ill be right back."

Apostrophes to Show Possession

If you could not use apostrophes to show possession, you would have to rely on long, tedious constructions such as "I drove the car of my father to the house of Ray to study for the test of tomorrow," instead of "I drove my father's car to Ray's house to study for tomorrow's test."

Making Nouns Possessive

There are two rules for making nouns possessive.

Rule 1: Add an apostrophe and *s* (*'s*) to form the possessive of singular nouns and of plurals that do not end in *s*.

Examples

the dish that belongs to the dog = the *dog's* dish
the pages of the magazine = the *magazine's* pages

the work of a day = a *day's* work
the flower garden belonging to Carlton = *Carlton's* flower garden
the toys that belong to the children = the *children's* toys
the office of my boss = my *boss's* office

PRACTICE 3   FORMING POSSESSIVES OF SINGULAR NOUNS

Convert the five expressions to possessives using *'s*.

1.   the glow of the flashlight = _____

2.   the blue shirt belonging to Charlie = _____

3.   the office of Dr. Bell = _____

4.   the career of the pianist = _____

5.   the schedule of next week = _____

* Grammar Alert!

When a singular word ends in *s*, it is also acceptable to use an apostrophe alone to make it possessive: *Mr. Jones'* job, *Dickens'* novels, the *boss'* office, the *crabgrass'* rapid growth.

Rule 2: If a plural noun already ends in *s*, add an apostrophe after the *s* to make it possessive.

Examples

the lawn belonging to the Smiths = the *Smiths'* lawn
the brightness of the stars = the *stars'* brightness

PRACTICE 4   FORMING POSSESSIVES OF PLURAL NOUNS

Convert the ten expressions to possessives using an apostrophe.

1.   the jobs of my sisters = _____

2.   the leashes of the dogs = _____

3.   the energy of the dancers = _____

4.   the determination of the athletes = _____

5.   the appearance of the cupcakes = _____

6.   the test grades of two classes = _____

7.   the keyboards of the computers = _____

8.   the overseas trip of the Joneses = _____

9.   the barking of the dogs = _____

10.   the movements of the actors = _____

PRACTICE 5   **FORMING POSSESSIVES OF SINGULAR AND PLURAL NOUNS**

Convert the ten expressions to possessives by adding *'s* or by adding an apostrophe after the *s*.

1.   the whir of the ceiling fan = _____

2.   the tick of the clock = _____

3.   the smiles of the children = _____

4.   the sale of Sports World = _____

5.   the disgust of Mrs. Bliss = _____

6.   the impact of the suggestion = _____

7.   the hairstyles of the women = _____

8.   the strong belief of Gina Terrino = _____

9.   the glow of the streetlights = _____

10.   the Web site of the college = _____

Distinguishing Possessives from Simple Plurals

To use apostrophes correctly, it is important to distinguish between possessives and simple plurals. A plural may be followed by a verb, a prepositional phrase, or by nothing at all. Words that show possession end in *s* like plurals, but they are immediately followed by something that is being possessed, as in "Mom's *homemade chicken and dumplings*" or the "*horse's mane.*"

Possessive (apostrophe used)	Plural (no apostrophe used)
a computer's hard drive	computers used in class
a day's work	days in a month
Mother's Day	Mothers Against Drunk Driving
a king's ransom	kings in the seventeenth century
the turtles' habitat	the mating habits of turtles
the tornadoes' fury	several tornadoes
the washer's spin cycle	the broken washers

PRACTICE 6   DISTINGUISHING POSSESSIVES FROM PLURALS

In each sentence, underline the noun that ends in *s'* or *'s*. If the noun is possessive, write *possessive* in the blank provided. If the noun is simply a plural, remove the apostrophe and write the corrected plural form in the blank. The first one is done for you.

parents   **1.** Sometimes I think my <u>parents</u>' are hopelessly old fashioned.

_____ **2.** The dog's expression was mournful.

_____ **3.** The speaker's voice was so soothing that Kim nearly fell asleep.

_____ **4.** Anthony visited several schools' before making his decision.

_____ **5.** Many years ago, most offices had typewriters' instead of computers.

_____ **6.** Amy had never liked the carpet's color.

_____ **7.** The Smith's host a neighborhood party every Fourth of July.

_____ **8.** The youngest employee in the library is thirty year's old.

_____ **9.** The manatee's large gray body moves gracefully in the water.

_____ **10.** The benefit's of a good breakfast include increased alertness and improved mental function during the morning hours.

Possessive Forms of Pronouns

Personal pronouns (*I, we, you, he, she, it,* and *they*) have their own possessive forms that never require an apostrophe. These forms include *my, mine, our, ours, your, yours, his, hers, its, their,* and *theirs*.

The pronoun that is the focus of the most confusion is *its*. Since the possessive form of a pronoun never takes an apostrophe, *its* is the possessive form, meaning *belonging to it*. *It's*, the form with the apostrophe, always means *it is* or *it has*.

Examples

The lawnmower seems to have lost *its* pep. (belonging to it)

It's too hot to mow, anyway. (it is)

That old paring knife has outlived *its* usefulness. (belonging to it)

It's time to buy a replacement. (it is)

PRACTICE 7 **CORRECTING APOSTROPHE ERRORS WITH *ITS* AND *IT'S***

Underline and correct the apostrophe errors in the following sentences.

1. "Its essential that you come to class every day," Professor Vanta told the class.

   _____

2. The house was old, and it's owner had not painted or repaired it for many years.

   _____

3. Ted is committed to getting in shape; its his first priority.

   _____

4. The salmon swiftly made it's way upstream.

   _____

5. Because Lindsay has not had time to finish her report, its sitting unfinished on her desk.

   _____

Proofreading for Apostrophe Errors

Apostrophes Incorrectly Omitted from Possessives

To find apostrophes incorrectly omitted from possessives, check each noun ending in *s* to see if it is followed by something it possesses.

✗ The *cars brakes* made a squealing sound whenever Vashti came to a stop.

Cars is followed by the word *brakes*. Do *brakes* belong to *cars*? Yes. But does the apostrophe go before or after the *s*? Look for clues to whether the original word (before it was made possessive) was intended to be singular or plural. The main clue in this sentence lies in the words *whenever Vashti came to a stop*. There is one driver, therefore also one car.

Brakes is followed by *made*, a verb, so it is plural, not possessive.

✔ The car's brakes made a squealing sound whenever Vashti came to a stop.

✗ The *employees paychecks* were small, but their work was strenuous.

Does anything belong to *employees*? Yes, *paychecks* belong to *employees*, but does the apostrophe go before or after the *s*? Since there is more than one paycheck, and since the pronoun *their* is used to refer to employees, the word *employees* is clearly plural. Therefore, the apostrophe goes after the *s*.

Does anything belong to *paychecks*? No, a verb follows the word, so *paychecks* is simply a plural.

✔ The employees' paychecks were small, but their work was strenuous.

PRACTICE 8   CORRECTING APOSTROPHE ERRORS

Supply the omitted apostrophe in each of the following sentences.

1. The driveways concrete surface had cracked in several places.

   _____

2. The speakers voice could not be heard clearly in the back of the auditorium.

   _____

3. The books ending was disappointing to many of its readers.

   _____

4. Sam and Elaine said they spent two weeks salary in one weekend.

   _____

5. The doctor said Elizabeths shoulder should begin to feel better in about two weeks.

   _____

Apostrophes Placed Incorrectly in Possessives

An incorrectly placed apostrophe is usually a confusion of singular and plural. As you proofread, target words ending in *'s* or *s'* and look for clues that tell you whether the word is singular or plural.

✗ For the landowner, the *tree's* beauty outweighed their value as lumber.

The pronoun *their* suggests more than one tree.

✔ For the landowner, the trees' beauty outweighed their value as lumber.

✗ The *buildings'* roof leaked and was in need of repair.

Only one roof is mentioned, so there is just one building.

✔ The building's roof leaked and was in need of repair.

PRACTICE 9   CORRECTING APOSTROPHE ERRORS

Underline and correct the apostrophe errors in the following sentences.

1. The airplanes' wings glinted in the sunlight as it flew overhead.

   _____

2. The twin's grade point averages are nearly identical.

   _____

3. Andre swept a days' accumulation of litter and cigarette butts from the side-walk in front of the restaurant.

   _____

4. At her husbands' urging, Valerie decided to enroll in college.

   _____

5. As the tennis player's skills improved, they enjoyed the game more.

   _____

Review Exercises

Complete the Review Exercises to see how well you have learned the skills addressed in this chapter. As you work through the exercises, go back through the chapter to review any of the rules you do not understand completely.

REVIEW EXERCISE 1

Convert the ten expressions in the exercise to possessives using 's or an apostrophe.

1. the beam of the searchlight = _____

2. the call of a mockingbird = _____

3. the opening of the museum = _____

4. the covers of the books = _____

5. the weed trimmer belonging to Jacob = _____

6. the craters of the moon = _____

7. a rest of three days = _____

8. the voice of Ms. Bradshaw = _____

9. the route of the truck driver = _____

10. the faded color of the blankets = _____

REVIEW EXERCISE 2

Each sentence has an omitted apostrophe in a contraction or a possessive form. Underline the error; then, in the blank, write the word with the apostrophe placed correctly.

_____ 1. After turning his ankle, Allen couldnt complete his run.

_____ 2. The restaurants lunch menu featured a variety of homemade soups.

_____ 3. Using an ice pack helped to ease the pain in Ronitas knee.

_____ 4. The tabloids headline read, "I Married a Space Alien!"

_____ 5. Amin stood on a dock at the rivers edge and watched the sun set.

_____ 6. "Work is important," said Dana. "But its my family that really matters."

_____ 7. Memos, notes, and papers entirely covered the desks surface.

_____ 8. The office buildings immense lobby was obviously created to impress visitors.

_____ 9. The letter said that Freds car payment was overdue.

_____ 10. A pirates treasure was said to be buried on one of the small islands.

REVIEW EXERCISE 3

Each sentence contains two omitted apostrophes. Underline the error; then, in the blank, write the words with the apostrophes placed correctly.

1. Phillip says that he hasnt had a good nights sleep in two weeks.

   _____

2. The hospitals smoke alarms were checked twice a month for the patients safety.

   _____

3. To the children waiting for Santas arrival, the clocks hands seemed to move slowly.

   _____

4. The students grades were not high enough for their instructors satisfaction.

   _____

5. "Ive put in two days work on this group project and not one person has helped me," Melissa said angrily.

   _____

REVIEW EXERCISE 4

Each numbered item contains two apostrophe errors, one omitted apostrophe in a contraction or a possessive form and one misplaced or unnecessary apostrophe. Underline the error; then write the correct form of each word below.

1. Lees garage is piled high with tools and bag's of fertilizer.

   _____

2. "Its been warm for October," said Max. "Usually, temperature's are in the fifties by now."

   _____

3. An old sofa and several bundles of clothes' sat on the porch, awaiting the Goodwill trucks arrival.

   _____

4. The cough remedys price was high, but it's performance was disappointing.

   _____

5. Tom said his VCRs feature's include a remote control and a preprogramming feature that he has never learned how to use.

   _____

REVIEW EXERCISE 5

Underline and correct the ten apostrophe errors in the restaurant review, writing your answers in the numbered spaces. Each numbered section of the review contains one error. Apostrophes may be misplaced, missing, or unnecessary.

[1]Restaurant Review: Eds R. K. Café

[2]When I told a friend I was reviewing Ed's R. K. Café on Interstate Drive, he whispered, "No! Havent you heard the rumors about how Ed gets his meat?" [3]I told my friend that rumor's were common in small towns, and I offered to treat him to dinner and put those rumors to rest. [4]There were no line's on Monday night at Ed's, and as we sat down, Ed himself came in with a large cloth sack. [5]He looked surprised to see customers but said, "Youre lucky I was just bringing in some groceries." [6]I decided on Steak Michelin, which I assumed to be a French dish, and ordered "Sunday Drivers Stew" for my friend, who had suddenly excused himself from the table. [7]When it came, the Steak Michelin, pounded very flat with some sort of tool that left an attractive zigzag pattern on it's surface, met all my expectations. [8]My friends' stew smelled delicious, and looked as if it contained several kinds of meat, but he said he was not feeling well and that he could not eat. [9]In any case, its a pleasure to recommend Ed's, which is close enough to the highway to be convenient for everyone. [10]Service is slow, but worth the wait, and the meat taste's wonderfully fresh.

1. _____

2. _____

3. _____

4. _____

5. _____

6. _____

7. _____

8. _____

9. _____

10. _____

CHAPTER 27

Quotation Marks

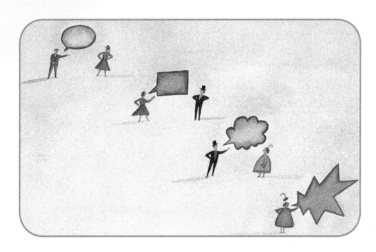

"Can I quote you?"

Quotation marks are visual signals that give a reader information that would otherwise have to be conveyed in words. They are a kind of acdemic shorthand that says, "Someone else wrote, said, or thought these words" or "These words are the title of a short work." Underlining and italics say, "These words are the title of a long work." Learning to use quotation marks, underlining, and italics adds another dimension to your ability to communicate within the academic world.

Quotation Marks to Signal Quotations

Direct Quotations

Quotation marks are used to signal direct quotation; that is, they are placed around the exact words that someone speaks, writes, or thinks. As you look at the examples, notice that when a comma or period comes at the end of a quotation, it is always placed inside the quotation mark. When a direct question is quoted, the question mark also goes inside the quotation marks.

Examples

"I'll pick up the dry cleaning on my way home," said Pat.

Keiko said, "I don't need to go to the gym. I stay in shape lugging all these books around the campus."

The child asked, "Why don't people have wings?"

"Did you bring the doughnuts?" asked David.

PRACTICE 1   USING QUOTATION MARKS WITH DIRECT QUOTATIONS

Place quotation marks around direct quotations.

1. I am sorry I'm late, said Al.

    _____

2. Is this something we need to know for the test? Karen asked the professor.

    _____

3. The bumper sticker said, If you can read this, thank a teacher.

    _____

4. Alicia said, I think there's a gas station at the next exit.

    _____

5. I get a headache whenever it rains, complained Rosa.

    _____

Split Quotations

Some direct quotations are split quotations. Below are two rules for splitting quotations.

1. When you split a sentence, use commas to set off the *tag* (such as *she said*) that tells who said, thought, or wrote the words you are quoting.

   "When you come through the door," Raven told her son, "please try not to slam it."

2. When there is a complete sentence before and a complete sentence after the tag, put a comma after the first sentence and a period after the tag.

   "I couldn't turn in my paper yesterday," Alex told the professor. "I wasn't here."

PRACTICE 2 USING QUOTATION MARKS AND COMMAS WITH DIRECT QUOTATIONS

Place quotation marks around direct quotations, and add commas where they are needed.

1. Your stock clerks need to be more careful the customer told the manager. This milk was expired when I bought it.

   _____

   _____

2. My job as a human cannonball is great said the circus performer. Business is booming.

   _____

   _____

3. If you can't say something nice Aunt Dolly said come over here and talk to me.

   _____

   _____

4. You have won third prize in a beauty contest the Monopoly card read. Collect $10.

   _____

   _____

5. For Mother's Day this year Charlotte told her husband I'd like a day of peace and quiet.

   _____

   _____

PRACTICE 3   USING QUOTATION MARKS AND COMMAS WITH DIRECT QUOTATIONS

Place quotation marks around direct quotations, and add commas or question marks as needed.

1. Are you new to this area the real estate agent asked.

   _____

   _____

2. I hate roller coasters said Anthony. I am afraid of heights.

   _____

   _____

3. Spreading his arms wide, the singer shouted Hello, Philadelphia!

   _____

   _____

4. I know you love your hunting dogs Janice told her husband but do we have to take them on vacation with us?

   _____

   _____

5. You have been preapproved for a $10,000 line of credit the letter began.

   _____

   _____

Indirect Quotations

An **indirect quotation** is a paraphrase. It repeats the essence of what a person said. It may repeat some or all of the words, but it is not a word-for-word quotation. The word *that* is stated or implied before an indirect quotation. An indirect quotation is not set off by quotation marks.

Examples

Ashley said that she needed a vacation.

Ashley said she needed a vacation.

The two examples above are indirect quotations. They do not repeat Ashley's exact words (Ashley did not use the word *she*). The word *that* is stated in the first example and implied in the second. Therefore, no quotation marks are used.

PRACTICE 4   IDENTIFYING DIRECT AND INDIRECT QUOTATIONS

On the line provided, label each quotation as direct (*D*) or indirect (*I*).

_____ 1. Ellen said, "I would have caught the ball if the sun had not been in my eyes."

_____ 2. Ellen said that she would have caught the ball if the sun had not been in her eyes.

_____ 3. The customer in the drive-through said he wanted extra ketchup.

_____ 4. The bumper sticker said, "In case of alien abduction, driver's seat will be empty."

_____ 5. "If you are going to lunch," said Zoe, "would you bring back a sandwich for me?"

_____ 6. Brandon said, "Here, Mom. I made this clay volcano for you."

_____ 7. Jan asked, "Has anyone watered the fern?"

_____ 8. Jan asked if anyone had watered the fern.

_____ 9. The salesperson told Bill that the tires should last for the life of the car.

_____ 10. Brad said that he could live without his car but could not get along without his bike.

PRACTICE 5   WORKING WITH DIRECT AND INDIRECT QUOTATIONS

On the line provided, label each quotation as direct (*D*) or indirect (*I*). Place quotation marks around direct quotations, and leave indirect quotations as they are.

_____ 1. Ray said, Mr. Bartlett, I can work nights but not weekends.

_____

_____ 2. Ray told Mr. Bartlett that he could work nights but not weekends.

_____

_____ 3. The headline read, Too Few Americans Exercise.

_____

_____ 4. Two out of three people surveyed said they were better off financially than they had been last year.

_____

_____ 5. Perry said, I wish I could afford a new truck.

_____

_____ 6. The article said Americans receive fewer vacation days than Europeans do.

_____

_____ 7. The child said she knew nothing about the broken cookie jar.

_____

_____ 8. I'm not in the mood to watch a video, said Theo.

_____

_____ 9. Would you like dessert? asked the server.

_____

_____ 10. The salesperson said that she could order any color we wanted.

_____

Quotation Marks, Underlining, and Italics to Set off Titles

Quotation marks, underlining, and italics act as academic shorthand to signal a title. Quotation marks are used around titles of short works or works that are contained within other works. The following types of titles are set off by quotation marks:

> *** Grammar Alert!**
>
> When you write *about* an essay, place the title of the essay within quotation marks. When you type the title of *your* essay on a cover sheet or at the head of the essay, do not use quotation marks.

1. Chapter title (short works contained within a longer work)
    "Subject-Verb Agreement"
    "Sentence Variety"
2. Essays
    "Barbie Madness"
    "Neat People vs. Sloppy People"
3. Individual episodes of a TV series (short works contained within the longer series)

"Phil Silvers: Top Banana" (in the series Biography)

"The Slicer" (an episode of Seinfeld)

4. Song titles (short works, often contained within a longer album of works)

"The Star-Spangled Banner"

"Georgia on My Mind"

5. Newspaper articles

"NFL injury list grows"

"Hungry for housing"

6. Poems

"I Wandered Lonely as a Cloud"

"Fern Hill"

7. Short stories

"Sonny's Blues"

"The Ones Who Walk Away from Omelas"

Underlining and italics are used to set off the title of a long work, a continuing work (such as a comic strip or television series), or a complete published work such as a pamphlet or brochure. Use underlining or italics with the following types of titles:

---

* Grammar Alert!

Italics are used instead of underlining in published materials, and modern word processors have italic capability. However, the MLA (Modern Language Association) recommends underlining for clarity.

---

1. Books

<u>The Color Purple</u>

<u>There Are No Accidents</u>

2. Comic strips (a series containing individual daily or weekly strips)

<u>Dilbert</u>

<u>Jumpstart</u>

3. Newspapers

<u>The New York Times</u>

<u>The Macon Telegraph and News</u>

4. Anthologies (collections) of poetry or short stories

<u>The Poem: An Anthology</u>

<u>Discovering Literature: Stories, Poems, Plays</u>

5. Compact discs

<u>La Pipa de la Paz</u>

<u>Hung Down Head</u>

6. Television programs

<u>Pop-Up Video</u>

<u>Inside the Actors Studio</u>

7. Movies

<u>E.T.</u>

<u>Titanic</u>

PRACTICE 6   USING QUOTATION MARKS AND UNDERLINING WITH TITLES

In each sentence, use quotation marks and underlining to set off titles.

1. Tonight's episode of Wild Discovery is entitled Cheetah.

_____

2. For next week, the professor assigned a chapter called Using Critical Thinking Skills in the book College Success.

_____

3. Rita's favorite song on Joan Baez: From Every Stage is Love Is Just a Four-Letter Word.

_____

4. From a book called Poetry: An Introduction, the class read The Ballad of Birmingham by Dudley Randall.

_____

5. The headline in the Wall Street Journal read Economy on the right track, but Sam did not feel any richer.

_____

Review Exercises

Complete the Review Exercises to see how well you have learned the skills addressed in this chapter. As you work through the exercises, go back through the chapter to review any of the rules you do not understand completely.

REVIEW EXERCISE 1

Rewrite the following sentences, placing quotation marks around direct quotations.

1. I need just one extra hour in the day, said Althea.

    _____

    _____

2. Patrick Henry said, Give me liberty or give me death.

    _____

    _____

3. I wish people wouldn't throw trash out their car windows, said Alphonso, especially since most of it seems to land in my yard.

    _____

    _____

4. You should have been at the game, said Claudius. We won fourteen to two.

    _____

    _____

5. The car's bumper sticker read, I may be slow, but I'm ahead of you.

    _____

    _____

6. The slip of paper in Gaia's fortune cookie said, Wherever you go, there you are.

    _____

    _____

7. I am sorry your goldfish died, said Andi's mother. Let's hold its funeral in the bathroom so we can send it back to the sea.

    _____

    _____

8. Let's pick up a copy of *Consumer Reports* before we buy a washer, said Nicole.

_____

_____

9. I like Joseph, but he's not very reliable, said Paula.

_____

_____

10. I wish I could lose weight without dieting, Betty sighed.

_____

_____

REVIEW EXERCISE 2

Rewrite the following sentences, placing quotation marks around direct quotations. Four of the sentences are indirect quotations that do not require quotation marks.

1. The loan officer told Brad and Lexie that she hoped they hadn't had to wait too long.

_____

_____

2. Why are your paws so wet? Alfreda asked her dog.

_____

_____

3. If he could have talked, Alfreda's dog might have said that he had walked through a puddle on the way home.

_____

_____

4. When she came back from the All-Night Moonlight Sale-a-Thon, Bernice said, Never again.

_____

_____

5. What is this disgusting-looking bug? asked Phillip.

_____

_____

6. Patrick said he had already finished his paper.

_____

_____

7. If I have to eat spaghetti one more time, said Nick, I'll turn into a meatball.

    _____

    _____

8. Too late, said his wife.

    _____

    _____

9. I've got it, said the worker as he grabbed one end of the sofa.

    _____

    _____

10. The disk jockey said that he would play audience requests for the next two hours.

    _____

    _____

REVIEW EXERCISE 3

Correct the following sentences, using underlining or quotation marks to set off titles.

1. Wendy took out a library book called Cold Mountain.

    _____

    _____

2. Before Chet left for the video store, his wife said she would leave him if he rented Men in Black again.

    _____

    _____

3. Chapter 10, Taking Care of Yourself, discusses stress and nutrition.

    _____

    _____

4. Meghan's Irish grandfather believes there's no sweeter sound than Danny Boy sung by an Irish tenor.

    _____

    _____

5. Luis bought an album by Los Fabulosos Cadillacs called Fabulosos Calavera.

    _____

    _____

6. Derek swears there is a country song called If My Nose Were Full of Nickels, I'd Blow It All on You.

   _____

   _____

7. The Complete Works of Shakespeare, Bjorn's text for English 210, must weigh at least ten pounds.

   _____

   _____

8. After new special effects were added to the 1970s movie Star Wars, it was brought out again for a new generation.

   _____

   _____

9. When it came out, the movie Titanic broke box-office records.

   _____

   _____

10. A small headline at the top of the page said No clues in hit and run.

    _____

    _____

REVIEW EXERCISE 4

In the following sentence groups, place quotation marks around direct quotations. Use underlining or quotation marks to set off titles. Do not place indirect quotations in quotation marks.

1. Karen said her trip over spring break was a disaster. The hotel claimed to have no record of our reservation, she said.

   _____

   _____

2. Give me just a minute to finish getting ready, said Aimee. You've already had an hour, said her husband.

   _____

   _____

3. Chloe bought a bumper sticker that read, I Never Eat Anything with a Face. That's disgusting, said Chloe's mother.

    _____

    _____

    _____

4. David clipped an article called Walk off pounds for good from Tuesday's paper. The article said that people who combine diet with exercise keep weight off longer than those who only diet.

    _____

    _____

    _____

5. Yesterday, Sophie bought a book called The Complete Idiot's Guide to Reaching Your Goals. It sounds like it was written just for you, her friend joked.

    _____

    _____

    _____

Eight Editing Exercises

**EDITING EXERCISE 1   Words Commonly Confused,
Fragments, Run-ons,
and Subject-Verb Agreement**

Find and correct the ten sentence errors in the paragraph below. In the blanks provided, write the number of the sentence in which you find each error, followed by your correction. Two of the sentences are correct.

2 errors in words commonly confused

2 sentence fragments

2 run-on sentences

4 subject-verb agreement errors

[1]I read an article not long ago that claimed that the weather effects the human body. [2]Since I can link both my headaches and my moods to the weather. [3]I can support the claim made by the author of the article. [4]My headaches begins with the drop in barometric pressure that precedes a storm. [5]The clouds roll in a throbbing pain that no aspirin can completely relieve begins on one side of my head. [6]As soon as the clouds dissipate. [7]My headache slips away like a forgotten memory. [8]Additionally, winter affect my state of mind like no other season. [9]With the falling of the leaves, my generally upbeat attitude begins to fall as well I slide into a gloomy mood. [10]According to the article, the changes in my mood is symptomatic of a condition called Seasonal Affective Disorder, or SAD. [11]Plenty of sunshine eventually lift my spirits. [12]The whether does play an important role in my well-being.

1. _____

2. _____

3. _____

4. _____

5. _____

6. _____

7. _____

8. _____

9. _____

10. _____

11. _____

12. _____

**EDITING EXERCISE 2   Commas, Words Commonly
Confused, and Comma Splices**

Find and correct the ten sentence errors in the paragraph below. Each sentence
contains an error.

1 comma omitted after introductory element

2 commas omitted in a series of three items

3 errors in words commonly confused

4 comma splices

[1]When I look back over the jobs I've held none of them taught
me more about responsibility and hard work than my summer job at
Tossi's Bakery. [2]My principle responsibility was to arrive at the
bakery at 5:20 every morning and prepare the machines and
the ingredients for the baker. [3]One Saturday morning I turned off the
alarm rolled over for just one more minute under the covers, and
drifted back to sleep. [4]On that day, disappointed customers did not
get there fresh bread and breakfast rolls when the bakery opened
at 7:00. [5]Ashamed of my irresponsibility, I promised Mr. Tossi that
I would never be late again, I never was. [6]I also learned too perform
hard physical work. [7]I hauled huge sacks of flour, sugar and other
ingredients from the storehouse in the back of the bakery to a
platform near the large machines that blended the ingredients into
dough. [8]At first, I dragged myself home each day and barely moved
until the next morning, however, I soon adjusted to the hard work.
[9]The huge bags of flour seemed lighter, the workday no longer
seemed to last forever. [10]My job at the bakery lasted just one summer, it
helped mold me into the responsible person that I am today.

1. _____   6. _____

2. _____   7. _____

3. _____   8. _____

4. _____   9. _____

5. _____   10. _____

EDITING EXERCISE 3   Apostrophes, Commas, Subject-Verb Agreement

Find and correct the ten sentence errors in the paragraph below. Each sentence contains an error.

1 apostrophe error

3 commas omitted after introductory element

6 subject-verb agreement errors

[1]At one time, seasonal displays and products appeared on retailers shelves near their actual season. [2]Halloween costumes and candy, for example, was placed on shelves a month or so before pint-sized ghosts and witches canvassed the neighborhood in search of as much sugar as they could carry. [3]In mid-January Valentine candy would appear, allowing sufficient time for children to purchase boxes of pastel conversation hearts and for adults to buy heart-shaped boxes of chocolate. [4]Traditionally Christmas displays appeared only after the Thanksgiving turkey had been digested. [5]Lately, however, stores seems to have lost their sense of time. [6]Halloween costumes and candy is on display from Labor Day through the end of October. [7]Christmas catalogs and advertisements begins to arrive in mailboxes in September. [8]By October, Christmas merchandise slowly appear on store shelves. [9]When Christmas items are removed in late December, the red hearts of Valentine's Day appears. [10]For retailers every day is a holiday.

1. _____   6. _____

2. _____   7. _____

3. _____   8. _____

4. _____   9. _____

5. _____   10. _____

EDITING EXERCISE 4   Pronoun Point of View, Pronoun Agreement, Subject-Verb Agreement, Pronoun Case

Find and correct the ten sentence errors in the paragraph below. Each sentence contains an error.

2 shifts in pronoun point of view

3 pronoun agreement errors

4 subject-verb agreement errors

1 pronoun case error

^{1}As an intern for a television station, I see firsthand how strangely some people behave when you point a camera at them. ^{2}Once, when I accompanied the camera crew to a local mall, we had trouble interviewing the manager because of all the teenagers who stood behind him, waving, grinning, and yelling out comments as if he or she were the reason the cameras were there. ^{3}Among my favorite assignments is street interviews. ^{4}When the interviewer tries to stop someone on the street to ask them a question, some people just shake their heads and walk on. ^{5}Other people look at their shoes and mumbles the briefest possible answer. ^{6}There is always at least one star-quality interviewee who looks directly into the camera and gives a polished answer that sounds as if they have rehearsed it for hours. ^{7}But the strangest people of all are the ones who act as if they has something to hide. ^{8}Once, when the camera operator and me were setting up the camera for the shot, a man covered his face with his jacket and actually ran from us. ^{9}Other camera-shy people cross the street to avoid you, as if they are afraid of being recognized on TV. ^{10}If there is one thing I have learned during my internship, it is that the sight of a TV crew and cameras make some people behave strangely.

1. _____   6. _____

2. _____   7. _____

3. _____   8. _____

4. _____   9. _____

5. _____   10. _____

EDITING EXERCISE 5 Subject-Verb Agreement, Pronoun Agreement, Comma Splices, Fragments, End Punctuation, Semicolons

Find and correct the ten sentence errors in the paragraph below. In the blanks provided, write the number of each sentence in which you find an error, followed by your correction. Two of the sentences are correct.

4 subject-verb agreement errors
1 pronoun agreement error
1 comma splice
2 sentence fragments
1 error in punctuation at the end of a sentence
1 semicolon error

[1]Reality television programming may be popular, it is anything but realistic. [2]One unrealistic version of reality TV involve a family living in a situation from the past. [3]Members of a family is placed in a Victorian mansion, a cabin in the woods, or a mud hut and expected to live as their ancestors did hundreds of years ago. [4]In the age of computers and microwaveable dinners, what is realistic about foraging for berries or pounding out laundry on a rock or an old-fashioned washboard. [5]Still another version of reality programming show the lives of celebrities. [6]On an episode of one show, a former model and her decorator, who is redoing the star's bedroom in pink and leopard, has a conference. [7]Then the celebrity and her entourage take off in a limo to Las Vegas. [8]Where she and her entourage stay in a huge hotel suite and visit casinos, bars, and strip clubs. [9]For most people; however, reality does not involve limos, decorators, or a lavish lifestyle. [10]True reality TV would follow a commuter through heavy traffic or show a parent rushing to get their children off to school. [11]Strangely enough, a true reality program might also feature people sitting in front of the TV. [12]And watching silly shows.

1. _____

2. _____

3. _____

4. _____

5. _____

6. _____

7. _____

8. _____

9. _____

10. _____

11. _____

12. _____

EDITING EXERCISE 6   Pronoun Case, Pronoun Reference, Irregular Verbs, Verb Tense, Quotation Marks, Comma Splices

Find and correct the ten sentence errors in the paragraph below. Each sentence contains an error.

1 pronoun case error

2 pronoun reference errors

4 errors in irregular verb form

1 shift in verb tense from past to present

1 error in quotation marks

1 comma splice

^{1}Walking around the block in my tree-lined neighborhood, I seen a white kitten sitting in the shade of an oak. ^{2}The kitten took one look at me, mewed piteously, and begun to follow me. ^{3}By the time I reached the end of the block, she is snuggling against my shoulder as I carefully carried her along. ^{4}I knew my husband did not want another cat, but by the time I reached my front door, I had figured out a way around this. ^{5}I sat the kitten on the porch and opened the door, saying to my husband, "Look what followed me home." ^{6}The kitten, later to be called Prudence, stretched her neck, taken a peek inside the living room, and bleated a cry for help. ^{7}My husband asked Did she really follow you all that way? ^{8}"I'll bet someone dumped her on the side of the road, and then they just drove off," I said, not answering his question. ^{9}My husband and me fed Prudence on the front porch for the next several days, just in case a neighbor knocked on our door to reclaim the kitten. ^{10}The knock on the door never came, Prudence entered the living room on the fourth day and never looked back.

1. _____

2. _____

3. _____

4. _____

5. _____

6. _____

7. _____

8. _____

9. _____

10. _____

EDITING EXERCISE 7   Capitalization, Verb Shifts,
Subject-Verb Agreement, Words
Commonly Confused, Adjectives
and Adverbs, Comma Splices,
Run-ons, Fragments

Find and correct the ten sentence errors in the paragraph below. Each sentence contains one error.

1 capitalization error
1 verb shift from past to present
1 subject-verb agreement error
2 errors in words commonly confused
1 confusion of adjective and adverb
1 comma splice
1 run-on sentence
2 sentence fragments

[1]Greek mythology shows that ancient greek gods took terrible revenge on those who opposed or displeased them. [2]When Tantalus, son of Zeus, displeased the gods, he was condemned to float for eternity in a beautifully lake. [3]If he bent to drink from the clear, sparkling water, it recedes from him. [4]If he reached for the luscious grapes hanging overhead. [5]They stayed just out of reach. Sisyphus displeased the gods by telling their secrets he was taught the meaning of frustration. [6]His task for all the years of eternity were to roll a huge, heavy rock up a steep hill. [7]When he had almost reached the top, the rock would invariably break loose and roll to the bottom, poor Sisyphus had to start again. [8]Arachne bragged that she could weave more skillfully than the gods theirselves. [9]She was sentenced to spend eternity spinning beautiful webs as a eight-legged spider. [10]With gods so cruel and imaginative. [11]It is a wonder that even mythological characters dared to oppose them.

1. _____

2. _____

3. _____

4. _____

5. _____

6. _____

7. _____

8. _____

9. _____

10. _____

EDITING EXERCISE 8   Fragments, Comma Splices, Words Commonly Confused, Run-ons, Apostrophes, Verb Shifts, and Irregular Verb Forms

Find and correct the twenty sentence errors in the essay below. In the blanks provided, write the number of each sentence in which you find an error, followed by your correction.

6 sentence fragments

2 comma splices

3 words commonly confused

3 run-on sentences

1 apostrophe error

2 unnecessary shifts from past to present

3 irregular verb form errors

¹When my wife and I were first married. ²I tried to interest her in fishing. ³I enthusiastically planned a Saturday trip to Waller Mill Pond, my favorite fishing spot. ⁴On the pond, only small electric motors were permitted large, noisy motors might frighten the fish and keep them from biting. ⁵Quiet, I explained to Maria, was essential for fishing, once we were on the pond, we would speak only in whispers. ⁶Maria did not seem very eager, I was sure that once we were out on the pond, she would enjoy fishing as much as I did. ⁷Little did I know that our first fishing trip together would also be our last.

⁸Saturday morning was perfect for fishing. ⁹Maria had seemed a little grumpy when I woke her at 5:00 A.M., but she smiled as I silently pointed to a group of ducks gliding across the ponds glass-like surface and a beaver gnawing a thick sapling near the banks of the pond. ¹⁰Tall pines lined the steep walls of the hills surrounding the pond, and the piece was

broken only by the occasional "ker-plop" of a fish jumping. [11]When I showed Maria the fat worms that I would use to bait the hook, she wrinkled her nose and turns away with a small exclamation of disgust. [12]I put a finger across my lips to remind her to be quiet she shot me an annoyed look. [13]Then reached for the paperback she had brought with her.

[14]I could hardly wait to get my line in the water. [15]I chosen a particularly fat and lively worm and baited the hook for my first cast. [16]I brought the fishing rod high above my head and flipped the rod to cast the hook the line never hit the water. [17]I felt resistance on the line and simultaneously heard a ear-shattering scream. [18]I had hooked Maria. [19]At the sound of her scream, the ducks spread there wings, lifting themselves above the noise. [20]The plump beaver looks up in alarm and waddled hurriedly into the water. [21]Maria was looking at her arm in horror, and I thought the hook had sank deeply into her flesh. [22]Luckily, the hook had only caught on her wristwatch. [23]Her horror was caused by the fat, slimy, and entirely harmless worm squirming on her arm. [24]After removing the hook from Maria's wristwatch and the worm from her arm. [25]I cast my line again. [26]However, at the sound of the scream. [27]The fish had undoubtedly fled to the shelter of the rocks and reeds below the surface of the pond. [28]Since the fish had swam off and Maria was still in an unusually grumpy mood, I decided it was time to head for home.

[29]On Saturdays, I still head to my special fishing spot, but I go without Maria. [30]Whenever I invite her to fish with me, she seems to have a shopping trip she can't put off. [31]Or an urgent need to visit her sister. [32]When I leave the house at 5:30 A.M. on a Saturday. [33]I am sad to think Maria is wasting her morning snuggled under the covers. [34]She does not know what she is missing.

_____   _____

_____   _____

_____   _____

_____   _____

_____   _____

_____   _____

_____   _____

_____   _____

_____   _____

PART 3

Readings

Barbie Madness

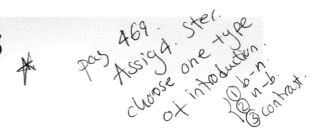

Cynthia Tucker

Since the 1950s, Barbie has been a part of the American culture. But critics say that Barbie is just one of the cultural influences that encourages young girls to pursue an impossible standard of physical beauty. Should parents worry? Cynthia Tucker explores the issue.

When I was 9 or 10, I was <u>steeped</u> in Barbie madness. So much so that I joined the Barbie fan club. My mother still has the membership document displaying my careful cursive writing alongside the scrawled block letters of a younger sister.

Too old to play with baby dolls, I was developing a <u>vicarious interest</u> in high fashion—a world to which Barbie allowed me access. Her overpriced collection of clothes included everything from bridal gowns to swimsuits, all accented by stiletto heels. In fact, her feet were permanently arched so that she could not wear sensible shoes.

She wore sheath dresses, capri pants, long gowns. She never got dirty; she never burst a seam (she never bent, of course); she never tripped over those heels.

Nor did she ever cause me to believe I would see many real women in the real world who looked or dressed like that. I had never seen a grown woman on the beach in high heels, and if I had—even at 10—I would have thought her nuts. Barbie was fantasy, one of the joyous escapes offered by childhood. My Barbie, white and brunette, never symbolized what I thought anyone ought to look like.

After nearly four decades of building a doll with a figure that, by one estimate, gives her measurements of 38-18-34, Mattel is preparing to release a new Barbie of less <u>fantastic</u> proportions. Many parents are breathing a sigh of relief that their daughters will no longer be subjected to such an unrealistic—and possibly damaging—cultural <u>icon</u>. Well, I have good news and bad news for those parents.

The bad news is, there will always be damaging cultural icons, plenty of unrealistic representations of women that emphasize youth and a weird voluptuousness/thinness, the combination of which defies physiology. If you think Barbie is the last of them, check out the *Sports Illustrated* swimsuit issue. Check out *Baywatch*. (The syndicated show sells well around the world. Sexism needs little translation.)

Now, for the good news: Parents will always have more influence over their children than any doll, any model, any magazine, any movie. Perhaps even more than their children's peers. Don't take my word for it—scientific research has confirmed it.

A recent study found that no matter a teenager's economic background, a 8
close-knit family helps prevent risky behavior and encourages educational excel-
lence. Might not attentive parents also provide protection against the sexist
influences that permeate the culture?

Children learn not just from their parents' rhetoric, but also from their 9
behavior. When a father leaves his family for a younger and more glamorous trophy wife, he gives his children a much more profound lesson about the value of
women than Barbie ever could. So does the mother who constantly applauds her
adolescent daughter's popularity with boys.

Years ago, Barbie's wardrobe evolved beyond *haute couture* to include profes- 10
sional attire. She also became more ethnically diverse. Now, the doll will get a little nip-and-tuck that widens her waist and de-emphasizes her chest (a bit).

But no matter what she looks like, Barbie will never be as important a role 11
model as Mom and Dad are. When Dad coaches his daughter's soccer team or helps
her build a treehouse, he gives her a measure of her worth that overshadows even
Barbie's bustline.

Building Vocabulary

For each question, choose the meaning that most closely defines the
underlined word or phrase as it is used in the essay.

1. The word steeped most nearly means
   a. drenched.
   b. made vertical.
   c. forced.
   d. indifferent.
2. The phrase a vicarious interest most nearly means
   a. an obsession that excludes everything else.
   b. a lukewarm interest.
   c. something that is enjoyed indirectly, through another person or
      thing.
   d. a dangerous interest.
3. The word fantastic most nearly means
   a. unreal.
   b. wonderful.
   c. damaging.
   d. beautiful.
4. The word icon most nearly means
   a. ambassador.
   b. god.

c. symbol.

d. destroyer.

5. The word <u>rhetoric</u> most nearly means

a. words.

b. actions.

c. parents.

d. behavior.

Understanding the Essay

1. The main idea of "Barbie Madness" is that
   a. Barbie is damaging to the self-image of young girls and should be banned.
   b. toys are just toys and nothing more.
   c. the influence of Barbie and other cultural icons is outweighed by the influence of parents on a child's self image.
   d. there is nothing unrealistic about Barbie.

2. When she had a Barbie of her own, the author
   a. considered herself too young to play with dolls.
   b. realized that Barbie was a toy, not a role model.
   c. wanted to be just like Barbie when she grew up.
   d. joined a fan club only because her little sister did.

3. If the author wanted to subscribe to the magazine least likely to show unrealistic images of women, which of the following would she choose?
   a. *Sports Illustrated*
   b. *Business Week*
   c. *Vogue*
   d. *Cosmopolitan*

4. How does Tucker support her statement that parents have more influence than the surrounding culture?
   a. She provides examples from her own life.
   b. She provides no support because her statement is obviously true.
   c. She cites scientific research and gives examples.
   d. She includes interviews with child psychologists.

5. The author would probably agree that a mother who wanted her daughter to be successful and well-rounded would
   a. forbid the child to play with dolls.
   b. teach her to use feminine wiles to get along in a man's world.

  c. insist that she go into a traditionally "male" field such as engineering.

  d. praise her daughter for her achievements and not for her looks.

Writing in the Margins

These questions encourage you to think not just about the essay but about the issues it raises. Your instructor may ask you to write down your answers, to discuss them in groups, or simply to think about them for class discussion.

1. In what ways does Barbie present an unrealistic image of women? Are there also toys that present an unrealistic image of men? Do you think these toys can harm the self-image of young girls or boys?

2. Tucker says that the messages that parents send with their own words and behavior overshadow any messages a toy could send. What example does Tucker give of a positive parental message? Which of her examples shows a negative parental message? Can you think of your own examples, both positive and negative?

3. In paragraph 9, Tucker uses the term *trophy wife*. Think about the meaning of the term *trophy*, and then write a sentence defining the term *trophy wife*. What does the term imply about a man's reasons for choosing the woman he marries?

4. Who are some of our cultural icons? What does each say about the things we value as a society?

Topics for Writing

Assignment 1: A Favorite Toy

Paragraph or Journal Entry

What was your favorite toy when you were a child? Write a paragraph or journal entry explaining what made it so special. This task will involve not just a description of the toy, but a description of how it made you feel. Did it capture your imagination, encourage one of your special talents, or take you to a fantasy world? Discuss.

Assignment 2: A Child's Self-Worth

Paragraph

What specific steps would you take as a parent to ensure that your child grew up with a healthy sense of self-worth? Write a paragraph outlining and explaining each step.

Assignment 3: Making Barbie Realistic

Paragraph

If Barbie's beauty, her fashionable wardrobe, and her dream house and car present an unrealistic image, then what would a reality-based Barbie be like? In a paragraph, describe what her appearance, clothing, and accessories would be like if she were truly realistic.

 ## Assignment 4: Stereotypes

Paragraph or Essay

A *stereotype* is a kind of misjudgment that attributes negative (and occasionally, positive) characteristics to a people simply because they are of a particular age, gender, religion, race, or socioeconomic group. Can you think of a television show, toy, video game, music video, or advertisement that presents a certain group of people (women, men, teenagers, members of a particular ethnic group, members of a particular profession) in a way that is narrow, stereotypical, or damaging? Write a paragraph or essay describing three of these stereotyped shows, toys, or advertisements.

Disorders R Us

Michael Skube

In the old days, says Michael Skube, people had character flaws. Today, they have disorders.

I have certain compulsions. One is to clean the coffee grinder every morning like 1
a man shining shoes. I wipe the cartridge that holds the grounds until it's spot-
less. Then I clean the grinders, picking away at every exposed ground of coffee.
I'd take the thing out and scrub them with steel wool, but I'm afraid I'd never get
it back together again.

The whole operation takes ten minutes, sometimes more. My wife wonders 2
about this, but it's time well spent. I don't want coffee the next day tainted by
stale grounds.

When I was a child, it was my job to wash the dinner dishes while my older 3
sister dried. It quickly became evident that I take an extremely long time to wash
and rinse a dish. I still do. I'm the master of the triple rinse. While I washed, she
stood by, rapping her fingers on the counter. One night she summarily ripped the
rag out of my hand, saying, "If you want to be here all night, I'm going to wash
and let you dry. I know you'll do a good job."

I wish you could see how dry I got those dishes. I know this is a disorder of 4
some sort. I just don't know which one.

There are so many. 5

Of all the countries on earth, we are the leader in disorders. The one most 6
hung up on pathology. If we don't have attention deficit disorder, we have one or
another kind of personality disorder. Or anxiety disorder. Or mood disorder. Other
cultures just don't seem to have the problems we do.

Or maybe they just don't have the psychiatrists and psychologists we do. 7

There is a tome called the *Diagnostic and Statistical Manual of Mental* 8
Disorders, and it's thicker than the repair manuals mechanics use. A recent edition
doesn't list just anxiety disorder; it lists eleven separate kinds. It lists seventeen
kinds of mood disorder. And eleven kinds of personality disorder. It lists disorders
by the hundreds.

The entire premise of therapeutic culture that pervades American life is 9
summed up in that one word—disorder. There is something wrong with us. We
need to be diagnosed and treated.

The corollary of this is that our problems—to the extent that they're actually 10
problems—aren't part of our character, they're medical. Once it's put that way,
we're off the hook.

Nothing we can do about it, except see the doctor and take our pills.   11

The epidemic of ADD cases is only the most visible example of the impulse   12
to pathologize more or less ordinary behavior. There are classrooms in which half
the students are on Ritalin. Kids are diagnosed and labeled if they're not
"on-task," teacher-talk for behaving like little soldiers, and they're diagnosed if
they concentrate too well. I know of a twelve-year-old girl who will read contentedly for hours. The teacher thinks something's wrong and told the parents
she thinks their daughter has ADD.

We should at least be honest and call these children patients.   13

By one recent study, fully one-fourth of the students in the nation's public   14
schools have a "learning disability." As you might expect, federal money plays
a part. When the Individuals with Disabilities Education Act went into effect in
1976, most schoolchildren it covered were physically impaired in some way.
Less than one-quarter had learning disabilities. By 1992, those with learning
disabilities represented fifty-two percent—2,369,385 disabled children—with
more than one billion dollars in federal money going to schools for programs to
teach them.

And their numbers are growing. We're identifying more disorders every day. It   15
doesn't require a perverse imagination to foresee a time when most people will
be disabled, with a minority of odd birds who don't have a label (a disability in
itself?).

People swallow this hooey uncritically. "Well, the psychiatrist (or psycholo-   16
gist or guidance counselor or whoever) diagnosed him, so it must be true." You
want to throttle these nincompoops as much as you do the charlatans who've
duped them.

Be grateful for skeptics like G. E. Zuriff, a clinical psychologist at the Massa-   17
chusetts Institute of Technology. In an article titled "Medicalizing Character" in
the Spring 1996 issue of *The Public Interest,* Zuriff wrote:

> Unlike physical disease, most psychological problems cannot be
> attributed to any known physiological pathology. Although we can
> safely assume that psychological problems are related to the central
> nervous system, the fact is that we know very little about the biolog-
> ical basis for schizophrenia, even less about anxiety and depression,
> and virtually nothing about the physiological causes of personality
> disorders.

All too often, a diagnosis is little more than an educated guess, and some-   18
times it's not that educated. I can make guesses as well as the next person. For
myself, I'm counting forty-two actual disorders, including No. 301.4 ("obsessive-
compulsive personality disorder"), all kinds of syndromes and quite a few com-
plexes. Is there a label for people who can't take psycho-babble seriously? I want
to label a few people, hard. If somebody can work "disorder" into it for me, so
much the better. It would give it a scientific touch. But it comes out to the same
thing: They're frauds.

Building Vocabulary

For each question, choose the meaning that most closely defines the underlined word or phrase as it is used in the essay.

1. The word <u>pathology</u> most likely means
   a. cultures.
   b. personality.
   c. disease.
   d. knowledge.

2. The word <u>premise</u> most nearly means
   a. theory.
   b. promise.
   c. property.
   d. problem.

3. The word <u>corollary</u> most nearly means
   a. opposite.
   b. therapy.
   c. diagnosis.
   d. result.

4. The word <u>perverse</u> most nearly means
   a. healthy.
   b. twisted.
   c. limited.
   d. required.

5. The word <u>skeptics</u> most nearly means
   a. academics.
   b. believers.
   c. doubters.
   d. experts in disorders.

Understanding the Essay

1. A good alternate title for this essay would be
   a. "Helping Kids with Learning Disabilities."
   b. "The ADD Epidemic."
   c. "Learning Disabilities: The Great Hoax."
   d. "What is 'Normal'? A Layperson's Guide to Diagnosing Common Disorders."

2. The opening example is intended to illustrate
   a. the author's obsessive-compulsive disorder.
   b. the kind of relatively normal behavior that is often labeled a disorder.
   c. how the author's childhood behavior has carried over into adulthood.
   d. the author's lack of tolerance for mess and dirt.
3. Which of the following is *not* true according to the essay?
   a. The *Diagnostic and Statistical Manual of Mental Disorders* lists eleven kinds of anxiety disorder.
   b. People in the United States have fewer disorders than those in other countries.
   c. In some classrooms, over 50 percent of the children are taking medication for ADD.
   d. Relatively little is known about the physical basis for psychological problems.
4. The essay implies that labeling behavior a "disorder"
   a. makes the behavior easier to treat and control.
   b. can foster a lack of self-esteem in those who are labeled.
   c. is less common in our culture than it used to be.
   d. encourages people not to take responsibility for what they do.
5. The example of the twelve-year-old who reads contentedly for hours while her teacher worries that she has ADD illustrates
   a. how well Ritalin works.
   b. the ridiculous lengths to which labeling can be carried.
   c. how all children should behave.
   d. the effectiveness of American schools.

Writing in the Margins

These questions encourage you to think not just about the essay but about the issues it raises. Your instructor may ask you to write down your answers, to discuss them in groups, or simply to think about them for class discussion.

1. The author asserts in paragraph 12 that there are some "classrooms in which half the students are on Ritalin." Based on your observations, is the statement true?
2. While the author clearly believes that we are too willing to label all kinds of behavior "disorders," others regard ADD and other disorders as real problems that can be treated medically. What kind of evidence

would it take to conclusively prove that one view or the other is correct? Does any such evidence exist, as far as you know?

3. Do you believe, as the author does, that diagnosis of disorders has been carried too far? Why or why not?

4. Discuss the author's statement in paragraph 10 that labeling problems as "medical" lets us "off the hook." What does the author mean? Do you agree or disagree?

Topics for Writing

Assignment 1: All in Your Head

Paragraph or Journal Entry

Have you ever had a disability or problem that was not taken seriously? Write a paragraph or journal entry about how the experience made you feel and how you resolved the problem.

Assignment 2: Close to Home

Paragraph

Have you ever been diagnosed with a learning disability? How did you react? Do you now accept or reject the idea that you have a disability? How has the diagnosis affected your academic life? (If the topic does not apply to you, feel free to write your paragraph about a close friend or relative who has been through the experience.)

Assignment 3: Faking It

Paragraph

If Skube is right that even normal behavior is labeled as a disorder and that such labeling allows people to avoid responsibility, imagine the possibilities. If you are habitually late getting up in the morning, perhaps you have "alarm clock resistance disorder." If you fail a test, perhaps it's due to "study avoidance syndrome" or maybe "success phobia." Think about your own self-defeating behaviors (or those of a friend) and invent disorders, syndromes, and phobias to explain or excuse those behaviors. Then write a paragraph explaining one or more of the "disorders" and how they affect your life.

Assignment 4: Coping with College

Paragraph or Essay

Learning disorders aside, most people find it difficult to cope with the demands of college. If a friend asked you for advice on meeting the demands of college successfully, what would you say? Write a paragraph or essay giving advice. You may confine your advice to academic life or you may broaden the topic to include balancing the demands of family and work against the demands of school.

All the Rage ("Road Warrior")

Dave Barry

You've heard of Road Rage. Humorist Dave Barry also explains Parking Lot Rage, Shopping Cart Rage, and other sources of anger that are all the rage.

If you do much driving on our nation's highways, you've probably noticed that, more and more often, bullets are coming through your windshield. This is a common sign of Road Rage, which the opinion-makers in the news media have decided is a serious problem, ranking just behind global warming and ahead of Asia.   1

How widespread is Road Rage? To answer that question, researchers for the National Institute of Traffic Safety recently did a study in which they drove on the interstate highway system in a specially equipped observation van. By the third day, they were deliberately running motorists off the road.   2

"These people are *morons!*" their official report stated.   3

That is the main cause of Road Rage: the realization that many of your fellow motorists have the brain of a cashew. The most common example, of course, is the motorists who feel a need to drive in the left-hand lane even though they are going slower than everybody else.   4

Nobody knows why they do this. Maybe they belong to some kind of religious cult that believes the right lane is sacred and must never come in direct contact with tires. Maybe one time, years ago, these motorists happened to be driving in the left lane when their favorite song came on the radio, so they've driven there ever since.   5

But whatever makes these people drive this way, there's nothing you can do. You can honk at them, but it will have no effect. People have been honking at them for years: It's a normal part of their environment. They've decided, for some mysterious reason, wherever they drive, there is honking.   6

I am familiar with this problem because I live and drive in Miami, which bills itself as the Inappropriate-Lane-Driving Capital of the World, and where the left lane is thought of not so much as a thoroughfare as a public recreational area, where motorists feel free to stop, hold family reunions, barbecue pigs, play volleyball, etc. Compounding this problem is another common type of Miami motorist, the aggressive young male whose car has a sound system so powerful that the driver must go faster than the speed of sound at all times, or else the nuclear bass notes emanating from his rear speakers will catch up to him and cause his head to explode.   7

So the tiny minority of us Miami drivers who actually qualify as normal find ourselves constantly being trapped behind people drifting along on the interstate at the speed of diseased livestock, while at the same time being tailgated and   8 occasionally bumped from behind by testosterone-deranged youths who got their driver training from watching "Star Wars." And of course nobody ever signals or yields, and people are constantly cutting us off, and *after a while we start to feel some rage, OK? You got a problem with that,* mister opinion-maker?

In addition to Road Rage, I frequently experience Parking Lot Rage, which   9 occurs when I pull into a crowded supermarket parking lot, and I see people get into their car, clearly ready to leave, so I stop my car and wait for them to <u>vacate</u> the spot, and . . . nothing happens. They just stay there! *What the hell are they doing in there?? Cooking dinner???*

When I finally get into the supermarket, I often experience Shopping Cart   10 Rage. This is caused by the people—and you just know these are the same people who drive slowly in the left-hand lane—who <u>routinely</u> manage, by careful placement, to block the entire aisle with a shopping cart. If we really want to keep illegal immigrants from entering the United States, we should employ Miami residents armed with shopping carts; we'd only need about two dozen to block the entire Mexican border.

What makes the supermarket <u>congestion</u> even worse is that shoppers are tak-   11 ing longer and longer to decide what to buy, because every product in America now comes in an insane number of styles and sizes. For example, I recently went to the supermarket to get orange juice. For just one brand, I had to decide between Original, Homestyle, Pulp Plus, Double Vitamin C, Grovestand, Calcium or Old Fashioned; I also had to decide whether I wanted the 167-ounce, 32-ounce, 64-ounce, 96-ounce or six-pack size. This is *way* too many choices. It caused me to experience Way Too Many Product Choices Rage. I would have called the orange juice company and complained, but I probably would have wound up experienc-ing Automated Phone Answering System Rage (". . . For questions about Pulp Plus in the 32-ounce size, press 23. For questions about Pulp Plus in the 64-ounce size, press 24. For questions about . . .").

My point is that there are many causes of rage in our modern world, and if   12 we're going to avoid unnecessary violence, we all need to "keep our cool." So let's try to be more considerate, OK? Otherwise it will kill you.

Building Vocabulary

For each question, choose the meaning that most closely defines the underlined word or phrase as it is used in the essay.

1. The word <u>bills</u> most nearly means
   a. currency.
   b. labels.
   c. charges.
   d. appropriates.

2. The word <u>emanating</u> most nearly means
   a. murmuring.
   b. coming.

c. trickling.

d. tinkling.

3. The word <u>vacate</u> most nearly means

   a. leave.

   b. remain in.

   c. enter.

   d. locate.

4. The word <u>routinely</u> most nearly means

   a. boringly.

   b. kindly.

   c. deliberately.

   d. habitually.

5. The word <u>congestion</u> most nearly means

   a. crowding.

   b. shopping.

   c. food.

   d. stuffiness.

Understanding the Essay

1. Barry's purpose in writing the essay is

   a. to analyze the modern phenomenon of Road Rage and to suggest solutions.

   b. to document recent research by the National Institute of Traffic Safety.

   c. to discuss several different causes of rage.

   d. to amuse the reader by poking fun at a serious subject.

2. In the essay, Barry does all of the following *except*

   a. sympathize with those who feel Road Rage.

   b. side with the victims of drivers with Road Rage.

   c. blame people who drive slowly in the left-hand lane.

   d. imply that drivers who feel Road Rage are the normal ones.

3. The tone of the essay is

   a. objective.

   b. angry.

   c. humorous.

   d. biased.

4. One type of rage *not* mentioned in the essay is
   a. Way Too Many Product Choices Rage.
   b. Car Dealership Ripoff Rage.
   c. Shopping Cart Rage.
   d. Automated Phone Answering System Rage.
5. Barry's persona in the essay is that of a person who
   a. is barely in control himself.
   b. has too often been a victim of enraged drivers.
   c. is trying to take a reasoned, logical approach to an illogical topic.
   d. does not care about the subject he is writing about.

Writing in the Margins

These questions encourage you to think not just about the essay but about the issues it raises. Your instructor may ask you to write down your answers, to discuss them in groups, or simply to think about them for class discussion.

1. Exaggeration of the truth is one tool of the humorist. What instances of exaggeration can you point out in Barry's essay?
2. Barry's humorous essay reflects a modern phenomenon that has become fairly serious. What are some of the ways that people lose control on the road and in other public places, and what are some of the reasons behind the phenomenon?
3. What driving behaviors strike you as most dangerous and/or annoying?

Topics for Writing

Assignment 1: Rage On!

Paragraph or Journal Entry

Do you have a pet peeve that drives you into a frenzy? It could be the woman who gets into the "fifteen items or less" line with twenty-five items, a fistful of coupons, and an expired debit card. Or perhaps it's the driver who tailgates you on the highway with his high-beams shining into your rearview mirror. What makes *you* angry? Rage on—in a controlled way—in a paragraph or journal entry.

Assignment 2: You-Name-It Rage

Paragraph

Write a paragraph describing a kind of rage that affects you. Use one of Barry's categories or, if you wish, make up your own.

Assignment 3: Driving You Crazy

Paragraph

Write a paragraph describing the kinds of drivers likely to incite road rage.

Assignment 4: Shop Till You Drop

Paragraph or Essay

These days, grocery stores are often cavernous places that sell not just groceries, but books, prescription drugs, housewares, and prepared foods. At some grocery stores, people can do their banking, pick up their dry cleaning, rent a video, and even work out. Malls, too, are becoming larger and more elaborate. On the opposite end of the scale, shopping from home through catalogs or computers is becoming more popular. A customer can order clothing, books, housewares, CDs, and computer equipment through mail-order catalogs or online sites. Even groceries can be purchased online. If given a choice, would you prefer shopping at huge malls and mega-stores or doing your shopping from home? Write a paragraph or essay telling why.

What If My Friends Hadn't Run?

Bill Pippin

What does it take to make an ordinary person pick up a gun and point it at another person? In this essay, a law-abiding family man recalls the day he picked up a gun in anger.

When I was a boy, I loved watching Gene Autry and Roy Rogers movies and then acting out my fantasies, galloping around the yard on a stick horse and shooting at bad men with my cap gun. On my 9th birthday, when Dad asked, "What'll it be—a bike or a .22 rifle?" naturally I chose the rifle. On the high plains at the edge of our little oilfield town of Lamont, Wyo., Dad showed me how to load my Remington single-shot and shoot at tin cans. In less time than it takes to eject a spent cartridge, that rifle was as familiar to me as a cap gun.   1

That summer of 1947, while my parents were away, I was hanging out near the house with my friends Donald and J.W., along with Donald's 4-year-old brother, Danny, looking for something to do. "I know," said J.W. "Let's play jujitsu."   2

"Yeah," I agreed, because it sounded like fun. That was before the two older boys started practicing the Japanese martial art on me, throwing me back and forth, trying different holds they'd seen in World War II movies or newsreels. Finally, I lost my temper and yelled, "Knock it off!"   3

They only laughed. By the time they got tired, I was dirty, bruised, outraged and crazy mad. "I'll show you guys," I said, gritting back tears. Stumbling into the house, I snatched my .22 out of the closet, then stood on a chair to reach the top shelf of the kitchen cabinet, where we kept the box of long-rifle shells. As I went back outside I slid one into the chamber.   4

When the two older boys heard the rifle bolt snap home, their faces paled. Donald grabbed Danny's hand and headed south, crow-hopping along as fast as his little brother's short legs would allow. J.W. took a threatening step my way but scampered off when I pointed the rifle at him and snapped, "Get outta here!"   5

The sight of those three fleeing in terror infused me with volcanic power. I couldn't resist firing a shot over their heads. The sharp crack sent J.W. rocketing past Donald, who then ran so hard little Danny skipped over the sagebrush like a rag doll. My laughter quickly sucked the fire out of my anger. A day or two later, my former tormentors and I were friends again, and the incident was forgotten.   6

My family moved away from Wyoming in 1951, but I returned with my wife, 7
Zona, a few years ago, when I took a new job in Cheyenne. This spring I was surprised by a call from Donald, asking, "Are you the Billy Pippin I knew in Lamont
fifty years ago?" I was <u>ecstatic</u> to hear from my childhood buddy. Like me, he'd
moved around a lot, and he now lives in Douglas, only a couple of hours away.
Soon after that, my now bald chum and his wife, Gwen, drove down to Cheyenne
to have lunch with Zona and me.

Sharing warm memories over iced tea and sandwiches was a blast: the tar- 8
paper shanties we lived in that lacked even electricity; our two-room school that
stood so close to an oil derrick you could hit it with a rock; the hot summer's
day we biked nearly 20 miles to Muddy Gap to skinny-dip for a brief hour in a shallow pond.

When I reminded Donald of the time I chased him with my rifle, he laughed. But 9
Zona and Gwen didn't laugh. They didn't even smile. In the awkward silence that
followed, Donald reached for a pickle, shrugging as if to say, "We were only kids."

That's true. But I've been thinking about it, and I don't honestly know what 10
I would have done that day in 1947 if my friends hadn't run. It troubles me.
I guess my saving grace is that I wasn't planning to hurt anyone; I just wanted
them to stop messing with me and chose the most effective deterrent I had at my
disposal—a gun. But I do know that what happened never would have if an adult
had been present, if my gun had been locked away or if my friends hadn't made
me madder than hell. I also know that "only kids" may serve as an excuse for
childish misconduct, but not for what I did. Certainly not for the kind of cold-
blooded <u>carnage</u> we've seen recently.

And on that sunny spring day, as Donald and I looked across the table at each 11
other, the seriousness of what happened more than 50 years ago hit me like a slap
in the face. I took a deep breath, <u>overwhelmed</u> by a rush of pure gratitude so powerful that for a moment I couldn't swallow. I was thankful that my role models had
been Roy Rogers and Gene Autry, not Sylvester Stallone and Arnold Schwarzenegger.
Thankful that my rifle had been a .22 single-shot, not an assault weapon. Thankful that after all this time Donald and I were still friends. Thankful that the memories we now shared brought laughter instead of tears.

When Donald and Gwen left, I gave them both a huge bearhug. More than 12
anything else, I was thankful that I could.

Building Vocabulary

For each question, choose the meaning that most closely defines the
underlined word or phrase as it is used in the essay.

1. The word <u>spent</u> most nearly means
   a. used.
   b. new.
   c. faulty.
   d. fresh.

2. The word <u>tormentors</u> most nearly means
   a. followers.
   b. friends.
   c. admirers.
   d. abusers.
3. The word <u>ecstatic</u> most nearly means
   a. understandable.
   b. joyous.
   c. resentful.
   d. reluctant.
4. The word <u>carnage</u> most nearly means
   a. childishness.
   b. pranks.
   c. bloodshed.
   d. innocence.
5. The word <u>overwhelmed</u> most nearly means
   a. unaffected.
   b. angered.
   c. overpowered.
   d. inactive.

Understanding the Essay

1. Which statement best expresses the essay in one sentence?
   a. When his friends torment him, an angry boy seeks a dangerous way of stopping them.
   b. A young man is forced to defend himself with a gun.
   c. A grown man finally confronts the horrible consequences that could have resulted from a childhood act of anger.
   d. A young man loses a friend when he points a gun at him, but is reunited with the friend in adulthood.
2. The author implies that the older boys who practiced jujitsu on him
   a. were violent bullies rather than true friends.
   b. were trying to teach him about the martial arts.
   c. were not really hurting him.
   d. were friends who were playing a little more roughly than usual.

3. What effect did the sight of his friends running in terror have on the author?
   a. He realized that pointing a gun at them was foolish and dangerous.
   b. He felt ashamed.
   c. He felt powerful.
   d. He never touched a gun again.
4. At the dinner table with his old friend, the author feels
   a. overwhelming gratitude.
   b. deep guilt.
   c. hidden resentment.
   d. slight boredom.
5. When he thinks of the incident, the author blames
   a. the fact that the gun was not locked away and no adults were present.
   b. his friends.
   c. himself.
   d. all of the above.

Writing in the Margins

These questions encourage you to think not just about the essay but about the issues it raises. Your instructor may ask you to write down your answers, to discuss them in groups, or simply to think about them for class discussion.

1. The essay suggests that the author, Bill Pippin, is now a responsible adult. If the childhood episode had turned out differently, how might his life have changed?
2. How often do you suppose acts of violence occur because an ordinary person, pushed to the limit, becomes angry and grabs a weapon? What is the solution?

Topics for Writing

Assignment 1: What If . . .

Paragraph or Journal Entry

Bill Pippin, the author of this essay, asks, "What if my friends hadn't run?" Most people have a "what if" story about a time when their actions brought them a heartbeat away from disaster. What's your "what if" story? Tell it in a journal entry or a paragraph.

Assignment 2: Should Guns Be Regulated?

Paragraph

Discussion of gun violence always brings up the question of regulation of firearms. Many other countries ban private ownership of handguns. Write a paragraph discussing whether the United States should make stricter laws regulating the ownership of firearms.

Assignment 3: Violence and the Media

Paragraph or Essay

The author mentions being "thankful that [his] role models had been Roy Rogers and Gene Autry, not Sylvester Stallone and Arnold Schwarzenegger." Do you believe that violence in entertainment media such as movies, television, video games, and music videos can influence young people to become violent? Answer in a paragraph.

Assignment 4: Reunions

Paragraph or Essay

If you could be reunited with one of your friends from elementary school, who would it be and why? Write a paragraph that describes your relationship with the person and your reasons for wanting to see him or her again.

Credits

Photo Credits

Index